The Times
Bedside Book

The Times

Bedside Book

Edited by
Philip Howard

with a Foreword by
Simon Jenkins

HarperCollins*Publishers*

HarperCollins*Publishers*
77–85 Fulham Palace Road,
Hammersmith, London W6 8JB

Published by HarperCollins*Publishers* 1991
9 8 7 6 5 4 3 2 1

A catalogue record for this book is
available from the British Library

ISBN 0 00 215948 1

Set in Linotron Times

Photoset by
Rowland Phototypesetting Ltd
Bury St Edmunds, Suffolk
Printed in Great Britain by
HarperCollins Manufacturing, Glasgow

Foreword

by **Simon Jenkins, Editor,** *The Times*

This is a book to be read in a moment of repose, a bedside book. A newspaper is a means of information, of opinion and of entertainment. It cannot legislate on when or in what spirit its readers pick it up, but *The Times* knows that in its columns, the highest standards are expected.

This collection must pass an even stricter test. As Pope said, 'Some praise at morning what they blame at night; / But always think the last opinion right.' Its contents must last the day, perhaps even mature with the setting of the sun. To merit reprinting in book form, an article has therefore to be more thoughtful and more witty than the normal run of column inches.

No topic is too serious for humour. A joke, a clever turn of phrase, an occasional pun give leaven to any argument and point to any criticism. Humour is the quickest path to the mind's comprehension of the world. This collection includes many of those *Times* contributors with an ability to raise a smile at the end of the day: Alan Coren, sage of Cricklewood; Craig Brown, craftsman of lateral whimsy; Matthew Parris, wit with a final sting. Humour of a different sort infuses Bernard Levin's writing, his sentences stretching ever tauter across the page until they snap in judgement; and our wittiest writers are often real correspondents, chuckling daily through the letters page. The events and public figures that have dominated newspaper pages over the last twelve months deserve some serious treatment from Robin Oakley and Anne McElvoy, among others; while Jan Morris and Philip Howard provide pieces with a more meditative tone.

A bedside table with them all gathered on top would not break under the strain. It would lift gently in the air and dance a jig. *The Times* is proud of them.

July 1991

Introduction

By definition, a daily newspaper has the shortest shelf life of any major industrial and artistic product. Its name proclaims its function, to spend its time doing nothing but telling some new thing. Today it must catch the fickle attention of the scurrying reader; tomorrow it is wrapping for fish and chips, or, more probably in these days of clean food legislation, litter for cats and lining for the budgerigar cage.

Before the last war Claud Cockburn applied for a job in the Washington office of *The Times*. The American editor invited the young man to write a 3000-word 'turnover' article about the state of the union: political, economic, social, and tragical–comical–historical–pastoral. Cockburn scribbled, and rewrote, and polished, and pulled out all his Pomposo stops, and then delivered his piece to the American editor in person. The great man read it through with maddening deliberation, and then turned to Claud, and pronounced: 'Young man, in this job you must always remember that you are competing for the attention of a little old lady [journalists have always been notorious for sexism] with two cats. On this occasion, I regret to tell you, the cats win.' And he tore Claud's masterpiece in half and then into quarters, and let the pieces flutter into his wastepaper basket.

As its form suggests, the 'news' used to be plural. Shelley, in a letter of 1821 wrote: 'There are bad news from Palermo.' John Thadeus Delane, one of the two great founding editors of *The Times*, asked William Howard Russell, his correspondent in the Crimea: 'What are the news?' Across the wires the electric message came: 'Not a damned new'.

Today the news has become singular, and the search for it

has become more professional and urgent. There is much more competition to spread the news than there was two hundred years ago, when *The Times* had a monopoly in the elusive stuff. The days when the public queued impatiently in coffee houses to read the news of the victory at Trafalgar in their only oracle, the single copy of *The Times*, have long gone. As soon as any noteworthy event happens anywhere on earth or in space, it is broadcast around the world by electronic media. The newspapers and other printed media have to follow up, flesh out and get right the news that readers have already heard on radio or seen on television or read on screen.

To watch a great newspaper like *The Times* about its daily business is a majestic and moving sight. We do not start work seriously until after lunch (and we all know what journalists' lunches are reputed to be like). During a hectic six-hour period, we write, sub-edit, design, headline, standfirst, illustrate, cut and print as many words as are in three novels of average length, to get them on breakfast tables from Penzance to Inverness by the following morning.

C'est magnifique, mais ce n'est pas littérature. It is not surprising that a daily newspaper, written at such a breakneck speed against the clock, should have occasional imperfections. Old fogeys, disgusted of Tunbridge Wells, sometimes complain that standards are slipping, and that *The Times* is not what it was. It was never perfect, dear boys. The cure for believing that *The Times* was once the arbiter of correct English and high literature is to go back and read those early issues of a hundred and two hundred years ago. Trollope (who eventually grew grudgingly to admire the *Jupiter*) was alarmed by its ungentlemanliness and indiscretion and bad English. The Fowler brothers, magnificent liberal pedagogues of *The King's English* and *A Dictionary of Modern English Usage*, took most of their examples of solecisms, elegant variation and how not to write from their daily newspaper. It was, of course, *The Times*.

It might seem contradictory to put something as ephemeral

as a daily newspaper between hard covers. But some of the writing earns a longer life than a mayfly, and always has. Russell's reports from the Crimea have stood the test of time. Since *The Times*'s foundation its pieces have influenced history and literature: leaders that brought down a government, letters from the great or the obscure that set the political agenda, fiery pieces of criticism . . .

Our best efforts go into the news – nothing is more exciting than the hot stuff of today's politics and sport. But, on the whole, nothing becomes stale more quickly: in a year's time we have moved on to new news. Accordingly, in a collection of pieces from *The Times*, the bias is slightly away from the red meat of hard news, and towards the fairy-dell department of features and comment. Humorous and witty writing, in which *The Times* is at present conspicuously rich, is timeless because it is not tied to any topical peg. The eternal arguments of art, literature and architecture keep for ever. The news passes in a flash. As the man said, *ars longa, vita brevis*: art is long, but the news desk wants four hundred words in ten minutes.

Nevertheless, the last year has been a good one for news: the fall of a prime minister, the shifting of the political certainties, a violent international war. The articles in this selection from *The Times* give a portrait of a notable year. They are both the abstracts and brief chronicles of our time, and a sample of writing in *The Times* that looks as if it will last and be read with pleasure ten years from now. I hope they will entertain, amuse, inform and even, occasionally, annoy. But to get the full flavour of the best newspaper in the world, you should read it daily.

Philip Howard, Literary Editor, July 1991

Better a cardboard box than Thatcher City

Barbara Amiel

A few years ago the manicurist in my local beauty shop mentioned to me that she was homeless. She had taken up with some fellow who turned out to be no good and, sure enough, one day the police came. They sealed off their flat, padlocked the doors and turfed her out. 'The police even took away my underwear,' she said. She was a decent woman, if a little thick when it came to men. She hadn't a penny to speak of. So I told her to move in with me for a bit, until she sorted herself out. I was a little embarrassed that I would be seen as a sort of shallow version of a caviar socialist. In fact, it worked very well. Some people are blessed with innate dignity, and she was one of them. We barely crossed each other's paths and my erratic hours were undisturbed. When she left my flat I missed her.

Some people worry about children in Africa, others about cats. As for me, well, I have a soft spot for the homeless. I was fourteen years old when I came back from school one day and saw all my possessions packed in a cardboard box next to the front door. My mother was very apologetic. 'Your stepfather and I,' she explained, 'just can't deal with you any more, so you have to go.' They had found me a room in a house on a council estate, and paid my rent till the end of the school term.

We lived in Hamilton, Ontario, then, and Canada was caught in a mean cycle of recession. My mother had emigrated to Canada in part to escape disapproval of a remarriage that broke religious and class taboos. But the work my stepfather had been promised in England did not materialize in Canada and now he was a young man with a ready-made family and no employment. I was a horrid little girl, always listening to classical music on the radio and lecturing my stepfather about his low tastes. I could not blame him for chucking me out, but I had never held a job and did not really know how I was going to make a go of it. When school ended that summer, they explained, I was on my own. They were going off to another city where my stepfather had work and my mother was pregnant again. They hoped I would be all right.

In fact, I was. I stayed a few months with Ken the garage mechanic and his wife with the thin dripping nose and whine to match. They had a wretched son who used to tease me about my having a moustache. Then I moved on. There was a succession of jobs working after school in fast food restaurants and on farms, factories and in department stores in the summers. Cheap labour does not lack job opportunities. My favourite job was working on the underwear counter in a Woolworth's store when I was fifteen. I had no bust and had never seen a brassière. I spent one week's entire pay on a padded bra in the belief that boys were attracted to what a girl looked like rather than what she had. My error was manifest on my first date.

The truth was that after the hurt passed and I had cried a bit, after I had got over the fright of sleeping in cellars underneath the furnace pipes, I came to cherish my freedom. Not having parents around was a tremendous advantage. I was a wild child, of course, with no manners or domesticity, but there was nothing, I believed, that I could not do. Later on in life, I would find out that this was not entirely true. Something decent died in me, or perhaps was stillborn: I would never manage to create a successful family life. Still, I think the gods struck a very fair bargain.

I think about those years whenever I read about the problem of runaway children. I still have that soft spot for their homelessness. Oh, I know it's not the same. I had the tremendous advantage of spending the first dozen years of my life as a nice middle-class girl in north London, while some of the kids on our streets today have known only alcoholism and violence, poverty and dirt. But a lot of the runaways I have spoken to in London share feelings I know so well. It *is* marvellously liberating to be away from the constraints of parents. It *is* better to live in a cardboard box than a strictly supervised Salvation Army hostel which may want you to wash behind the ears or sing a hymn. But the question remains. A fifteen-year-old is a fifteen-year-old. He or she is a child, no matter how much more street-wise they are than we were. What are we, as a society, going to do with them?

The numbers of these homeless children are increasing. The magnitude of the problem is a direct consequence of certain social policies and social developments. Although we do not have any precise breakdown ethnically, socio-economically or racially on these children, I think it is probably fair to say that the majority of them will come from those sorts of families most affected by the direction our society has taken vis-à-vis the family: that is, more of them will come from the single-parent families which our social policies support and from communities which do not censure loosely structured relationships. Many of these communities are minority cultures and we are afraid to criticize them lest we be seen as being prejudiced.

Mind you, we would have had a certain number of runaways, no matter what direction our society had taken. But the numbers will always vary according to the social factor, which can be anything. If we had a real depression now and there was genuine, widespread poverty rather than the relative poverty we have today, that, too, would increase the numbers. As it is, the numbers of runaways at the moment are increased by the utter destructiveness of our policies towards the family. We have undermined the family's authority and reallocated its powers. Our school systems encourage children to demean their parents' values, while at the same time we have admonished parents not to discipline their children except in ways acceptable to the state. We have discouraged

3

families through our tax laws and made illegitimate pregnancies acceptable through our benefit system.

Some of these changes are probably for the good, but whether they are or not, are they reversible in favour of policies that would strengthen the family? We could, for example, make divorce more difficult, rather than our current inclination to make it easier. I cannot embrace Auberon Waugh's suggestion for a punitive bachelor tax – fearing, as I do, a punitive spinster tax which I can ill afford – but I see his point. All the same, I simply do not think we can turn the clock back in this manner. And even if we could, it would take too long to re-establish the cohesion of the family.

Who, then, is going to act *in loco parentis* for these children living on London's streets? The answer to that is perfectly clear: it is going to be the state – the community – because it cannot be anyone else. How to do it is the only real question to be debated. Will it be done in a so-called 'conservative manner', or will it be done by the so-called 'liberal approach'? Will we support Mrs Thatcher in her £15 million programme to provide spankingly neat hostels for the homeless, who will be charged under vagrancy laws or the new 'crime' of squatting if they don't move into Thatcher City? This will undoubtedly injure some people, but it might slow down and discourage the process of running away from home. Or will we tackle the fifteen-year-olds by giving them pocket money, counselling and other liberal measures which will make it more comfortable for some, but will only aggravate the problem?

I have no doubt that the conservative approach would have been worse for people like me, but probably better for most others. Anyone who has some inner resources and discipline, as well as a small ability to self-start at fifteen years of age, will not thrive under Mrs T's schoolmarmish approach. The trouble is that we have so undermined the concept of self-reliance in our society that it is all but extinct among our young runaways. On the other hand, the liberal approach would have suited me to a t. Alas, I suspect it is hopeless for

4

the sort of people who have only the urge to leave home and not the wits to get a job, a room to live in or to attend school. And while I admit that I have done absolutely no scientific study of the matter, I have absolutely no doubt in my mind that the helpless outnumber the self-reliant by nine to one.

Those people to whom Labour speaks today of giving pocket money, to make running away at fifteen more easy, are very likely to be our peace disturbers and welfare charges tomorrow. I suppose we will tolerate the difficulties they cause for a time, but in the end we will have to crack down on them. The problem with too much liberalism is that eventually it leads to totalitarian-type measures – identity cards, and passports withheld, and mass conscription of bullies and hooligans into some kind of an army. How, we will ask, did it all happen?

The answer is simple: we could have avoided the whole mess if we had not diluted the family before we had something to put in its place. I suppose I shall have to brush up on contemporary vernacular and take a couple of the kids in.

29 June 1990

How the profligate bankers can be called to account

Bernard Levin

If there is a banker, reasonably well disposed to me, reading this, I have a request to make. Would he be so kind as to lend me three or four hundred million pounds, as soon as possible and at latest by the weekend? (On further reflection, I think I would like the full half-billion; no point in spoiling the ship for a ha'porth of tar, eh, ha-ha-ha?) I don't have any of what I think experts call collateral, but I am certainly willing to sign a paper committing myself to repay a reasonable proportion of the sum in due course – with the obvious proviso that if I lose the lot I shall have nothing to pay, so the loan will have to be (again, I am not entirely sure about the nomenclature) 'written off'.

As for the purpose of the loan, I was thinking of putting some of it into a most promising enterprise I have recently heard of: the technicalities, of course, I do not understand, but the point of it is to extract moonbeams from cucumbers. The rest I intend to put into the care of a gentleman I bumped into the other day, a Mr Cornfeld. (His forename, too, is Bernard, a delightful coincidence, and we got on splendidly. Within the hour he was insisting that I should call him 'Bernie' – he assured me all his friends do!)

Ah, yes, you will say, Levin's in a merry mood again. So he is; but what exactly is the difference between my nonsense and the daily reality as it unfolds in the financial pages? Let us start at the top, with the serious financial difficulties in which Mr Donald Trump has found himself. It is not necessary to go into the details of his plight, or how he got into it; in any case, I would not understand the intricacies, and you would not

6

understand my exposition. Just suck this very ripe plum, and mind you get a hankie first, or the juice will run down your chin:

> Bankers who are owed millions of dollars by Donald Trump . . . agreed yesterday to keep him out of the bankruptcy courts . . . all but one bank signed an agreement . . . to provide a $20 million bridging loan enabling Mr Trump to pay interest on bonds . . . Over the next 30 days the banks will complete the paperwork for the balance of a $65 million rescue package . . . the deal will go ahead with . . . the . . . 70 banks that had agreed to defer . . . payments on $850 million of Mr Trump's $2 billion bank debts . . .

The most urgent and important words in that report – at any rate the most urgent and important to you and me – are 'all but one bank signed', and it therefore behoves me to name, with a 99-gun salute, this noble maverick, this magnificent loner, this shining example. It is the West German Dresdner Bank, and my advice to all those of you who have money to invest is to put every penny you have into its care, confident that it will be carefully looked after, and will grow at a reasonable rate. As for the 70 other banks which rushed to sign the loan agreement, go and stand outside any of them, and when you see a lorry unloading thousands of cucumbers, *run*.

Do not believe that such goings-on are limited to the United States; as far as my reading about such matters goes, British banking is actually worse. I had a lot of fun with Ferranti not long ago (a great deal more than the shareholders did), but such horrors can be found wherever you look. I see, for instance, that the Securities and Investment Board is urgently seeking the key to the stable door, following the B&C crash. All sorts of remedies are being touted: institutions may even have to be more careful about where they put their clients' money or may have to limit their deposits to 10 per cent in any one bank – good gracious! Indeed, a far more revolutionary principle is being discussed: firms may be obliged to tell their clients just what they have done with their money – imagine! Why, Barclays have already had to set aside £100 million against their loans to B&C – think of it!

And what about Coloroll, which went down the sluice a few weeks ago £300 million short of a pop-up solvency? Yet here is what a representative of the receivers said, when asked whether the crash might bankrupt some of Coloroll's suppliers: 'It depends on how deep the creditors are in and how well they have read the tea leaves over the past months. They were given enough warning.'

Oh, they were, were they? Yes, they were: hear also a representative of Kleinwort Benson, the merchant bank, on the disaster: 'Anyone who goes out and buys textile assets at the current time has got to be half-baked if they pay a high price, because there's no sign of an upturn.'

My opening request is beginning to look perfectly possible; if I could only discover who Coloroll's bankers were, I bet I could persuade them to stake me. After all, the receiver, and the man at Kleinwort's, had no interest to declare, and they apparently had no doubt that Coloroll had been doomed long before the shutters came down. So why didn't Coloroll? Why, indeed, didn't Mr John Ashcroft, the boss ('His severance payment is still being negotiated')?

Aha, cry those (Arthur Scargill is one) who would solve problems of this nature by nationalizing the whole of business: the bankers and capitalists can do nothing but oppress the working classes; put the assets into the hands of the sons of toil, and prosperity will come galloping over the horizon, will it not? Alas, not necessarily. Listen to this enchanting sentence: 'The accounts of . . . the Transport and General Workers' Union reveal an £8.7 million deficit for 1989, but the general secretary, Ron Todd, yesterday denied that the union was facing a financial crisis.' Very well; who were the TGWU's bankers, and what has become of the discreet cough behind the hand?

Never mind discreet coughs; what has become of the principle of not throwing good money after bad? I buy no shares, neither do I sell them, but if I did, and one of my investments was doing badly, I would probably get rid of it. I say 'probably', because close inspection of the shares might well suggest, on good grounds, that they had a real chance of rising again. But if I learned that the company whose shares I held was borrowing substantial sums of money from banks in order to pay the interest on its bank loans, I would get the hell out of the shares at whatever price they would fetch, and if I then discovered that the company was borrowing more money to enable it to pay the interest on the interest, I would get the hell out of the bank in question as well.

I do not know the solution; I am by no means sure that I know the problem. Amateurism? Leave it to good old Fred? Lack of training? Insufficient penalties for failure? Insufficient rewards for success?

Pass. But perhaps I can offer a practical suggestion. When the crash comes, the experts always announce that the 'secured creditors' (which almost invariably means the banks and big institutions) will get their money, though the small shareholders, unsecured creditors and the staff will get nothing. What about legislation which inverts that pyramid?

5 July 1990

. . . *and moreover*

Alan Coren

This morning, I shall have to proceed with particular caution. For mine is a highly sophisticated readership, and I say this not simply to butter it up; although, admittedly, it can't hurt to butter it up a bit, given where its sophistication might very well lead it, should my particular caution not come up to snuff. That is because my readership is so sophisticated that it knows what the Delphic audience did to Aesop when they took against the moralistic tone of his witterings. They chucked him over a cliff.

Ever since then, those with a fable to offload have had to proceed with particular caution. Doing it somewhere cliffless is a good start, but the best thing is a good finish and a good finish means: no moral. Nothing in italics at the end, pointing the audience towards the homiletic pith. That is what got up their noses at Delphi. Nobody likes being told what they are supposed to have understood.

So what follows is just a fable. Make of it what you will. You will get no help from me. It is called *The Fox and the Cellphone*.

There was once a man who found himself, on a sunny July morning, standing on Kentish Town Railway Station. Kentish Town Railway Station is part of Network SouthEast, which is what the man himself wanted to be, only nothing came to net him and work him towards Cricklewood. He had been standing on the platform, alone, for twenty minutes, and this conjunction of time and solitude bothered him not a little, because he had seen *North by Northwest* and – being a susceptible sort of a man – he kept squinting up at the sky, just in case a biplane had any plans to dive on to him. You never knew, it was a funny old world, and just because you were going south by SouthEast, it didn't mean you shouldn't remain on your guard.

At the twenty-first minute, the man became aware of something approaching, down the track. It was not a train, it was not even a biplane coming in at zero altitude, it was a fox. It was trotting alongside the live rail, with a rat in its mouth. When it saw the man, it stopped. The man knew there was no point in asking it whether it had seen anything of the 10.14, because foxes have got smarter since Aesop's day and they know that if they open their mouths to speak, their food will drop out and they are not going to be caught that way twice.

Something, however, did speak. It said 'bloody hell', and when the man turned, he saw that he had been joined by another man, thirty-ish, snappily suited, who must have just come up the stairs from the booking-office. 'Look at that,' he continued. 'I think I'd better tell someone about that,' and he ran down the stairs again. At the clatter, the fox turned, and began trotting back the way it had come.

The second man returned, flushed, clearly angry.

'They don't give a toss!' he cried. 'They say they get foxes here all the time. I pointed out all the risks, but they don't give a toss.'

'More than their job's worth, no doubt,' said the man from Cricklewood, in jocular vein, for he did not wish to offend the stranger, who, despite the smart cut of his jib, might well be a homicidal crop-duster who had parked his biplane round the corner to divert suspicion.

'Not only could it cause a derailment,' said the stranger, 'it is a dangerous and verminous animal. We have,' he added, 'just moved in here. We've got small children! I'm phoning the council.'

Whereupon he opened his briefcase, took out a portable telephone, and began punching buttons. That he knew the council's number was not lost on the first man: here, clearly, was someone who got things done.

But not always. For, after a moment or two, the stranger

11

swore, and shook the phone. 'Sodding battery's flat,' he said. 'Can you believe it?'

The man from Cricklewood might have replied, had the train, at that moment, not appeared, encouraging the distant fox to hop delicately off the track and disappear. He might also have wondered which of his two new companions was the more likely to survive in Kentish Town. But he would not, of course, have said anything, because the area was unfamiliar to him, and could well have a cliff somewhere.

13 July 1990

An Englishwoman on Broadway

Sheridan Morley

These have been the best and worst of times for Maggie Smith. In the past six months she has been made a Dame of the British Empire and (possibly of more immediate commercial advantage) won a Broadway Tony award for her current performance there as the eccentric architectural preservationist in the comedy written for her by Peter Shaffer, *Lettice & Lovage*. In the past eighteen months, however, she has also been nearly blinded by a thyroid condition and temporarily crippled by a bicycle-riding accident in the Virgin Islands.

Happily, the physical and ocular disasters have not destroyed a bewildered sense of humour: 'really quite extraordinary', she said of the honour, 'especially as I had been off the stage for a year. Maybe the palace now gives awards like that for medical rather than theatrical survival.' A few months earlier, she had telephoned one of the West End producers of *Lettice & Lovage* in some amazement at the news they were to replace her with Geraldine McEwan: 'But darling,' she told the manager, 'you can't be going to have Geraldine. She's got such a funny voice.'

Apparently oblivious to the fact that her own voice has been the funniest in the business since the demise of Beatrice Lillie, Dame Maggie continues her uncertain but usually triumphant progress through a life and career which she views with an astonished kind of disbelief, as though they belonged to some altogether different human being.

Having elevated her perpetual state of worry to an art form in itself, our latest dame has achieved comparatively early in life (she was born Margaret Natalie Smith in Oxford fifty-five

13

years ago) that peculiarly English type of benign but regal eccentricity which a grateful nation used to applaud in such earlier theatrical dames as Thorndike and Evans only when they had reached their middle seventies. But there is ice and steel here too: within days of her arrival on Broadway for the currently sold-out run, Smith made it clear to her American management that they had chosen the wrong New York theatre, the wrong leading man and the wrong stage cat. The leading man (Roderick Cook) left abruptly in rehearsal, the theatre remains standing, but the cat is still fighting for its stage life having been roundly abused by Smith at the awards ceremony for overacting.

Smith is now so secure a phenomenon on Broadway that it is surprising to recall that it was as recently as the end of 1988 that her round of troubles started. She had just completed a long and triumphant West End run in *Lettice & Lovage* when she and her husband, the playwright Beverley Cross, went with their friend Joan Plowright, Lady Olivier, for a holiday in the Virgin Islands.

'Joannie had to leave before us, so Beverley and I bicycled along the cliffs to wave her boat goodbye. I'd forgotten that American bicycles have their brakes on the pedals, so the next thing I knew I was flying over a cliff into a huge cactus. Some passing tourists were very kind: one asked me when I was supposed to be opening on Broadway, another had liked *Jean Brodie*, and the third got me into a nearby hospital where it became immediately clear even to me that I wasn't going to be opening on Broadway for some considerable time. Then, when I got back to England for treatment on my back and shoulder, I began to develop a quite separate thyroid condition, so for a while I was touring doctors' offices in Harley Street looking like a blind hunchback. All in all, I was jolly glad to see the end of the Eighties.'

But even in crisis, Smith remains the most resolutely down-to-earth actress I know, with the possible exception of Katharine Hepburn, who once told me, in all seriousness, that the reason she had refused to quit MGM during the worst

14

of her studio years in the Thirties was that 'when one had to change trains in Chicago, one found one always needed the man from Metro to deal with the baggage'. A porter might have been the better career option, but Hepburn, like Smith, always regarded the actual planning of her career as about as unnecessary as the planning of an earthquake, or any other act of God.

Smith may well be the most stylish and accomplished light comedienne of her generation, but she is also a player queen capable of sudden and breathtaking forays into the classics, and one who takes the resolute view that acting is something to be done rather than discussed.

Peter Shaffer, who first wrote two short plays for her back in 1962 (*The Private Ear* and *The Public Eye*) and then returned a quarter-century later with *Lettice & Lovage*, reckons that 'she is quite simply unique, a sort of national treasure', and the crucial importance of preserving national treasures, however inconvenient, gothic, baroque or idiosyncratic they may prove to be, is precisely what his latest script is all about.

But as she emerges, blinking myopically, into the glare of the Broadway lights, the American press is discovering to its amazement that Smith grants interviews with all the frequency of the late Greta Garbo. It is not that she has anything especially intriguing or scandalous to hide in her private life: true, she is married to the writer who was her first Oxford love, and has only lately achieved domestic stability after a once-golden marriage to Robert Stephens went spectacularly wrong, at about the same time as their joint careers, back in the middle Seventies. But friends and colleagues are bidden on pain of instant excommunication not to chat about her to the media, largely because she considers the intrusion of journalists to be about as acceptable as having a motorway driven through her bathroom. It is simply a matter of personal privacy, and the belief that acting for stage or screen is enough of an effort and an end in itself, without the crucifying need to discuss it on talk shows.

15

'I watch all those actresses banging on about themselves and their traumas on television, and I'm always somehow amazed at the way they can keep talking without getting overcome by the boredom and pointlessness of it all. I mean, who cares why people want to act or have to act: why don't they just get on and do it? People in other careers don't keep stopping to tell you all about why they started or what makes them do it, they just press on regardless. I rather like that.'

Though not, therefore, the easiest or most willing of interviewees, Smith has occasional insights into her own elusive art which are worth an hour or two of more traditional backstage chatter and self-analysis: 'I seldom go to see other actresses in plays,' she once told me, 'because it always seems rather like trespassing.' On another occasion I asked what she most hated about acting, apart from having to do it every night: 'The way it ends so totally, with nothing to put on the wall or in the bookcase. Just a lot of yesterdays, and then you have to start out all over again.'

She started out at the Oxford High School for Girls: the daughter of a local pathologist, she progressed through the backs of crowds in end-of-term plays ('a pinhead I was, all eyes and teeth and average at everything') to local college productions, one of which took her to an early Edinburgh Festival and thence to a small cabaret theatre at the back of Leicester Square, where she was spotted by an American revue producer called Leonard Sillman.

As a result of that, Maggie Smith made her Broadway début as one of the *New Faces of 1956*: 'That was all very bizarre, and frankly terrifying. I'd been hired as a singer–comedienne, but as soon as I arrived in New York they made the discovery that I wasn't all that funny and couldn't sing at all. So I finished up just introducing all the other people in the show and crying a lot in lifts, because I didn't know anybody in New York until Julie Andrews came over to do *My Fair Lady* and started being jolly kind to me.'

Career details after that are best obtained from the reference books rather than the dame herself ('one went to school,

16

one wanted to act, one started to act and one is still acting' rates as one of her more detailed autobiographical summaries to date), but life on Broadway must have improved somewhat during *New Faces* because she considered making a life there, until the offer came along of another London revue for which she returned home to join Kenneth Williams in *Share my Lettuce*. Returning home has never been that easy for her: once, when she got back from long classical years at Stratford, Ontario, I asked her what had most changed in her absence and was treated to a memorable thirty minutes on how garage owners now insisted on locking themselves up with their cash registers, instead of standing by their pumps, where they might prove more useful to passing motorists in distress.

In her revue years with *Share my Lettuce*, there were moments when she seemed almost to become Kenneth Williams too, echoing that high-camp voice of a Lady Bracknell and apparently challenging him for the West End grotesque-of-the-week award. But it soon became clear that she had something altogether more classical in mind, and after a run of Shaftesbury Avenue comedies she was among the first to join Olivier's National Theatre in 1964. It was there, coming on stage in Noël Coward's own revival of his comedy of appalling country-house-party manners *Hay Fever* to announce 'this haddock is disgusting', that she carved out a moment in high comedy which many with better lines have failed to equal. The line now haunts her in the way that Lady Bracknell's handbag was always to haunt Dame Edith Evans.

It was Alan Brien, reviewing Smith in a less-than-wonderful comedy about venereal disease called *Snap*, who may well have come closest to the truth of her high-comic timing. 'All those knees and elbows and pointed toes, like an umbrella in a thunderstorm, or a sleepwalking bat, or a spider escaping from treacle, keep us continually watching her in a spirit of incredulous delight. She seems forever enmeshed and tangled in her own clothes and in her own ideas, blinded by her hat, struck dumb in mid-sentence, falling over her own

17

ankles, colliding with her own syntax. Hers is an extended music-hall act, a unique circus turn.'

But there has always also been, at the heart of her work, an essential chilliness; and even her Desdemona to Olivier's Othello managed to suggest that in only slightly different circumstances it could well have been she who strangled him. During the rehearsals, Olivier had once been unwise enough to criticize her apparently insufficiently rounded vowels. Waiting until he had laboriously covered himself in total body-paint for the evening performance, Smith put her head around his neighbouring dressing-room door at the Old Vic to enunciate, all too perfectly, 'How now, brown cow.'

Until now, Smith's Broadway career has been a less than raging success: ten years elapsed after *New Faces* before she returned with *Private Lives*, which had already gone dangerously over the edge into self-parody, and then ten more before a curious flop with Tom Stoppard's *Night & Day* which, Smith reckons, foundered on the failure of a New York audience to grasp the deep, spiritual, English significance of Cash's name tapes to a school mother.

Now, however, she is back in triumph, with a comedy about conservation being performed amid the bomb-site ruins of what once was a thriving Broadway theatre district.

'Noël Coward once told me it was no good just being a hit in New York, you have to be a smash hit, and luckily we seem to be just that. But what this last year of trekking around hospitals and doctors has taught me is that it's no use trying to plan anything very much, apart from whatever it is that you happen to be doing at the time. You just have to take what comes, and avoid the depression that starts whenever you suddenly think that you might not be able to work again. I've been through a very black tunnel lately, and when you come out on the other side into the lights of New York, you are bound to have to blink a bit. Also, Lettice is the most exhausting character to play: once she starts talking she never shuts up, and she demands more energy than any Shakespearean King.'

Precious few high-comedy actresses this century have achieved what the late Kenneth Tynan used to define and celebrate as high-definition performance, which is another reason why, to see Smith whole, you have to see her on stage. Somehow the camera, whether film or television, seems to back away from her as if afraid that fuses could get blown. Besides which, she has never been too good with technology of any kind; during her first BBC radio audition she almost set fire to Broadcasting House:

'I was smoking away nervously, put my cigarette down on a piano, and then while I was at the microphone out of the corner of my eye I saw it roll on to the felt floor and soon there was an awful lot of smoke everywhere, so I thought I'd better just leave the building quietly and I haven't been back much since.

'As a result, I seem to do lamentably few plays by living dramatists: indeed my husband never ceases to amaze me by being a living dramatist, like Shaffer. Somehow I always expect them to be dead, like Shakespeare. It leads to a lot less trouble in rehearsal if they have the grace to be deceased.

'But even in the classics, the trouble for an actress is that there's no glissando, just one appalling leap from Juliet into Lady Macbeth and then the grotesques: I somehow don't see myself as Dame Maggie, battling valiantly on into my nineties as old crones, but on the other hand there's really nothing else I have ever wanted or been able to do. The problem is that nobody in the London theatre seems to be in charge of anything any more, just a lot of little groups all carrying on as best they can. I suppose I was very lucky to have Olivier at the National and Robin Phillips at Stratford Ontario for years telling me what I should be playing next. I can never think of a part for myself unless someone just tells me to go ahead and do it and stop worrying. In fact, of course, one never stops worrying, but at least when you are in rehearsal you know what it is you are actually worrying about, and I do find that such a relief.'

14 July 1990

19

If the cello had eyes

Richard Morrison

The same old story: British yobs behaved abominably again. A national occasion ruined by the mindless few. Coins thrown at the players. Toilet rolls, too, or 'streamers of excessive width' as they were delicately described at the time. Disgraceful scenes had jeopardized Britain's international standing. 'Hooliganism was rather too evident,' thundered *The Times*. 'High-spirited gratitude must not be confused with sheer bad manners.'

That was the Last Night of the Proms – forty years ago. Throughout the starchy Fifties, prim guardians of the nation's morals complained that the country's most celebrated music festival – the summer-long season of Henry Wood Promenade Concerts – degenerated on its last evening into a chaotic shambles of singing, cheering and ad libs from all corners of the Albert Hall.

Why were these banner-waving, foot-stamping youths not doing their national service? How dare the BBC allow them to react noisily all over that sanctum of middle-aged sobriety: the classical music concert?

Some people blamed the chief conductor of the day, Sir Malcolm Sargent. With his carnation and charisma both in full bloom, and his speeches full of impeccably manicured witticisms, Sargent revelled in being at the centre of classical music's most famous stage. He may not have been too wonderful a conductor (when Karajan came along, Beecham dubbed him 'a kind of musical Malcolm Sargent') but he knew how to milk an audience. Orchestral players, who take an extremely sardonic view of conductors with pretensions, called him 'Flash Harry'.

All very different from the man who founded the Proms in 1895, and conducted them for fifty years: Henry Wood. Orchestral players called *him* 'Old Timber'. Solid chap, Sir Henry, and considerate with it. Knowing that brass players had a habit of nipping out for liquid refreshment in items that did not involve them, he had an alarm bell installed in the nearest pub, operated by a buzzer on his stand.

Suddenly, in the early Sixties, people stopped fretting about how unruly the Last Night was becoming. It became clear that television audiences abroad regarded the whole eccentric spectacle as a treasurable demonstration of British whimsicality.

But then the thinking classes started to worry about the nationalistic side of it all: those people waving Union Jacks; those squirmingly jingoistic words, 'make me mightier still', 'We shall build Jerusalem', 'Britannia, rule the waves'; those Elgar and Parry harmonies, as solid and reassuring as a Victorian nanny. Was it not all a touch imperialist?

During the late Sixties, even some of the conductors began to have doubts. The sensitive and not at all flashy Colin Davis, who succeeded Sargent as the BBC Symphony Orchestra's conductor, described 'Land of Hope and Glory' as 'smacking a bit of Earl Haigery and sending millions to the slaughter'. In 1969, the BBC management, catching the *Zeitgeist* of 1968 only twelve months after the rest of the world, removed Elgar's *Pomp and Circumstance* March No 1 from the last-night programme on ideological grounds. Such was the ensuing row that the BBC allowed it to be played anyway, but as an encore.

Since those heady, revolutionary days, the Last Night has been left more or less untouched. So on September 15 this year seven thousand pairs of lungs, many belonging to people wearing funny hats and clutching balloons, will hurl out 'Land of Hope and Glory'. They will do it not because they are all rampant nationalists, but because roaring a tune at the top of your voice, and still not hearing yourself, is one of the finest physical thrills known to mankind. (We music lovers lead sheltered lives.)

The real trouble with the Last Night of the Proms, however, is that it bears almost no resemblance to the preceding 65 nights. Many of the students packed in the arena on the Last Night will have been coming to the Albert Hall every evening for the previous eight weeks, not to shout but to stand as still as statues, sometimes in a swelteringly hot and, let us be frank, unfragrant atmosphere. During that time, they will have absorbed music like blotting paper absorbs ink: Beethoven's symphonies and medieval masses; electronic plinks and plonks; steel bands and Wagner operas; plump tenors and intense pianists; classics and first performances, some of which may also be last performances.

This is the greatest crash course in music ever devised, and all for £2.50 a night – or £2 if punters forgo all visual contact with the performers and clamber high into the Albert Hall's gallery. First, however, they must endure The Queue.

Some can tell what is on the Prom programme any night by noting, at around 6.30pm, the end of the queue. If it has scarcely straggled down the steps towards the Royal College of Music, the programme probably includes daunting chunks of contemporary Danish organ music. If it stretches along Prince Consort Road, some romantic symphony is to be played by a decent orchestra. With a top-ranked soloist as well, the tail of the queue will be round the corner in Queen's Gate. On some occasions, a shady-looking gent will probably approach with an offer to sell a pair of £20 seats for £80. Refuse disdainfully. What makes the Proms unique among concert series is that the patron who pays least money – the promenader – gets the finest position in the house.

Well, there is something else as well. Great performers are great performers because, over and above their natural talent, they have almost a superhuman commitment to their art. When they come to the Proms, they look out at that sea of expectant, eager faces, belonging to teenagers who have queued outside for hours to be standing where they now stand. The performers know that they have finally found an audience whose commitment to music matches their own.

When the leading American orchestras come to the Proms, even their tough, long-serving senior players cannot but gawp open-mouthed as they come on to the platform. Admittedly, the average age of the audience at a symphony concert in Philadelphia or Chicago is about 109. But it is more than the youth of the Proms audience that startles them.

There is, for instance, the Brits' weird and wacky sense of humour: the time-honoured shouts of 'heave-ho' when the piano lid is raised; the way that the audience sings a coarse A flat, when the orchestra is trying to tune to a natural. Then, most importantly, there is the utter stillness during the performance itself: no fidgeting, no whispering, definitely no whoopee cushions. And finally, there is the roar of acclaim, such as lesser audiences reserve for footballers or rock stars.

That atmosphere seems to nurture high drama. By macabre coincidence, on the same day Soviet tanks rolled into Prague, the USSR State Symphony Orchestra was playing at the Proms. The tension and the tempers were snapping like high-voltage cables in a storm. BBC television news focused cameras and powerful lights on the audience – an open invitation to interrupt the music. Yevgeny Svetlanov, the conductor, refused to start until they were removed. They were.

A further grotesque irony emerged. The Russians were playing Czech music: Dvořák's Cello Concerto. You've stamped all over the Czech capital and Czech freedom, we thought; now you are about to maul Czech culture as well.

Nothing could be further from what happened. The soloist that night was Mstislav Rostropovich, friend of the dissident scientist Sakharov, public protector of the proscribed Solzhenitsyn, and himself destined to flee his homeland six years later. He played the cello concerto as the world's finest preacher might speak at the world's saddest funeral. If his cello had eyes, they would have wept.

Other memories are less traumatic. In 1970, the arena

suddenly filled up with hippies and strange aromas for the first appearance at the Proms by a pop group ('The Soft Machine' – RIP).

Will the Proms continue forever the way they are? Certainly not. Musicians can tell when spring has arrived, not by listening out for cuckoos but by watching the uproar when the BBC announces its new Proms season, and vested interests denounce its latest aberration or omission.

People have been walking out of new music at the Proms since at least 1930. In the 1960s, there were rows about foreigners conducting at the Proms (bizarrely, none had done so until 1962). Later that decade, the BBC was under fire for the amount of Stockhausen and Boulez inflicted on the faithful. Yet in the arena they lapped it up.

In 1980 the musicians' strike threatened to scuttle an entire Proms season – something the Blitz had never achieved. The season eventually started in mid-August. Robert Ponsonby, then the BBC's controller of music, once remarked wearily: 'I have sometimes thought that I should like to run the world's *smallest* music festival.'

14 July 1990

Incitement to covetousness

John Julius Norwich

The magic begins before you even get there, with the first sight of W. H. Playfair's cool, honey-coloured Ionic portico, low and unassertive but quietly distinguished amid the rich greenery of Princes Street gardens: the Royal Scottish Academy facing it like its own Doric reflection, the castle and its ramparts towering up behind. The prospect is quintessential Edinburgh – and more than enough to provide that *frisson* of expectation that I remember on my very first visit to the National Gallery of Scotland. It has never failed me since.

Once I am through the entrance door, expectation gives way to exhilaration – prompting, every time, the inevitable question: though all great galleries lift the spirit, why is this one more enjoyable than any other? There are, I think, three reasons. First, it is conceived on a human scale. To enter the Louvre, or the Kunsthistorisches Museum in Vienna – or, heaven knows, the Hermitage – is to be set adrift in a vast ocean of genius in which we are made to feel very insignificant indeed. We may – we must – restrict ourselves to just a few rooms, but that only arouses an uncomfortable feeling that we are missing some masterpiece just beyond the point at which we stop. The National Gallery of Scotland, by contrast, seems to have been made to measure: big enough to satisfy, but never to satiate. We leave it after a couple of hours knowing that we have seen, not just a quantity of pictures, but a *collection*: something that we can conceive as a single entity, of which the building in which it is housed plays an integral part.

Which brings me to the second reason. Just as a painting needs a frame, so a collection of paintings needs a setting worthy of it; and no gallery on earth provides a better one. The recent spectacular redecoration, completed only a year ago, swept away the sanitized, post-Festival-of-Britain decor that had for the past twenty years drained the gallery of all its life and colour, and set about restoring Playfair's magnificent rooms to an approximation of their original appearance when the building was first opened in 1859. Fortunately there exists a charming watercolour painted only a decade or so later (and now displayed in the gallery) showing claret-coloured walls, Dutch weave grey-green carpet, geranium-red pedestals for the sculptures and grained oak cornices and skirtings – precisely the scheme ordained by David Ramsay Hay, a protégé of Sir Walter Scott, for whom he decorated Abbotsford. All these features have been brought back, and the result is a triumph: warm and rich and sumptuous, showing off to perfection some of the loveliest pictures in the world.

As for those pictures themselves, they are set neither in a single line as in recent years nor in the wall-to-wall, carpet-to-cornice jigsaw style so inexplicably favoured in the high Victorian age, but in the classical and infinitely more civilized manner of the eighteenth century: frequently two deep, with those designed for over doors hung accordingly and large full-length portraits at the above-the-chimneypiece height for which most of them were originally intended. Below them, the general atmosphere of opulence is increased by occasional pieces of superb furniture together with pedestalled busts and other assorted sculpture, all relating in style and date to the paintings that they set off to such advantage. In the central interstices between the octagonal galleries have been set two smaller ones, mysterious and sombre like shrines, their walls dark brown with flashes of gilding, their floors laid in shining polychrome marble. One is devoted to Poussin's great series depicting the Seven Sacraments; the other, more secular, takes the form of a tiny princely *Schatzkammer* containing – among other treasures – two small Rembrandts, a glorious Rubens sketch of Jacob and Esau, and an *Interior with a Young Violinist* by Gerrit Dou for which I would willingly commit murder.

And so to reason number three. I have always judged pictures by the degree to which they arouse not my admiration but my covetousness; and again and again in Edinburgh I find it almost impossible to keep my hands to myself. If that mad, astronomically rich collector that we are always reading about really exists, forever gloating over his secret hoard of stolen but unsaleable treasures, I can only say that I see his point entirely. Given the money, I find myself musing, would I not follow his example? Wall space might admittedly be something of a problem; but even without it, that little Corot of Ville d'Avray would be a considerable improvement on Aunt Florence's watercolour of Tintern Abbey – and anyway, wouldn't that Velazquez of the *Old Woman Cooking Eggs* just fit in over the mantelpiece? In most collections, such thoughts are inspired by perhaps half the pictures; in Edinburgh, I long for the lot – even if the largest canvas in Scotland, Benjamin West's tersely entitled *Alexander III, King of Scots, Saved from the Fury of a Stag by the Intrepid Intervention of Colin Fitzgerald*, does have to go into the garage.

If I were allowed to select only a few favourites, which would they be? High on the list would be Titian's *Three Ages of Man*, Bernardo Bellotto's view of the Ponte delle Navi in Verona and Baron François Gérard's portrait of *Madame Mère*, sitting beneath the bust of her son Napoleon with a worried look in her eyes; and I should probably also have to demand Reynolds's wondrous triple portrait of *The Ladies Waldegrave* – painted for their great-uncle, Horace Walpole – and Gainsborough's oddly suspicious-looking *The Hon. Mrs Graham*. Throw in Raeburn's *Colonel Alastair Macdonell of Glengarry* and the Van Dyck sketch of the baby daughters of Charles I and I shall be more than satisfied.

So far, at least, as the ground floor is concerned; but the ground floor is not all. Though most of it rises the full height of the building, at the two ends the ceilings are lowered to allow for additional upstairs hanging space; and this we ignore at our peril. Room A1, at the north end over the entrance hall, contains all the gallery's pictures dating from between around 1300 and 1527: roughly speaking, from Giotto to the death of Raphael and the sack of Rome. Here, against hangings of green brocade, we find Quentin Matsys's haunting *Portrait of a Man* (unaccountably awarded a rose, cross and halo in the eighteenth century), Holbein's astonishing *Allegory of the Old and New Testaments*, Raphael's *Holy Family with Palm Tree* and the lovely *Madonna and Child* that is attributed to Verrocchio and once belonged to Ruskin. Stunners, all of them, but my mind is made up. Thank you: Gerard David's three enchanting predella panels showing *Three Episodes from the Life of St Nicholas* will do very nicely.

At the south end, another staircase – and the staircases, incidentally, are small *tours de force* in themselves, adorned with groups of eighteenth-century plaster busts from the antique that had been in store for a century until they were disinterred a couple of years ago – leads up to five more small rooms dating from 1971–2, each hung in a different colour, in which smaller pictures from 1710 onwards are arranged not by schools but chronologically. Here is Boucher's dazzling portrayal of Madame de Pompadour and – everybody's favourite Christmas card – Raeburn's *The Rev. Robert Walker, Skating on Duddingston Loch*; here too are Canaletto and Guardi, Corot and Courbet, Bonnington and Boudin, Gauguin and Van Gogh.

Yet we are left in no real doubt as to the star of the upstairs show; for there in the centre of the end wall, dominating the whole enfilade, is the portrait of *Lady Agnew of Lochnaw* by John Singer Sargent – a work of such style, elegance and sheer panache as effortlessly to earn the artist a place in that pantheon where Reynolds and Van Dyck are of the company.

On my last visit, with Lady Agnew acting on me like a tonic, I was ready to descend to the new wing – in fact a subterranean extension to the east – in which a suite of eight rooms is exclusively devoted to Scottish art. Alas, it was closed, doubtless for rehanging – a misfortune on which I instinctively seized as a splendid excuse to return as soon as possible. But who needs an excuse? Great galleries need no justification to visit them; and the National Gallery of Scotland is a very great gallery indeed.

21 July 1990

Forget gender,
the play's the thing

Benedict Nightingale

The play *Earwig*, just arrived at the RSC's Pit, concerns a team of dramatists uneasily collaborating on an upmarket television series. It also shows us extracts from that series, which involves a serious writer impelled by debt to write soap operas surreptitiously. Then we see snippets from one of those soaps; it turns out to combine *Neighbours* at its flimsiest with *Coronation Street* at its folksiest.

So what is new? We should now be used both to multi-layered plays and to plays attacking the mass media. Yet only recently *Earwig* would have been impossible. It is not just that its author is a woman, Paula Milne. It is that its most impressive characters, in both the play and the play-within-the-play, are women dramatists, too. Moreover, they end the evening by deciding that the place for a creative talent is not television but the stage.

Ten years ago that would have been akin to a cat expecting a warm reception in Battersea Dogs' Home. The encyclopedia *Contemporary Dramatists*, published in 1977, contains essays on 135 British and Irish playwrights, only 13 of them women. Of the 250 plays presented between 1956 and 1975 at that epicentre of new drama, the Royal Court, barely a dozen were by women.

Nor was that anything new. A few women playwrights emerged after the Restoration, prime among them Nell Gwyn's redoubtable friend, Aphra Behn. There was a brief blossoming of female talent in the Edwardian era, though nobody now remembers Githa Sowerby or Elizabeth Baker, author of a case study of suburban tedium called *Chains*. But overall, the contribution made by women to the history of drama has been not so much thin as anorexic. In 1982, the feminist critic Michelene Wandor could only mourn 'the fact that a theatrical tradition of "great" writers does not have a single woman in it'.

How things have changed. Women dramatists, if not yet in the majority, are at last arriving in impressive numbers. They contributed 16 of the 49 plays presented at the Royal Court in the past three years. More and more names seem worth including in the encyclopedias and anthologies: Pam Gems, Julia Kearsley, Timberlake Wertenbaker, Sue Townsend, Ann Devlin, Charlotte Keatley, Clare McIntyre, Christina Reid, Shirley Gee. And, in Caryl Churchill, the sex has a dramatist well on her way to winning Wandor's critical gong, 'great'. Witness her *Top Girls*, her *Fen*, and the marvellous play about revolution in Romania whose run at the Embassy Studios is just ending, *Mad Forest*.

Why did women writers, so dominant in the novel, stay clear of the theatre for so long? Why have they now belatedly arrived at the continuing feast, and what dramatic victuals have they brought for the diners to consume?

Enter the feminist critic, her answers naturally depending on her ideological hue. Sue-Ellen Case, American author of *Feminism and Theatre*, would pre-empt the discussion by disputing its premises. For her, only male bias explains why we honour the woman-hating Aeschylus as the founder of drama instead of Hrotsvita, a tenth-century nun who wrote six brief plays on Christian themes. The history of drama, she thinks, consists of a few unfairly forgotten female writers, and hordes of men balefully propagating false images of women. Didn't that over-rated Shakespeare show 'powerful misogyny' by casting a male as Lady Macbeth and letting him cry 'Unsex me here'?

But there are cooler voices among the ranks of both the 'radicals' and 'materialist feminists'. Roughly, the first group thinks women are different from men and probably better, since they are more sensitive, intuitive, caring and peaceful.

31

The materialists believe women are essentially the same as men, but are browbeaten into thinking and behaving differently. Both camps would claim the sex has long been exploited by the 'patriarchy'.

Materialists would argue that the theatre has always been controlled by men, and for much of its history, exclusively peopled by them, too. Women dramatists would have felt they were invading an ancient club whose leather chairs bore the dents of generations of male buttocks.

Writing a novel is a private activity, getting a play produced a more public and collaborative one. Women playwrights would have been sucked into a sweaty male world of disputes, telegrams, anger and a reputation for unsavoury morals. A woman dramatist needed to be a bruiser, yet also risked being called a whore, as Aphra Behn frequently was. No wonder they were not exactly in abundant supply.

To this 'materialist' thesis, the radicals have added the idea that there is something off-puttingly masculine about most traditional dramatic forms. Sue-Ellen Case, at one of her pottier moments, argues that the pattern of tragedy is foreplay, excitation and cathartic ejaculation, a climax quite unlike the 'multi-orgasms' enjoyed by women. A more moderate view might be that for the past 150 years, most plays have been more rigidly structured and more social in their themes than most novels. The theatre has not been the place for the emotionally intricate.

Well, well. It is true that drama has become more flexible with the decline of the 'well-made play'. Twenty years ago, it would have been hard for Caryl Churchill to write either *Cloud Nine*, in which men and women swap roles by way of demonstrating the complexities of gender, or *Top Girls*, which opens with a surreal party whose guests include Pope Joan and Chaucer's patient Griselda. Yet Churchill, like other women, has written more conventionally. And was Chekhov, a man, crasser and cruder than Clemence Dane, Dodie Smith, or Lillian Hellman, women all?

Actually, Hellman herself saw no problem. 'I don't write

with my genitals,' she said, with her usual bluntness. Yet her example seems instructive. It was becoming a bit easier for women to battle their way to success in the Thirties and Forties, but they still needed to be pretty thick-skinned. It took another three decades for women more generally to acquire the confidence necessary not merely to compete in the theatrical marketplace, but to find the drama itself compatible. The American dramatist, Marsha Norman, says that playwrights have to understand and control men and women in action and conflict, and only recently has women's self-image begun to tally with that job description.

Men cannot fairly be accused of reducing all their women characters to (in Case's words) 'merchandise in a world of male exchange' or 'cultural courtesans'. Nevertheless, it is hard for them fully to identify with the opposite sex. Now, at last, audiences are getting a sense of how some of the silent 51 per cent feel about themselves – and about men.

True, there have been inevitable excrescences as the more self-conscious pioneers have tested their ideological muscles. Americans have had to tolerate a lot of stuff like Cappy Cotz's *In Search of the Hammer*, in which witches steal magic ironmongery from the wicked Reagan and imbue it with 'the power of the matriarchy'. I winced at a feminist play called *Mama's Gone A-Hunting*, which showed Mozart's kid sister elegantly improvising the Fortieth Symphony only to be elbowed aside by that incompetent plagiarist, beastly Wolfgang. Sarah Daniels's work has been seen at major theatres, but those who refuse to see men solely as pornographers, rapists and women-loathing sadists may feel it owes more to wishful paranoia than observation.

Yet we have only to compare this with the best of Gems, Wertenbaker, Devlin or Churchill, to see how unrepresentative it is. Not that their work lacks punch when it ponders the implications of belonging to the less powerful sex. A man could not tell us what Andrea Dunbar's *Arbor* and *Shirley* show: how it is to be young, poor and female in our rougher cities. Nor could he communicate the special sense of threat of Gilly Fraser's *I Can Give You A Good Time* or Julia Kearsley's *Waiting*, both set in Yorkshire Ripper territory. Nor could he talk as authoritatively about a woman's sexual awakening as Sharman Macdonald's *When I Was a Girl*, nor create the feelings of camaraderie which permeate Clare McIntyre's *Low Level Panic*, or Nell Dunn's *Steaming*, with its embattled women in their endangered public baths.

Nor could even the great O'Casey have come up with quite the slant on Irish agonies Ann Devlin achieved in her marvellous *Ourselves Alone*. Who, she asked, is suffering most among the Catholics of Ulster? The women, of course, and not so much from British soldiers as from the despotism of their own men. She even dared drop the suggestion that the wife of the 'martyr' Bobby Sands was so terrified of his violence that she felt safe only when he was dead.

After all, why should women playwrights have to concentrate on women's problems? When they begin to write about each and every aspect of life, they can be said definitively to have arrived; and that does seem to be happening.

The best plays transcend gender – and, in any case, *what is* gender? There is something superficial about categorizing the great dramatists, those capable of creating a Medea or a Cleopatra or a Phèdre, straightforwardly as male or female. When they wrote, Euripides, Shakespeare and Racine were *men and women*, a mix of understanding and intuition, mind and feeling. There is no reason why women dramatists should not penetrate as fully beneath the human skin.

21 July 1990

34

Times chess man cracks 'missing woman' riddle

Raymond Keene

I was contacted at the end of last week by Detective Superintendent Roy Fletcher of the Lancashire constabulary with the most bizarre request I had ever encountered. Superintendent Fletcher had arrested a man, a computer expert from Seaford, East Sussex, who was suspected not only of having defrauded his girlfriend of her substantial life savings amounting to £27,000 but also of having disposed of her body sometime in January this year at an unknown location in southern Ireland. The suspect refused to indicate to the police where the body was concealed, although he did admit freely to having buried the woman. The only clue he would give the constabulary to the victim's whereabouts was, as Superintendent Fletcher put it to me, a chess diagram and a sequence of chess moves. Superintendent Fletcher knew of me through my chess contributions to *The Times* and asked if I would help to crack the deadly code. I asked him to fax the chess diagram and the moves, which he promptly did.

I had expected that a conventional chess diagram with recognizable chess moves would probably represent the co-ordinates of some point on a map and that the chess pieces in the diagram would stand for the players in this legal endgame. What came through on the fax lines did not justify my initial optimism. It consisted of two pages, one with a crudely drawn map entitled 'Area for Game', while the other page consisted mainly of a very obscure series of unconventional chess moves with the heading 'Timescale for Game'. Initially, these two sheets made about as much sense to me as if they had been written in Babylonian cuneiform. The 'Area for Game' sheet consisted of three amorphous anonymous blobs (one of which had even been crossed out) which could have represented anything, from a pond, a lake or a farm or an estate to a country. The sole connection with chess, apart from the title, was the word 'Black' scrawled in the left hand corner. The other page was almost as bad. References to a black king, queen and pawn and a white king and pawns were again the sole chess connection immediately apparent.

I was beginning to think that it was going to be insoluble, but at this point I drew heart from my recollection of a Sherlock Holmes story, 'The Dancing Men', in which Holmes breaks a singularly barbaric and recondite code which utilizes little figures of dancing men. This case was redolent of that fictional forerunner. Confronted with the dancing men Holmes said: 'These hieroglyphics have evidently a meaning. If it is a purely arbitrary one, it may be impossible for us to solve it. If, on the other hand, it is systematic, I have no doubt that we shall get to the bottom of it.' These words acted as an inspiration.

There appeared to be yet one more literary reference, whether by accident or design, in this curious conundrum. Looking at the sequence of moves, all of them above the line across the centre of the page appeared to be made by black. As is well known, in chess black and white, the two opposing

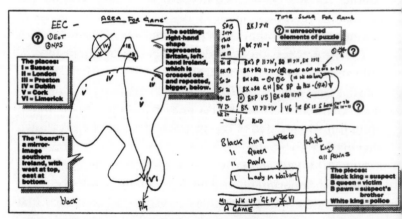

The 'board' and moves supplied to the Lancashire police

forces, must move alternately. This curious monopoly of moves by one side reminded me of the chess problem at the start of Lewis Carroll's book *Alice through the Looking Glass*. In this the heroine Alice enters a looking glass world of reflections and mirror images peopled almost entirely by chess pieces. The mirror image motif is an important one, and will recur with great significance. As Lewis Carroll observed in his preface, 'the alternation of black and white is perhaps not so strictly observed . . .'

Now, fortified by literary allusions, let us look at the page 'Timescale for Game'. In the left hand column at the top we see a series of days of the week with dates attached. They start with Saturday 13 January 1990 and run through from top to bottom to Wednesday 24 January. This is the period in which the action takes place. Next, there is a reference to chess pieces. Without knowing what these pieces refer to there was no hope of further progress. I deduced that the black king should refer to the suspect, that the black queen signified the victim while the black pawn was, in all probability, the suspect's brother who, as the police had told me, had been in Ireland accompanying the duo. The game is initiated by the arrow indicating that the black king writes to the black lady-in-waiting. I deduced that the lady-in-waiting must refer to the status of the victim before the game begins, i.e. she is waiting for the game to start and once it has started she appears as the black queen. I operated on this assumption throughout the remainder of my analysis.

The next thing to establish was the identity of the white king and the white pawns. Since white opposes black in chess one has to seek a possible opponent for the suspect and it can only be the police. It is interesting to note that the suspect has chosen the black pieces for himself and that he has decided that in this case, contrary to all the rules, black will move first.

Now I looked at the game moves. In discussion of the document, Superintendent Fletcher had suggested to me that the first line opposite Saturday 13 read 'BK17V1'. On this assumption the code is uncrackable. I came to the conclusion, upon which all the rest of my work is based, that the symbol which appears to resemble a seven is in fact a vector sign indicating movement from one place to another. Treating all apparent sevens as vectors in this fashion means that we can start to read off some of the lines of moves. Thus the line opposite Saturday 13 would appear to read 'Black king moves from 1 to 6'. The next line down opposite Tuesday 16 January then reads 'Black king moves from 6 to 1'. This is all well and good, but what do the figures 1 and 6 represent? To determine this I had to shift back the focus of attention to the sheet labelled 'Area for Game', consisting of the three hideously anonymous blobs.

What if the triangular blob on the right were to represent the UK mainland while the crossed out round blob on the left were to be a crudely drawn representation of Ireland which the suspect had then rejected as inadequately detailed for his purposes of taunting the police with the conundrum of locating the victim's body? In that case the large blob which dominates the centre of the page suddenly becomes a representation of the section of southern Ireland in which the drama took place. It should be noted that the UK mainland indication is, as one would normally expect, on a north-south axis. The map of Ireland, however, has been revolved so that east is at the top and west is at the bottom. By carrying out this rotation the map begins to make sense.

Having identified the outlines as countries, the numbers now fit neatly into place. We know that the suspect lived in East Sussex, that the victim lived in Preston and that Dublin, Cork and Limerick figured in their journey. I now deduced that I on the 'Area for Game' page represents Seaford, II represents London, III is Preston, IV is Dublin, V is Cork and VI is Limerick.

Why are there on the map two IVs and two Vs? As is well known, there is only one Dublin in Ireland and only one Cork. I attacked this problem by treating the map of Ireland as a chessboard. The line drawn from London to Limerick in this case not only acts as the trajectory of a journey but also as a dividing line between the two halves of a chessboard which are mirror images of each other. In modern chess notation, the algebraic variety as used in *The Times*, a grid reference system gives one name only to each square of the total of 64, be it a1, c4, e5, g8 or whatever. In the old-fashioned descriptive chess notation, which *The Times* abandoned in 1986, each square had two names, depending on which side of the board one was situated. There were two King Five squares, there were two Queen Four squares and so on. It seemed to me therefore that the suspect had taken a large section of the map of Ireland and reduced it to a chessboard with black playing on the left adopting the principles of the old descriptive notation.

Armed with this information I now tried to decipher the game. The game proper starts after Wednesday 17 January when a black line is drawn across the page. The arrow pointing upwards above that indicates a preparatory phase for the game when the suspect may even have travelled to Limerick, or arranged for someone to do so on his behalf, indicating premeditation of the dark events which were to follow.

Thursday 18 January: Suspect's brother travels from London to Dublin, victim travels from Preston to London, suspect travels from Seaford to London.

Friday 19 January: Suspect and victim travel from London to Dublin (victim makes a telephone call to say 'we are in Dublin').

Saturday 20 January: Suspect and victim use victim's credit card both to obtain cash and in some way to enable them to hire a car. I identified circles as indicating some sort of financial transaction while V appeared to relate to a credit card transaction. The police later confirmed that there were six Visa card transactions during this period. I believe the C referred to the hiring of a car.

Sunday 21 January: The suspect and his brother inflict grievous harm (GH) on the victim. The words 'do this' seem particularly sinister in this context. The brackets with V34 indicate two further uses of the Visa credit card to obtain cash.

Monday 22 January: Suspect and brother use Visa card for the fifth time to obtain cash. Suspect and victim (who may by now be dead) travel to Limerick or its environs.

Tuesday 23 January: The suspect returns to Dublin and uses the Visa credit card for the sixth time. The suspect considers himself safe or successful. The hired car is sent back and the suspect and his brother return from Dublin to London.

Wednesday 24 January: The macabre game is at an end.

What has white been doing all the time? 'Move 1, white king and white pawns search back and forth between Dublin and Limerick.' This confirms the suspect's dismissive attitude towards the British police and the Irish Garda as he sees them fruitlessly thrashing around between the two conurbations.

Where does this place us in locating the body? It is my firm belief that the body is located at HG some miles probably to the north-west of Limerick. The initials HG are a grotesque mirror image reflection of GH grievous harm on Sunday 21 January. They may also refer to a small isolated location, such as a farm, bog or even landmark with such initials. There is also an indication so simple it can be overlooked, namely 'her grave'. Finally, Superintendent Fletcher tells me that both suspect and victim are devout Catholics, so in this sense HG may refer to 'hallowed ground'. If the suspect's psychology is as I read it, his bizarre sense of humour and sense of intellectual superiority may well have led him to inter his victim at night in the grounds of a local church.

Superintendent Fletcher seemed delighted with the advances made over the weekend and armed with this new information his men should receive a fresh boost in their morale. I am reminded of one more Sherlock Holmes story 'The Retired Colourman' in which the great man says 'Amberley excelled at chess – one mark, Watson of a scheming mind.' I hope in this case that the schemes of the suspect will be duly frustrated. *23 July 1990*

Shadows of the pyramid peak

Ronald Faux

Zermatt in the Swiss Valais is dominated and made rich by a mountain. The Matterhorn overshadows the town, infiltrating every corner of life, luring tourists who arrive on the rattle-track railway that clatters up the Mattertal from Brig.

The mountain's formidable pyramid shape, made famous on generations of tin lids, greetings cards and chocolate wrappers, has become as famous as the man-made pyramids of Egypt. Even when the Matterhorn's dark tilted head and razor ridges are obscured, its presence may be just as evident as the clouds break up and boil against the great north and east faces, or stream in plumes from the 14,691 ft summit.

The notoriety of this daunting peak lies not just in its impregnable appearance but in the tragedy that marked its conquest. Zermatt recently celebrated the 125th anniversary of the first ascent of the Matterhorn. From shop windows and tourist haunts stares the sombre poster image of Edward Whymper, the British artist who became obsessed with climbing the mountain and led the first ascent.

On 14 July, 1865, Whymper, with a party of English alpinists and their guides, reached the summit. It was the great moment in what had become the golden age of alpinism, but it was overshadowed by what happened on the descent.

Roped together and scrambling down the steep rocks overlooking the huge north face of the mountain, Douglas Hadow, the least experienced member of the party, slipped, and the others were dragged after him.

Lord Francis Douglas, the Rev Charles Hudson, Hadow and the Swiss guide, Michel Croz, fell 4000 ft and perished, but the rope linking them to the rest of the party broke, saving the others' lives. Whymper and two local guides, the Taugwalders, father and son, survived. They watched, horrified, as their companions slid to their deaths. The accident caused a furore. Queen Victoria questioned whether alpinism should be outlawed, there were dark rumours about how the rope came to break, and Whymper's explanation in a letter to *The Times* drew such attention to the mountain that life changed irrevocably for the small community that lived in its shadow.

The Matterhorn casts a very large shadow. Sinking below the last steep stretches above the Hörnli hut at dusk, the setting sun throws a gigantic wedge of darkness into the valley 4000 ft below. The black shape advances down the Mattertal, swallowing a glacier's edge, pastures, woods and hamlets, and finally Zermatt itself.

A freezing wind rattles across the mountain's ribs. It is easy to understand the superstitious fear that Zermatt folk once had of this beetling peak, the haunt of restless bad spirits.

To modern alpinists the Matterhorn does not rank very high, although Whymper's footsteps are followed every season by thousands of visitors. They pay their guides £260 for the privilege of attempting the summit, which is marked by a huge iron cross scarred by lightning strikes.

What appears from a distance to be an indestructible fang becomes at close quarters a very rotten tooth. The east face is swept by avalanches, and the north face is dangerously exposed to stone fall when the weather is anything but perfect. The Zmutt ridge is a fine, soaring line reaching north-west above the Zmutt glacier, but it is beyond the reach of the average visitor to Zermatt, and neither the Furggen nor Italian ridges attract many ascents. The Hörnli is the popular line, protected now by fixed ropes in the area where Whymper's party fell.

Getting the mountain into shape, so to speak, for the 125th anniversary celebrations was a close run thing. The delayed start and late finish to the winter season left a heavy weight of snow on the east face and along the lip of the ridge, making it treacherous. Five climbers – a Japanese woman, two Germans, an Austrian and a Yugoslav – were killed in separate accidents while attempting the Hörnli in the three weeks before the July 14 celebration.

Twenty guides made the mountain safe by landing on the summit by helicopter and clearing the route and fixing new safety ropes for the town's distinguished invited guests. Bruno Jelk, head of the Zermatt mountain rescue service, says: 'People imagine the Hörnli is an easy way up, but the record proves it is not.'

Four of every ten rescues in the valley take place on the Matterhorn, even though Zermatt is surrounded by 13,000 ft summits. Last summer there were thirty-three accidents and nine rescues on the north face alone. The victims were people who simply became exhausted or were trapped by a change in the weather. Mr Jelk has rescued 600 people over the years and is acknowledged throughout Europe for his skill at extricating trapped climbers from cliffs.

'Once it was very difficult, often dangerous to carry casualties down on a stretcher, but the helicopter has changed that. An injured climber can be picked up on the mountain and be in a hospital bed within half an hour of falling. One man I remember lost an arm. It was torn off in an avalanche, so we packed it in ice in a rucksack and sent it with him to hospital, where the surgeons sewed it back on.'

Others have been less lucky. The guides estimate that since Whymper's day, at least 500 climbers have died on the Matterhorn. Twenty have never been found after disappearing into the crevasses that ring the mountain. Even so, people still imagine there is an easy path to the summit. Richard Andenmatten has been a guide for thirty years and has climbed the Matterhorn 650 times; his grandfather once guided Winston Churchill on a climbing expedition in the Valais. 'It is incredible how many people come here who are unfit and untrained, yet they still try to climb the mountain without a guide,' he says. 'No one can stop them, but many things can go wrong, especially with the weather.'

People become lost and stray on to dangerously loose areas, disorientated in cloud that may suddenly creep around the ridge. It is more than 3000 ft from the Hörnli to the summit, and with the cold, the wind and the mountain's exposure and steepness, an unfit climber may easily weaken.

Mr Andenmatten's quickest time to the top and back was four hours, climbing with a very fit young American. Normally the round trip takes eight hours. All kinds of people at varying levels of fitness are drawn to the challenge of the Matterhorn: either compelled by its magnificent shape or because they want to prove something to themselves. One American was seventy when he tried – and failed. Then he went into training, and at seventy-eight soared up it on the end of Mr Andenmatten's rope.

Most visitors to Zermatt are content to take one look at the Matterhorn and let their imaginations do the rest. The town that Whymper and his companions would now hardly recognize enjoys two high seasons a year: for winter skiers and summer climbers.

It has grown from a remote backwater into one of the most prosperous corners of Swiss tourism. Although it was outside investment that built the railway linking Zermatt to the outside world, much of the control over the hotels, ski lifts and restaurants remains local.

In the early days, British alpinists stayed at the home of the local curate, who persuaded his brother, Joseph Seiler, a soap and candle maker in Sion, to take over the only hotel in the village. The luxury hotel chain which resulted is now run by Christian Seiler, in the fourth generation of the family.

'Tourism brings in 350 million francs [£140 million] a year to this town, which has a permanent population of only 4500,' says Mr Seiler. 'That is an awful lot of wealth per head.' How much is due to the Matterhorn? Everything.

The Seiler group includes the Monte Rosa Hotel, which was the original building taken over by Joseph Seiler and is named after another of Zermatt's neighbouring giants. There is a plaque to Edward Whymper on the outside wall, and many reminders inside tell of the hotel's long association with the early years of British alpinism.

The Zermatt museum has relics from the 1865 tragedy in the Whymper room: strands of the hemp rope that broke, saving the lives of Whymper and the Taugwalders, the hat and rosary of Michel Croz, and fragments of clothing found on the glacier where the victims fell. There is a boot of Hadow's – unsuitable for climbing mountains – Hudson's prayer book, and a boot belonging to Lord Francis Douglas, whose remains were never found.

For the guides in the Zermatt bureau the Matterhorn is both a way of life and a livelihood, rearing up above the town like some enormous cash register.

Amadé Perrig, head of tourism, admits that Zermatt holds on to its ostensibly village atmosphere with difficulty. More than 100 hotels and guest houses straddle improbably steep plots worth a fortune per square metre. Cars are banned and must remain in garages on the outskirts. And yet he can still say: 'I have good health and God's blessings. Things change, people change – but the mountains, they never change.'

28 July 1990

45

Violent steps on strongman Saddam's pathway to power

Hazhir Teimourian

and

Juan Carlos Gumucio

The conquest of Kuwait is one more stepping stone in President Saddam Hussein's strategy to become the undisputed leader of the Arab world. At the age of fifty-three, he is well on his way. His readiness to use violence has served him well, so far.

Saddam Takriti, orphaned early, was set on his present path at the age of seven, when he was sent to school in the central Iraqi town of Takrit with a loaded pistol in his pocket. The pistol was bought for him by relatives and was a reflection of a violent society which had little regard for legality. According to his authorized biography, President Saddam first went to prison in 1958, after the overthrow of Iraq's Hashemite monarchy, for the murder of a teacher, his uncle's communist opponent in Takrit's local parliamentary elections.

He developed a reputation as a meticulous and daring assassin and was chosen by the leaders of his party, the Socialist Arab Renaissance (Baath) party, for an attempt on the life of General Abdel Karim Qassim, the then military dictator. This was apparently in collusion with the government of Colonel Gamal Abdel Nasser of Egypt and, according to the biography, the young Saddam regarded the assignment as a great honour.

The five-man gang bungled the ambush, even though Qassim travelled with almost no protection, and Takriti fled to Syria. He stayed in Syria for six months before going on to

Cairo to study law. The memorabilia of this and his other terrorist actions are now on display in the museum of the Baath party in Baghdad.

Saddam Takriti returned to the country after the overthrow of Qassim less than three years later and was immediately engaged in a number of plots against the Baathists' partners in the government and his personal rivals inside the party. The authorized biography says that at one stage in 1964, after the military had ousted their Baathist coalition partners from the government, he planned to burst into the cabinet room at the presidential palace 'and machine gun everyone, military or civilian'. The plot failed because a fellow conspirator inside the palace was transferred.

During the next four years he was engaged in protectionism, forcing contributions to the party from members of the public and the accumulation of secret caches of weapons for his party's street fights with opponents. He rose quickly through the party by intimidating or eliminating his rivals. He also planned for the eventual successful takeover of power in 1968, when he became the effective strongman of the regime. During this period he issued an order forbidding the use of surnames by citizens. Thus Saddam Takriti became known as Saddam Hussein (after the personal name of his father). The widest interpretation of the law was that he wanted to make it difficult for people to see how many members of the cabinet were his relatives from Takrit.

Two of his most notorious acts since then have been the invasion of Iran in 1980, and the decision to bomb the Kurdish city of Halabja in northern Iraq with nerve gases. The latter atrocity killed more than 4000 civilians in a single afternoon in March 1988. Yet a combination of the Arab lobby at the UN and a number of communist and western governments ensured that he went unpunished. Indeed, soon after the worst of the chemical attacks on the Kurds, Britain doubled the size of the exports credit guarantee to Iraq to £320 million. Observers of Iraqi politics believe that episode convinced President Saddam that, as long as Iraq had money to spend abroad, all avowed concern for human rights in the world would remain mere hypocrisy.

Few things can better illustrate the monumental proportions of his personality cult than the sun-dried clay bricks forming the new walls of Babylon. 'This glorious city was rebuilt in the era of our beloved leader, Saddam Hussein', the Arabic calligraphy reads.

The reconstruction of Babylon is only one of Saddam's obsessions. He flies there twice a month not only to inspect the works at the ancient city but to pay less-publicized visits to an adjacent compound just outside the ruins, where the hanging gardens of Babylon are thought to have existed centuries ago. No one would of course discuss the nature of the works taking place there, but Iraq's worst kept secret is that President Saddam is building his new multi-billion dollar palace.

This would perfectly match his vision of grandeur: the project contemplates a residence reminiscent of the Tower of Babel, with water flowing into fountains and gardens from a diverted river. If it is ever completed, it would certainly be a fitting place for a man who sees himself no longer as the president of a modern nation, but envisages himself as the new emperor of the Arab world.

3 August 1990

A liquid love affair rekindled

Philip Howard

Enthusiasm is not a London emotion. London pride is a sentimental song, and a scruffy pink saxifrage. Cocky cockney chirpiness in adversity is the mode for Londoners, and the nearest we come to animation these days is when invited by an inarticulate voice to leave the Underground, because the train is being taken out of service for a piece of incompetence that passeth all understanding. We show enthusiasm then – for filleting the staff, if there were any of them around. But a funny thing has happened this summer. We have rediscovered our enthusiasm for our river.

It is partly the heat, and partly the wicked congestion of travel across London on or sub-terra firma. Suddenly the Thames has become again what it was for most of London's history: our high street. The new waterbus and taxi services are not just the nicest ways of crossing town, but also the fastest. For a generation the buildings on the banks of the Thames have been a disgrace, from the multi-storey car parks of the City to the concrete boxes of Vauxhall. Suddenly, imaginative new buildings are emerging from the scaffolding along the forty miles of the London river, from the ziggurats of the Isle of Dogs to the neo-Georgian triumphalism of Richmond. There are decent places to eat and drink, and to sit and stare at one of the great river scenes of the world, on both banks of the Thames. Why, just opposite *The Times* on the south bank, with fizzy water in beautiful blue bottles – but, aposiopesis, Philip. Why ruin a Thames treasure by telling everyone about it?

The divorce between Londoners and their river was always a mistake. There were several reasons for it, the main ones being the death of the docks, and the absence of any planning more imaginative than could have been organized by Guy the Gorilla. And come to think of it, Guy would have been better than what we got, since he is safely stuffed in the Natural History Museum. I was present at the divorce. Pretty well my first job at *The Times* as cub reporter was to write the colour piece (descriptive prose with epithets) of Sir Winston Churchill's funeral. Quite unexpectedly, as the launch carrying the coffin pulled out from Tower Pier, the forest of cranes at Hay's Wharf and Butler's Wharf suddenly all dipped their long necks in a last goodbye, as all the sirens wailed. The dockers had come in, spontaneously and unpaid, on their Sunday off, to salute the bulldog Brit. I disgraced myself by blubbing dreadfully. It was, as they say, the end of an era; and it marked the end of the docks.

For twenty-five years the docks decayed. The riverine buildings were brutalist tower blocks. The water in the Thames became so dirty that if you fell in, you probably died of poisoning before you drowned. In our scurrying way of scratching a living, Londoners turned their backs on the river which is our reason for being here.

It is instructive to ask why the Thames is the most famous river in the world. Other rivers such as the Nile and the Amazon (and even the confluent Ob and Irtysh in the Soviet Union) are twenty times as long, and roll down a hundred times as much water. Other cities also stand on famous rivers. New York stands between an ocean and a New World rather than on a river. The focus of Florence on the Arno is a single old bridge. Parisians have a love affair with their Seine. The relationship between Londoners and the Thames has always been a working one.

The Romans founded London where it is because it was the convenient front door for ships into the heart of the big green island. They could sail and ride on the flowing tide fifty miles inland until they came to dry land. Twenty centuries ago London's first historian described us as 'a colony much frequented by merchants and trading vessels'. The Venerable

Bede called us 'a market for many nations coming to London by land and sea'. Trade and money up the London river made us. The Thames runs down the adventurous history of England from the beginning; and the poets, painters, and architects, who followed their patrons and their audiences where the money was, made the river famous.

The Thames flows through English literature as symbol and refrain from Chaucer to T. S. Eliot. The exception is Shakespeare, who never got over being an Avon boy. Spenser built his great spousal verse *Prothalamion* around the haunting incantation: 'Sweet Thames, run softly, till I end my Song.' The cure for disbelief about the fame of the Thames is to look up the entries for it and other rivers in any dictionary of quotations in any language. The Thames is a running character, symbolizing the passage of time and the darker side of London life, in the novels of Dickens, who at the age of twelve thought that his life had come to an obscure end in a blacking factory at Hungerford Steps, where Embankment station stands today. At a lower level, the river haunts the works of Edgar Wallace as symbol of danger. A Thames pea-souper is a leitmotiv that the game's afoot for Sherlock Holmes.

As with poets, so with painters. Canaletto's views of the Thames, with the buildings, sky, water, and passing show shimmering in a more northerly blue than his beloved Venice, strike me as just as lovely as his Venetian scenes. Monet painted one of his greatest series on a single subject around the Thames in the heart of London, to observe the transformation of the river city under changing light and atmosphere. Turner, too, was obsessed with the changing light and texture of the London river.

The Thames is not merely a source for painters: it is a good place for looking at paintings. In this year of the rediscovery of our river, we have opened two great new riverside galleries facing the high street of London at Somerset House and the new Turner Galleries at the Tate. The Thames in London is the stage for another peculiarly English art form: the stately

51

house. Because of our long, curious history, the banks of both sides of our river, from Greenwich to Hampton Court, are congested with more extraordinary palaces than any equivalent stretch of river in the world. You could Pevsner your way happily and profitably, seeing beautiful and historic buildings, for all of August, from Kew Palace to Ham House, and from Syon down to Lambeth. I have not yet been to see the renovated Queen's House at Greenwich, castigated by purists as the Royal Disneyland. I must, I must. The right way to enjoy London is from and on its river. Twice a day it brings the wild smell of the North Sea into the heart of the great city. It is liquid history, and liquid literature, and liquid art. One of the most moving views on Earth is from Hungerford footbridge looking down river. And it has been great fun. I could go on wittering about the Thames all day. But the sun is shining outside. The Thames is just at the gates of News International. If I scurried out, looking like a man on very urgent business from on high, I believe that I might just catch a boat from Wapping Steps – like so many Londoners before me.

4 August 1990

No way to keep intruders at bay

Charles Wintour

Finding an effective remedy for unjustified 'physical intrusion' by the press clearly gave the Calcutt Committee on Privacy and Related Matters a massive headache. In the longest and most carefully argued chapter of its report, the committee reviewed the existing laws of both England and Scotland, together with proposals for reform which had been made to it, and finally plumped for the creation of new laws making certain forms of physical intrusion a criminal offence.

The committee was clearly much influenced by *Sunday Sport*'s truly monstrous invasion of the hospital ward in which Gorden Kaye, the actor, was recovering from brain surgery. It was also worried by harassment of private individuals, often at times of emotional stress or bereavement. There were many other instances of an individual's privacy and property being invaded, often on dubious grounds. When such offences occur few people would argue for a policy of unadorned 'benign neglect'.

However, Calcutt's definition of the new criminal offences made it clear that they were directed at journalists. The first was 'entering private property without consent . . . with intent to obtain personal information *with a view to publication*'. The second was 'placing a surveillance device on private property without consent . . . to obtain personal information *with a view to its publication*'. The third was 'taking a photograph or recording a voice of an individual on private property, without his consent, *with a view to publication* with intent that the individual shall be identifiable'.

Why should a particular act be a crime if carried out for

journalistic purposes (irrespective of motive) but not if carried out for any other purpose? This is the sensible question which the Newspaper Society, representing the regional and local press, has just asked the Home Office. A film or drama critic has the same rights of free speech as any member of the public – and no more – when he reviews a show. A leader-writer has no God-given right to defame an individual, however passionately he may wish to condemn his behaviour. Journalists in this country draw their strength as representatives of the public from the very fact that they themselves are ordinary citizens, in no way singled out from the rest. Once they are subject to special laws, they will demand special privileges, too. The result could lead to even greater tension between the press and Parliament than exists already.

But why bring in the criminal law at all? Calcutt says this is necessary 'because only the criminal law can guarantee prompt relief (i.e., arrest or removal) to the victim and provide a sufficient deterrent to the intruder'. This underrates the possibility of toughening up the civil law, and the effect that one or two successful actions brought under the civil law would have. The Calcutt report draws attention to the Conspiracy and Protection of Property Act 1875, 'which makes it an offence persistently to follow someone about, to watch or beset a person's house, business or workplace or the approach to it . . . with a view to compelling him to do something he does not wish to do'. This could cover a journalist attempting to pressure someone into giving an interview he does not wish to give. For some unexplained reason, Calcutt says 'it is unlikely that the act would be invoked against the press'. Surely it would be better to try that path rather than bring in the criminal law?

Calcutt does, of course, propose that it would be a defence if the act was done 'for the purpose of preventing, detecting or exposing the commission of any crime, or other seriously antisocial conduct; or for the protection of health or safety'. The committee thought that the phrase 'in the public interest' was too broad to be useful. But what can be said of 'seriously antisocial conduct'? In the detailed argument Calcutt says revelations about the private life of a public figure would be justified if his behaviour 'adversely affects his public duties or is so hypocritical that the public is likely to be seriously misled'.

But can a dose of political hypocrisy always be classed as 'seriously antisocial conduct'? Could politics survive without it? There would surely be even more argument and scope for confusion in the courts than if the phrase 'public interest' was used.

The Newspaper Society has done well to open up the debate on this aspect of Calcutt. The Newspaper Publishers Association, speaking for the national newspapers, is also reviewing the whole report and will be making its comments known. David Waddington, the home secretary, while accepting the creation of new criminal offences 'in principle', is showing a welcome disposition to hear further argument on the detailed proposals. One hopes that the television world is not so absorbed by its own problems that it fails to realize the threat which Calcutt could pose to all investigative reporting, in whatever medium.

29 August 1990

Crimes of Peter Rabbit

Leader

As the Middle East totters on the brink of war and governments strive to fend off economic recession, an encouraging
glimmer of light shines through the darkness: *Times* readers
have rediscovered Peter Rabbit.

An item in *The Times* Diary three weeks ago reported that
while Noddy was being taken to the cleaners – golliwogs and
spanking sessions have been censored – Beatrix Potter's most
celebrated hero was to star in a £12 million film. The producer
assured his public unequivocally that Peter was morally and
ethically squeaky clean.

But was that so? His biographer described him as 'very
naughty'. Readers have pointed out that he not only dis-
obeyed his mother but along with his young cousin, Benjamin
Bunny, was a habitual thief and mischief-maker – despite the
whippings dealt out by Bunny Senior.

Correspondents who have leapt to his defence have argued
that Peter was below the age of criminal responsibility.
Though guilty, it would seem, of two offences, namely criminal damage and theft (of Mr McGregor's lettuces, radishes
and French beans), his youth should have saved him from the
full majesty of the law. Justice would best be served,
suggested one reader, by Mr McGregor seeking compen-
sation against Peter's mother under the small claims procedure in the county court.

On the other hand, the aggrieved Mr McGregor should
beware of pressing his case against widow Rabbit, who could
file a counter-claim against him in respect of the loss of her
late husband's support. How far Mr Rabbit was the author of
his misfortune would probably be the principal legal issue if

the case were heard under the Fatal Accidents Act. But the evidence that he was 'put in a pie by Mrs McGregor' would probably sway the court against the plaintiff – and in favour of the widow. The consequent damages payable by the gardener would far exceed the cost of his own vegetables.

Peter Rabbit was not alone in setting a poor example to our children. Squirrel Nutkin and Tom Kitten were young tearaways and Samuel Whiskers a bit of an old rogue. Jemima Puddleduck was more sinned against than sinning. She was always such a bad sitter that her eggs had to be taken away at birth and placed in care. But perhaps poor Jemima was a frustrated careerist for whom the farmer should have provided a crèche.

Winnie the Pooh was obese, lazy and illiterate. William Brown was in most respects worse. As for Alice, the object of Lewis Carroll's infatuation, she would have taken sweets from any stranger. Confronted by a bottle inscribed 'Drink Me', Alice resisted the temptation only momentarily. After tasting it – 'it had a sort of mixed flavour of cherry tart, custard, pineapple, roast turkey, toffee and hot buttered toast' – she promptly drank it.

It seems hardly surprising that after next swallowing a cake marked 'Eat Me' she started seeing caterpillars smoking hookah pipes, sitting on magic mushrooms. Alice in wonderland was desperately in need of moral guidance. And as for that young chalet maid, Snow White . . . How successive generations of British children have turned out as well as they have is to be marvelled at.

1 September 1990

This land is my land

Charles Bremner

With drums pounding and a chorus chanting a hypnotic dirge, a group of Sioux Indians shuffles around a tall cottonwood tree with slow, rhythmic steps. Following a ritual almost as old as the hills, the men and women circle a young man as he leans back, gazing at the sky, while he pulls taut a cord that ties him to the sacred tree. The tether is attached to two thongs inserted under the pierced skin of his chest, which is bare, like those of all the men in the dance. As the music builds to a crescendo, the youth strains at the cord, leaning ever harder back until, suddenly, his flesh gives under the strain, the rope springs free and blood spills down his chest, reaching his long red loin-wrapping.

The young man is purified, and another volunteer will soon take his turn at the blood sacrifice. The elders of the tribe, watching with their families from pick-up trucks, nod their satisfaction as the dancers move off for ritual cleansing in the sweat lodge, the igloo-like tent beside a tepee where they roast in the steam that crackles off red-hot rocks. It is impossible not to be moved by the intensity of the sundance, a four-day ceremony of spiritual renewal, a fertility ritual from the days when these Indians invoked the blessings of their creator, the provider of the buffalo that they hunted. The sundance is the central rite of the Sioux year. It is also the act by which the survivors of the once great tribe of hunter–warriors reaffirm their pride in their nationhood.

We had come more than one hundred miles from Rapid City, through the empty Bad Lands and across the burning prairies of South Dakota, to watch the sundance on a hillside in the Pine Ridge Reservation, the home of the Oglalas, the largest branch of the Sioux, or Dakota, nation. The ceremony, now repeated several times every summer, symbolizes the revival of Indian pride that began in the late Sixties.

Outsiders are not very welcome, and suspicion reigns, as ever, between the races. 'It's the devil's work,' warned a white rancher who stood outside one of the dozens of small missionary churches that stud the reservation. 'It's witchcraft, and bad things happen.' The dance, he recalled, had been banned by the United States government until the early Thirties.

The sundance is a good starting point from which to understand the renewed frustrations of the Sioux and other tribes, from the Mohawks in the east to the Navajo in the west, as America marks a century since the close of the Indian wars – that period when the white man lived by General Sheridan's dictum: 'The only good Indian is a dead Indian.'

This year, the Indians have awoken the interest of a usually neglectful America with a rash of demands and protests. In Arizona, the Hopi and Navajo have become involved in a bitter dispute with a coal company over underground springs. The Indians claim the water is holy to them, and theirs by right under their treaties with the US government. In Connecticut, just outside New York City, the courts have just ruled that 400 acres of land is Indian country, belonging to the Schaghticokes. In Canada, Mohawk Indians have attracted considerable support for their campaign to prevent a golf course being laid out on what they regard as sacred tribal lands near Montreal, even though their blockade of a road bridge led to a shoot-out with police.

In March, the leaders of twenty-eight tribes signed a treaty designed to repel what they regard as a movement to grab their lands and destroy their sovereignty. It was the kind of mutual defence alliance that the old leaders such as Crazy Horse, Pontiac and Tecumseh dreamed of, but never forged in their unequal struggle with the white man.

One hundred years ago this December, the whites sealed their supremacy at a little hamlet called Wounded Knee, a few miles across the dried-out prairies from the sundance site. There, in late December 1890, American soldiers panicked and slaughtered Chief Big Foot, an octogenarian who had resisted the treaties that most other Sioux bands had accepted, along with up to 300 of his people, mainly women and children. They had surrendered their arms and were camped under army protection, waiting to join the rest of the tribe in the reservation.

The dreams of the Sioux died along with the bodies that froze in the snow. 'The nation's hoop is broken and scattered. There is no centre any longer, and the sacred tree is dead,' lamented Black Elk, an Oglala Sioux who, as a youth, was with Crazy Horse when he defeated Custer at Little Big Horn in 1876, and lived on to survive the great chief Sitting Bull and tell the tale of Wounded Knee.

Few landscapes convey so great a sense of melancholy as the plains of Pine Ridge, a reservation some 50 by 100 miles, home to 18,000 Oglala Sioux. At Wounded Knee, there is no visitors' centre or grand edifice: only a nondescript monument by a little white church. But the pain endures among the people of the reservations. The memory of their confinement through defeat and treachery in the second half of the nineteenth century is still too strong.

'For seven generations, our children have been born with these horrible memories in their minds,' said one Oglala in his thirties. 'We have not yet had the wiping-away of tears.' Tillie Black Bear, an Oglala whom I watched having her arms pierced in the sundance ceremony, recalls how her great-grandfather described arriving at the massacre site, where the bodies had been left for two days in the snow. 'He came up on the scene and he wanted to cry. It was absolutely terrible. He saw everyone he knew, dead.'

For most of the past century, the 1.5 million Native Americans have been the country's most silent minority: a race that declined into despair, ignored by the outside world, resented by the states they inhabited and patronized by the federal bureaucrats who ran their affairs and subsidized them.

Seventeen years ago, after the civil rights movement and the awakening of Sixties idealism, the conscience of America was jolted by a second battle of Wounded Knee. Militants of the American Indian Movement (Aim), seeing themselves as the true heirs to Crazy Horse but regarded by many of the tribal elders as extremists from outside, held off the FBI and heavily armed troops for ten weeks. About sixty people died in shootings on the reservation over the next two years. Leonard Peltier, an Aim leader, is still in prison for the murder of two FBI men, despite a campaign by international human rights groups and several congressmen, who see him as a victim of injustice.

In the aftermath of the second Wounded Knee, a new spirit was born among younger Sioux and other Indians across the country; textbooks were rewritten and schoolchildren learnt that Native Americans were far from the 'redskin' savages of popular legend. Their cause faded in the Reagan years, and the misery continued. A new generation is on the warpath, seeking solutions to the social collapse that has brought them poverty.

Alex White Plume was a young schoolteacher at Wounded Knee when the militants took over. Now, as executive of the Oglala tribe, he is one of the leaders of the campaign to redress the wrongs suffered at the hands of what appeared to the Indians as a powerful but corrupt race. 'We really feel bad that Columbus got lost and landed out here, and brought all kinds of diseases and all kinds of people with ill minds,' he says. 'We see the white men as strange people. You can't trust them. For the past 498 years we have been lied to and given diseases and cheated. We've been killed and murdered.'

He has a point. Modern historians estimate that war and disease killed up to 80 per cent of the Indian population in the United States well before the final battles of the nineteenth century.

While the elders of some tribes pursue the old-style politics of dependence on the Bureau of Indian Affairs, some of the younger men and women, such as Mr White Plume and Ms

61

Black Bear, are talking of autonomy. Among other things, they want a separate currency for the reservation, and want it to be an area governed by tribal law, answerable only to the federal government, not to the states. The activists are planning to approach the United Nations with grievances, the foremost of which for the Sioux is ownership of the Black Hills, the holy land of the tribe.

The Sioux were granted title of the Black Hills by treaty in 1868, and then evicted in 1877 when gold was discovered there. The 5,000 ft pine-covered mountains, near Rapid City on the western edge of the plains, are home to Mount Rushmore, the cliff-face presidential sculpture, and to a national park saturated with theme parks, side shows and other diversions, including war-painted Indian 'warriors' who dance for the tourists.

In 1980, the Supreme Court described the eviction of the Sioux as 'the most ripe and rank case of dishonourable dealing in American history'. A New Jersey senator has been trying, against heavy opposition, to win recompense for the tribe. While some Sioux are pressing for a financial deal, Mr White Plume and the activists insist they want no money for the land. 'The Black Hills are mine,' Mr White Plume says. 'We just want our land back, and we don't want the US to be able to wipe out their guilt.'

You hear the same confidence across the reservations, from the people at Lakota College, founded in the Seventies, to the KILI radio station, the only one in America owned by Indians, which broadcasts a diet of rock 'n' roll and community news from high on the hill overlooking Wounded Knee.

Mr White Plume, aged thirty-eight, is convinced, like many of the more devout younger generation, that the culture of the original Americans has much to teach the rest of the country – and even the world. The Indians saw themselves as stewards of their land, appointed to guard it for future generations. When they killed buffalo, they ceremonially asked forgiveness of their 'brother', the animal. Their modern descendants contrast this with the destruction of the environment inflicted by the newcomers.

With concern over the environment, and interest over the past couple of years in alternative, or New Age, spiritual movements, the Indian tradition is winning sympathy, particularly in Europe. Mr White Plume's wife had just left to attend a seminar in Italy, and groups have come this year from Germany, Switzerland and elsewhere. In Rosebud Reservation, close to Pine Ridge, Ms Black Bear says she is a little irritated by the 'white people who come out and live for a year, and then they decide they want to sundance and then they want a sacred pipe'.

The Indian view of the world has been winning a wider following with the emergence of a much-revised version of America's most cherished national myth: the conquest of the West. Gone is the old image, perpetuated by John Wayne and all the legends, of the heroic struggle of the individual homesteader against savage nature and tribes. Instead, the frontier is being seen as a place of rapaciousness, racial strife and vast disparities of wealth.

When hundreds of thousands rushed westwards in pursuit of America's 'manifest destiny', the native peoples were devastated and nature was raped. The settlement of the Great Plains, the unfertile steppeland between the Missouri to the east and the Rockies in the west, is now seen as an environmental disaster. The extermination of some sixty million buffalo over thirty years, and the seizure of unsuitable land for cattle and crops, inflicted what many see as America's biggest ecological catastrophe.

Populations on the plains are now dwindling as people leave for other states. Over the past year or so, a body of experts, largely at east coast universities, has alarmed many in the region with a proposal to take about 140,000 square miles of the economically depressed Dakotas, Nebraska, Wyoming and Montana, and restore it to the wildlife and the Indians as a 'buffalo common'.

Down in Pine Ridge and the neighbouring Rosebud Reservation, they have little time for such lofty schemes. It is more urgent to find a way out of the cycle which has kept the tribes in poverty and generated many socially destructive ills, notably alcoholism. For a while the American government and the churches tried to turn the Indians into white men, taking their children away to religious and state boarding schools and encouraging them to assimilate as small-holding farmers.

Teachers punished children who spoke the Lakota language and, to bury their dead, Indians had to join a church. In 1934 forced assimilation was abandoned. The federal Bureau of Indian Affairs continued to oversee the tribes, which were regarded as 'domestic dependent nations'. In the early Seventies, President Nixon decided to foster tribal autonomy, and in 1983 President Reagan ordered the promotion of stronger tribal self-government, with the BIA adopting a less visible role. Big tribes such as the Sioux and the Navajo have strong tribal authorities, including courts and police forces.

But the critics, including many prominent politicians, say nothing much has changed. Last year a Senate investigation concluded that the reservations were afflicted by nineteenth-century poverty and dependent on a government administration pervaded by fraud, waste and mismanagement.

Around Pine Ridge, which lies in America's poorest county, the poverty is almost as visible as in the South Bronx of New York, that national yardstick for social dysfunction. Although far from squalid by third world standards, the scene is a stark contrast with the tidy prosperity to be found in the white-settled stretches of South Dakota. Prefabricated housing dominates the human settlements, many of them surrounded by wrecked cars. For a workforce of 10,000 men there are only 2,300 jobs, says Mr White Plume, who works from an office in the tribal administration in the centre of the township. He thinks education and renewed cultural life can pull the tribe out of its malaise. More and more Oglalas who grew up with English are learning Lakota and returning to the reservation after education elsewhere, he says.

Jeaneen Grey Eagle, the thirty-six-year-old director of

Project Recovery, an outfit which tries to tackle the consequences of rampant alcoholism, presents a gloomier view. With no money for treatment centres and only $132,000 a year from the government, she says she is fighting a losing battle. Ms Grey Eagle says about 90 per cent of the people of the reservation have been touched by the problems of alcohol, and about 25 per cent of babies are born with foetal alcohol syndrome. The hope, she says, lies with the new sense of Indianness, which 'gives the young something to hold on to'. The people want to work, she says, 'but we can't help them find a job'.

Many are more hopeful than Ms Grey Eagle. Take Tim Giago, a veteran journalist brought up on Pine Ridge, who came back to the area ten years ago and founded the *Lakota Times*, a thriving English-language weekly based in Rapid City. He has little time for the pessimists who see the Indians and their culture as doomed. 'We are going to have to stand up as a nation. We must say we are no longer a reservation. We are the Oglala Lakota nation.' Some tribes, notably the Mescalero Apaches of New Mexico and the Warm Springs reservation in Oregon, have made themselves self-sufficient. In some other tribes again, federal grants to business have been pocketed by officials.

Mr Giago says the revival of spirituality is the key to escaping social collapse. 'Young people are turning back. I see light at the end of the tunnel.' It was Mr Giago who challenged George Michelson, the governor of South Dakota, to proclaim 1990 the year of reconciliation, a time to 'put all the hatred and anger behind us'. Mr Michelson took up the challenge, and has attended tribal pow-wows and initiated a number of events on the theme.

White America still has a long way to go in appreciating the contribution of the Indians. Mr Giago recalls a tourist who bumped into Wilbur Between Lodges, the Oglala vice-president, and asked: 'Where can we see some real Indians?'

The lack of rancour among the Indians is remarkable to an outsider. But this year they want some attention and symbolic

65

redress from the country. In December, Alex White Plume is to lead a big seven-day memorial ride to Wounded Knee, following the trail of Big Foot's band. Tillie Black Bear, a forceful young grandmother, is campaigning for the return of eighteen Medals of Honour and twelve other decorations awarded to US soldiers for bravery in the Wounded Knee 'battle', an event in which most of the 25 dead soldiers are believed to have been killed by their own bullets and shrapnel.

The Indian activists are also lobbying hard to subdue the planned celebrations in 1992 of the 400th anniversary of Columbus's 'discovery' of America, and they want the country to discard the demeaning caricatures of Indians that are found across white culture – from countless brand names to football teams such as the Washington Redskins and the Atlanta Braves.

Standing in a field by the little St Francis missionary settlement on Rosebud, where she grew up, Ms Black Bear says patience and endurance are part of the Indian spirit. 'We know that our lives are not just for us to do what we want with. I know I am here to share my life with others.'

1 September 1990

The Booker's baneful influence

John Gross

Ladbroke's are offering 4–5 on *Wuthering Heights*; Joseph Conrad has been passed over three times in a row; the smart money is on *Sense and Sensibility* . . . No, it won't do.

In recent years, a new glumness has been added to the onset of autumn. It's the Booker Prize again: shortlists, shortening odds, interviews, inspired leaks, the televised dinner, the Oscar-like moment of truth, the rushed-through reprint.

I suppose that, in principle, anyone who cares about literature ought to be grateful, especially for those reprints. In a world where serious fiction is hard to sell, the Booker has created new interest and curiosity. In a world where life for most serious writers is a struggle, who can object to a scheme that steers a little more money their way? Certainly the advent of the prize must have aroused fresh hopes in authors' bank managers everywhere.

So why the depressed feeling?

It is not the choice of winners that is the big problem. Some have been good, some less good, some the obvious product of compromise. But life being what it is, that is only what you would expect. No, it is a question of atmosphere, of the *kind* of interest that is being encouraged. The more publicity the prize has attracted, the more it has been sending out the wrong signals.

The great reward for writing a book is being read. Everything else ought to be secondary. Competitions, on the other hand, are about winning; and as the circus surrounding the Booker has grown, it is the verdict that has come to seem all-important. The novels themselves – their actual contents – are a comparatively minor issue.

As for the novelists, they are reduced to the level of mere contestants. A degrading spectacle, at its worst: the literary world has never been short of jealousies and rivalries, but it is surely better if they are not systematized, if ambition and disappointment are not spelt out quite so openly. And while most Booker candidates preserve a decent degree of detachment, or at any rate keep their feelings to themselves, there is still something uncomfortable about seeing them paraded around and lined up for a race that only one of them can win.

Not that winning is an unmixed blessing, either. You acquire, briefly, a specious celebrity; you pop up in gossip columns, or attract the loving attentions of *Private Eye*. For most of the novelists I really admire, past or present, going through the prize-winning rites would have involved a positive loss of pride.

Against this, there are all the extra copies that are sold. But even here, the result can ultimately cut both ways. If the winning novel is a deserving one, or has popular potential, fine. But if it is a dud (they do occasionally get by), or if it is worthy but esoteric, thousands of purchasers who don't usually buy hard-cover novels are going to think a long time before they pay good money for another.

Once upon a time things were different. British literary prizes used to be modest affairs, generally commemorating little-known names. The winner got a pat on the back and a cheque for a small, curious sum, something like £109 3s 7d. Even in those days there were occasional flurries of ill-feeling, but it was a point of general satisfaction that we did not go in for the kind of skulduggery that was supposed to surround the Prix Goncourt.

By contrast, Booker and the other big prizes mean business; and the more there is at stake, the fiercer the competition is bound to be. But it is not so much Goncourt-style politics that seems to me the danger, as the spread of an American-style star system.

In America, ever since the days of Hemingway, big novelists have been big names, up there with the giants of entertainment and sport. If they are not careful, their books start counting for less with the public than their miscellaneous opinions, their opinions start counting for less than their personalities (in the show-business sense of the word), their personalities start counting for less than the size of their advances. And if they get involved in punch-ups, literal or metaphorical, those are what count most of all.

One inevitable consequence of this preoccupation with fame is an extreme competitiveness. Everyone knows who the seeded players are; most people have a pretty good idea of whether last season's number one seed is currently number two. There is an intense respect, even among those who make a show of denying it, for the visible symbols of success: earning power, movie rights, rankings on the bestseller list, and, of course, awards and prizes too. I have heard a Nobel prizewinner – in the course of a speech accepting another prize – complain that he had not been awarded that year's Pulitzer prize.

We have not gone as far as that over here. But you only have to watch arts shows on television or read interviews with the writer of the month to see the signs. There is another side to it, too – less scope for the books that do not win prizes, in the end perhaps less chance of being published. It is all part of the centralization of culture. People are told what to think; a few brand-names dominate the shelves.

The Booker Prize has become a fixture as no other literary prize before it. (I should perhaps add that I have been a judge myself, and found it, for the most part, an agreeable experience.) But as another contest comes round, I find myself recalling Henry James's advice to a young man who told him that he wanted to be a novelist: 'The word you must inscribe on your banner is Loneliness.' There is not much room for loneliness under the arc lights.

13 September 1990

The tourist trap

Geoffrey Moorhouse

The summer holidays weren't funny in the Yorkshire Dales. The convoys of coaches and cars were so dense that a journey from the A1 to the top of Wensleydale, which can be done in less than an hour, took almost twice as long. The market place in Hawes – Pevsner's 'compact grey little town with an intricate pattern of streets' – resembled Blackpool promenade from mid-morning each day. A neighbour of mine, stuck in a sweltering traffic jam, caught my eye and shook his head wearily as I walked past. 'I think they're breedin' this year,' he said.

Tourism is a dirty word to many inhabitants of the Dales, and it will not have any defenders at all if it continues to expand at the rate it has recently grown. August has always been the time, above all others, for locals to take cover round here, but every week is now much the same all the way from April to October's end. Quite apart from the traffic choking country roads that were never intended to take such volumes as these, several things make us feel we are being overrun by an army of occupation.

Once there was a balance between the claims of those who live and work here and those who visit the Dales for recreation. Most of the latter were walkers and cyclists, and almost without exception they had a care for the country and the interests of those belonging to it. The motorized columns of today are of a different calibre.

Whenever possible they avoid the car parks that were expensively constructed specifically for them, but become . . . let us say *testy* . . . when they are blocked in after leaving their vehicles inconveniently elsewhere. They can also be rude when our village shopkeepers do not jump to it with the expected alacrity. They drop their garbage in our intricate streets and they stuff discarded cans into our dry-stone walls. But the worst thing of all about them is that they are now too many by far. We find ourselves outnumbered by people in Bermuda shorts, interested in nothing so much as where the next snack is coming from. The farmer in his four-track is becoming incongruous, his natural habitat dominated by yuppies in Range Rovers, refugees from suburbia who insist on bringing part of it with them on a towbar, and coaches bearing trippers from Newcastle and Leeds. The loudest noise of summer (when low-flying Tornadoes are having a day off, that is) is not the rumble of a tractor, bouncing down a lane. It is the tearing din caused by half-a-dozen motorbikes whose riders are having fantasies about competing in a grand prix. These are not among the expectations raised by James Herriot, whose televised yarns have done as much as anything to bring the tourists here. I cannot see what pleasure all these visitors now get out of the Dales, when what they mostly see is each other, *en masse*.

Here I must declare an interest of my own, quite apart from the fact that my home is in the middle of all this. Among my books are three that describe journeys I have made, and there are others whose topics have been places abroad. I may, therefore, be accused of inciting tourists to foul someone else's backyard, while wishing my own to remain inviolate. I don't think there is an adequate reply to that charge, except, perhaps, to doubt that Wallace Arnold will ever take his coachloads anywhere near the Saharan Well of Asler, which I missed in a sandstorm, all but catastrophically; and not many people will see Calcutta, even after reading of my enthusiasm for it, as an alternative attraction to Venice, Bangkok or Benidorm. But my antipathy is not an isolated, northern English rural one. The residents of Bath, I see, have lately taken to hosing down open-topped tourist buses because they are sick of amplified commentaries booming past their garden gate throughout each day. For years now, the Indians of Goa have been hurling rotten fish and other filth at western hippies who have colonized their beaches.

The danger is that in this frame of mind one is tempted to say that everyone should stay at home, which is plainly preposterous, and would not be desirable even if it could be arranged. It is not as though every place lined up by the tourist boards is irreparably damaged by visiting hordes. Nothing much more destructive can be done to, say, London and New York by outsiders that hasn't already been wrought by their own citizens. There are other places whose brilliance remains somehow undiminished in spite of their incorporation in the entertainments business, and Niagara is a case in point.

God knows we have done our best to ruin it over the years, with souvenir shops and other 'tourist facilities' surrounding that tremendous cavity. The natural phenomenon, however, has 'em all licked. Most of Lake Erie still pours over the Horseshoe Falls as though it were going to quench fire in the belly of the earth.

Halfway down and just behind the cataract is a gallery, where the spray splashes your face and bubbles up your nose, and you are elated and frightened and transformed by the sheer power of it all. Sober and middle-aged couples who have come looking unhappy and awkward in the regulation oilskins and gumboots begin to giggle and act the goat under this influence. Children who have followed parents nervously are so intoxicated that they try to stand on their heads. The same goes for those who take the launch which sails below the falls and into its spray, rocking and lurching under the tumult as though it will never make it back to the landing stage. I defy anyone not to feel that man's contribution to Niagara is just a little small.

Moreover, it is the chemical pollutions of industry that threaten the Taj Mahal much more than the tens of thousands who make a beeline for Agra each year. Indeed, this is (perhaps uniquely) a case where the visiting crowds actually emphasize the merit of a tourist attraction. There are many things to wonder at in the mausoleum Shah Jehan built for Mumtaz: the perfect proportions of the building, the texture of the marble, the sumptuous patterns of inlaid semi-precious stones. But one thing above all others causes the visitor to pause and meditate. It is this: because the Taj was constructed high above the River Jumna, with nothing in sight behind, it appears from the gatehouse to be floating on the edge of infinite space, to be drifting off into nothingness. This is a stunning sensation in India, where no landscape is totally unpopulated, no person is ever utterly alone. The tourists thronging the foreground help to create the sensation of the Taj Mahal by pointing up the emptiness behind. Without them it would be an almost sterile edifice, as may be seen by anyone studying the posters which show it without anyone in sight.

Would that the natural triumphs and the historic monuments towering above the holiday trade were more common than they are. Instead, I fear, there are places which have so far survived the great exploitation, but which now teeter on its edge and may never be the same again. I am profoundly grateful that I saw Prague long before the mixed blessings of the past few months. The freedom the Czechs now enjoy and the manner of their getting it was never more deserved by anyone. But this very release, and the fame of its happening, has meant that the city has been overcrowded with foreigners as never before this summer. I don't blame them, and part of me wishes I had been there, too; for, ever since I saw Prague in the sweet, sad, stirring days of 1968, I have thought it a bewitching model of what European civilization at its best is capable of. How long now, though, before that heavenly skyline above the Vltava is spoilt by the addition of a Hradcany Hilton and other luxurious accommodations, which will alter the composition that has stood in perfect harmony for centuries? Can anyone who knows the place visualize the desecration of the Old Town Square when it has become a parking lot for scores of tourist buses, which is doubtless the fate awaiting it, if it hasn't already happened in this first summer of happiness?

Leningrad, too, I suspect, is bound to be transformed when the Soviet Union gets its act together and manages to attract the necessary investment. Given that it contains one of the world's greatest treasuries of art and two mighty Bolshevik totems (the cruiser *Aurora* and the Smolny Institute) as well as Peter the Great's sublime panorama beside the Neva, Leningrad could be in for concentrated rubber-necking on a Roman scale. Like Prague, it has been accustomed to tourists for years, but never in such quantity that they have defaced the place. It has avoided this pitfall through the inadequacies of communism, including the crummiest catering industry outside black Africa. It would not be amusing if these cities were now to lose their precious character as a result of seduction by the unhindered blandishments of capitalism.

Who, then, is this creature we have spawned and must now, I think, be wary of? Someone once asked me if I saw some finicky distinction between a traveller (implicitly myself) and a tourist, and immodestly I said I did. For one thing, the traveller does not expect the comforts of home as a top priority wherever he goes and would be prepared to doss down anywhere – if need be in the open air – if it meant the difference between seeing and missing sunrise over the Ganga at Varanasi, or the Byzantine mosaics at the Kariye church in Istanbul. This proposition would not even be a starter among most holidaymakers, and there are other differences. The traveller does not expect or even want to be (literally or metaphorically) carried by some agency or operator, but gets a part of his pleasure from planning, arranging and fending for himself; out of ascertaining as much as he can before he leaves home, so that he will know what to look at and for when he reaches his destination, his imagination having been engaged beforehand.

The tourist is quite otherwise. He is not disturbed by the proximity of other tourists when he regards a building, a landscape or simply passing humanity, because he does not contemplate so much as gawp unreflectively. At home he will spend semi-comatose hours in front of his television set, but will think it laborious to read a book. He is, therefore, quite happy to follow a group leader's upraised brolly and to be addressed at regular intervals, because this saves him the trouble of finding out for himself beforehand, and he lacks the curiosity to do so anyway. He is essentially a spectator on wheels, whether he goes forth *en famille* in his own vehicle or is otherwise conveyed in a gang. He is not discouraged by mobs of people like himself cluttering the view. The traveller, ideally, would like to be the only one of his kind.

By now, I should think, Mr William Davis will be composing his letter to *The Times* to repudiate all this nonsense in the name of the British Tourist Authority. He will, if he repeats himself as usual, quote the annual cash value of tourism to the national economy and he will insist that the only need is to manage things a bit better by diverting holidaymakers from areas they are inundating and coaxing them to places which have so far missed out on the tourist bonanza. I am sure Bill Davis can manipulate many things, but I doubt whether even he could persuade the hordes who are now despoiling the Dales under the stimulus of James Herriot to commune with George Orwell instead at Wigan Pier. Or convince the busloads who make life a misery to the people of Chipping Camden and Broadway that they will get just as much of a kick out of Barnsley or West Hartlepool. And whether or not he could perform such feats is irrelevant. In this part of the world something irreversible will happen soon unless action more drastic than 'management' is taken.

We need, above all, to limit tourism and in certain places that means we must actually start to discourage it until it has returned to acceptable levels. This is not a revolutionary idea, though it will provoke cries of outrage as if it were. In London and many other cities, after all, it has long been the custom to limit traffic by erecting bollards, parking meters and other devices for the benefit of pedestrians and householders among others; in order, according to the jargon, to protect the environment. One effective way of limiting the flow of tourists, as defined above, might be the abolition of newspaper travel sections, which not only pride themselves on finding more and more virgin territory to exploit while repeatedly publicizing the already exploited, but do everything else to give the tourist a sendoff short of booking his ticket for him. I am not sure that life's passengers should be encouraged to that extent. If someone has the wit and curiosity to find out these things for himself then good luck to him: if not, perhaps he deserves to stay at home.

Everywhere now groaning at the thought of another tourist season will find its own way of imposing local limitations. I have no doubt at all about the best way of saving my own patch from destruction by the holiday industry. There has been some talk of conceivably re-opening the railway which once ran the length of Wensleydale to join the Midland main line – the Settle to Carlisle, as it is now known – above Hawes. Trains pottered from one village to the next with passengers until 1954, with freight a little longer, but most of the line has been closed, its tracks torn up, for a quarter of a century. It would take a colossal expenditure to restore it, and my fear is that the only potential investors are people who wish to bring yet more tourists in. Yet, if the Wensleydale line ran again, it would be possible to eliminate the biggest bugbear of all, the vehicles that convey the invaders. Construct one car park beside the A1, another beside the M6, and forbid all but local and service traffic to go any further. Visitors would have to take the train and the minibuses awaiting them at every station. Other than this, there would be no way of getting about except by bike (hired, perhaps) or on two feet.

Doris Lessing has remarked that the world would be much safer in the hands of its most primitive peoples than if it is left to the mercies of the so-called civilized races. She points out that sophisticated societies tend to have no sense of a future beyond the lifetimes of their grandchildren, whereas the aborigines of Australia, and other primitives, simply see themselves as part of a continuum without a definable end:

and that they, therefore, cherish the earth as something that must sustain those who follow them in perpetuity, just as it has been preserved from the beginning of time to benefit us.

This is the antithesis of an attitude that has lately prevailed in the Dales, at any rate. That thrilling triumvirate of Whernside, Ingleborough and Pen-y-ghent, which the Victorians thought of as mountains, have been gradually weathering into their twentieth-century outlines ever since the Ice Age, changing imperceptibly over very long periods of time, except for the occasional rock fall caused by extraordinary frost or storm. In the past couple of years it has become necessary to *reconstruct* parts of each hill, where narrow tracks have become bogs a quarter of a mile wide, where slopes have fragmented away, where ugly scars have been left visible for miles. And why? Mostly because a national tabloid, wishing to inflate its circulation, has organized an annual Three Peaks race which has caused hundreds of runners at a time, from all over the country, to rip away the topsoil with their hard soles.

When we have reached the stage where we must rebuild our ancient landscapes with artificial substances in the name of mass entertainment, the time has come to call a halt; just as it is also time to reduce other hazards before they damage the inhabited parts of the Dales beyond repair. If it were left to those whose families have dwelt here for generations, I do not doubt that the consensus would now insist that enough is enough. The people who have been most active in promoting tourism hereabouts are noticeably not Dalesmen at all, but outsiders who have scented rich pickings in running hotels and selling things, and seem to have little thought for anything but making as much money as possible out of the place. The Dales families have always understood that there is a balance to be maintained, between a useful income from tourism and the need to protect their inheritance from its excesses. Like Doris Lessing's primitives, they are rooted in the land and feel an instinctive obligation to hand it on to posterity in the condition they have received it themselves.

But it would be humbug to minimize my more selfish concern. A metropolitan friend of mine, a man whose substance partly comes from inciting tourism, came to stay for the weekend. He was obviously irritated by my Nimby attitude, which he could not have disdained more if it had come from Nicholas Ridley himself. He thought I was being unreasonable, especially – gesturing around the barren hillside we were on – when there seemed so much space to spare.

'OK,' I said, 'but see what you make of this. I have a small portable fairground organ, a beautiful instrument, but rather loud. It is a steady little earner, and I can make £50 a day by passing the hat round whenever I like. Next Easter, I am going to set it up outside your house in Holland Park, west London, and play it continuously from breakfast until sunset, every day without fail until the clocks go back again. I bet I make a bomb, but what do you think about it?'

My friend didn't even stop to think. 'I'll call the police,' he said. I expect William Davis would, too.

22 September 1990

The slippery slope to a bottomless pit

Matthew Parris

When I was a little boy, and before my parents gave up their ideas of a strict upbringing, I was forbidden to say the word 'bottoms'. Or rather I was forbidden to say it in a rude way. The result was that I wanted to say it very much.

Sometimes I would sit alone in the safety of my room saying 'bottoms, bottoms, bottoms' just for the excitement of it. At the dinner table my younger brother and I found ways of not quite saying bottoms but of suggesting it: using formulas which kept just within the letter of the rules.

Yesterday at Blackpool David Blunkett MP, Labour's local government spokesman, found himself in a similar predicament. The word was not bottoms, however, but something far more shocking: two words in fact, 'domestic rates'.

Ooh, that was fun! Can I say it again? Domestic rates. There. Now I've said it twice. But here's a curious thing: Blunkett never did. Domestic rates are, of course, Labour's proposal for financing local government. The idea is to return to the old system, with knobs on. But was he saying so? Was he heck!

He said almost everything else. He said what a Labour government was *not* going to do. They were not going to carry on with the poll tax. For emphasis, he said what a Labour government would abolish. They would abolish poll tax. The country cried out for the abolition of poll tax and abolish it he would. They would definitely, indubitably, certainly, abolish poll tax. It was beyond all question that they would abolish poll tax.

He said when they would abolish poll tax. He said why they

would abolish poll tax. He said how they would abolish poll tax and in what stages. He slalomed down a verbal ski slope, gathering speed, ducking and weaving, repeating himself, adding riders to what he had already said – about poll tax – sliding faster and faster towards the great big rock which he, and you, and I, and the whole of the Winter Gardens, could see waiting there for him.

If poll tax was to be abolished, what was to replace it? 'We will implement our proposals, stage by stage.'

The rock loomed larger. There were to be two stages, he said. *First*, Labour would abolish poll tax. '*Then*' – we gasped: the rock was surely on us now? – 'in order to get rid of the poll tax within twelve months, we will . . .'

Now, at this point, my printed text of his speech says 'reintroduce the rates'. Perhaps it was the hubbub of a noisy hall, perhaps Mr Blunkett was gabbling, or perhaps he lowered his voice a little here: but I did not make out this phrase. I did hear him proceed quickly to a passage about immediately removing from poll tax those poorer people who only pay 20 per cent.

Then he moved on to say that Labour would improve the rebate system. Of what? He added that they would 'remove capping'. Of what?

There would be no restrictions on capital investment, he said. Seven families in ten would be better off. There would be a 'new valuation'.

Under what system? New valuation of what? Slowly it dawned on us. The rock was behind him and receding fast. He had skirted it, slid past and we blinked. We had left the poll tax, and Mr Blunkett was now talking about the new system, the D******* R**** system. We had jumped. Without his signalling it, we had moved to a discussion of life in the future – life under the nameless thing.

David Blunkett was skiing effortlessly now, coming in on the final slope, his peroration.

'Looking to the future, we need boldness, confidence, optimism . . .'

Yes, David, but isn't there something else we need? This speech has only four seconds to run . . .

Blunkett swallowed hard. Out with it, man . . .

'FairratesforafairerBritain.' And it was over.

A strange desire seized me. I wanted to leap on to the rostrum, grab the microphone, and yell: 'Domestic Rates! Domestic Rates! Bottoms! Bottoms! Bottoms!'

4 October 1990

Opening the door on Abbott

Alan Franks

If ever there was a parliamentary victim of the curiosity factor
and its fickle side-effects, it was surely Diane Abbott. Three
years after her election to the troubled London constituency
of Hackney North and Stoke Newington, she remains now
what she was then, Britain's first and only black woman MP.
While most new members are in the business of acquiring
prominence, Ms Abbott has actually shed a fair amount of
hers, and if things continue in this vein she could even attain
an honourable obscurity by the age of forty.

It is all relative, for her particular prominence was of the
kind that cannot endure, depending as it did on her novelty.
She also happened to be something of a gift, with her gold-
threaded plaits like designer dreadlocks, her power-dressing
which parodied the male, her frankness about sex and her
fabled temper. Just as alluringly, her political lineage was
based firmly in the 'loony left' of the London Labour party.
This meant she not only caught all the odium then being
directed at the Livingstone tendency, but also members of her
persuasion were blamed by sections of her own party for
electoral defeat.

Here was a confluence of stereotypes that the media could
not resist. Yet here, too, was a genuinely significant moment
in British politics. Whether Ms Abbott was being evaluated as
a candidate whose success coincided with the moment, or
whether as a voice in her own right, the fact remained that she
was a genuine first. Although the publicity became too
hysterical, and the bleeding of prejudice too rabid to make
such comparisons seem anything but mock-heroic, her name
was in the history books as indelibly as those of Lady Astor,

who, in 1919, was the first woman to take her seat in parliament, and Sharpurji Saklatvala, the Parsee lawyer who sat for Battersea, first for Labour and then as a communist, between 1922 and 1929, and who was the first member identifiably from the ethnic minorities. When Ms Abbott took Hackney with a majority of 7,000 she became part of the first intake of members from the Afro-Caribbean communities.

She did not, indeed does not, behave with a conventional British sense of history, but would argue that there is no particular reason why she should. In the early months she seemed faintly appalled by the institution she had joined, and that attitude has not altogether gone. She looked brash and inept, like someone drunk on exposure; the only expectation she seemed to comply with was the one that said she would clash vigorously with anyone who disagreed with her. All this may be history, but it is important, for Labour was about to enter one of the most difficult periods in its own position on black representation, and this, ironically, at the very time when the class of '87 (Ms Abbott, Paul Boateng, Bernie Grant and Keith Vaz) had given the communities a potentially greater advocacy in the Commons than ever before.

Last year, when Ms Abbott attempted to set up a parliamentary black caucus, along the lines of the congressional group in the United States, she received a hostile reception from senior Labour members who were apprehensive that a 'party within the party' would itself appear racist. Yet when the caucus petered out a few months later, the reasons had as much to do with internal division, and the non-joining of Mr Boateng, the only one of the four to sit on the Labour front benches. What was to have been her apotheosis appeared to have become her nemesis.

For the time being she is, at thirty-seven, just another MP (although she did stand unsuccessfully for Labour's National Executive Committee this week). She has a place on the treasury select committee and the overwhelming workload of a constituency even more hard-pressed than the Paddington of her childhood. It has all happened in reverse. 'I remember meeting John Smith in the taxi queue,' she says, 'and he said it was a good thing to come in during the party's time in opposition. Most MPs, even the stars such as Gordon Brown, spend years in obscurity. When the media interest fell away, it came as a terrific relief. For the first six months it was overwhelming, and they were all the same questions. I was reminded of whatever it was that Dr Johnson said about a woman preaching being like a dog on its hind legs; the remarkable thing is not how it does it, but that it should do it at all.

'I had that glare from day one. What really surprised me was the extent to which some of my own colleagues in the party had absorbed the stuff in the press, and half believed it; that the London left really was loony. I was in the tea room once, and this Scottish MP, Labour, said to me: 'You don't belong here,' in a way that made me feel taken aback by the aggression.'

Ms Abbott's is a peculiar articulacy, all flinty London vowels and then long, quite classical constructions, perfectly executed at colossal speed. She can puncture each style with the use of the other; right in the middle of a literary allusion comes a flurry of those words which the press denotes with asterisks. If you take them as they are intended, this is not profanity, but emphasis. It is also a pointer to the past which brought her to this present, and to the story of a poor black girl's double-edged obsession with the establishment. For she is already well versed in obscurity, in much the same way as was Thomas Hardy's Jude.

By the time she was at secondary school, her parents, a metal worker and a nurse, immigrants from Jamaica in 1951, had moved four miles to the northwest of London; this hardly landed them up the tracks in the blameless heart of Metroland, but in the white, lower-middle-class suburb of Harrow. Her own Christminster, the horizon towards which her dreams inclined, was not Oxford, but Cambridge, where she had been one day on a school outing, 'and seen people there in striped scarves, gods and goddesses, people from another state of being'.

By now it will be clear that Ms Abbott was not, to use her own words, 'scraped off a playground in Brixton' and brought to parliament. Far from it; she did make it to Cambridge, despite having to study for her exams in the painful wake of her parents' divorce, and in the belief that her teachers did not consider her to be Oxbridge material. Yet, in that first blaze of 1987 publicity, as in the lesser coverage since then, you could have read copiously about her and still not known that she had read history at Newnham College; it was as if the intellectual credentials were an inconvenience in her portrayal. She was occasionally referred to, tantalizingly, as being Harrow-educated, which was true as far as it went. The school was, in fact, Harrow County School for Girls, the sister institution of the one which was shaping her political contemporary, Michael Portillo, the local government minister.

The figure now cut by the first black woman MP is one of those peculiar English hybrids. It is no criticism to say that for her credentials and her political rhetoric she mines at the very seam, black poor and urban, from which she dug herself out with her own bare hands; nor to say that the daughter of such an unpropitious neighbourhood now dresses up to her part in public life because her constituents expect her to trade on equal terms with the genetic toffs. But the inevitable cost of all this has been that there are two mobilities at play. Sometimes they seem to be counter-marching; here a cosy feature on her dress sense and personal style ('she applies Saint Laurent's "Opium" in winter, a tea-rose scented oil in summer'); and there a howl of rage about health cuts in Hackney. Yet all the while there is proving to be as much consistency as there is apparent contradiction, even if that consistency springs from her being just about the most dedicated model of minorities: black for a start; then the only black girl visible in Harrow; then the only one at Newnham, then at the Home Office, and now in the Commons.

When she looks to her roots to confirm her own posture,

she finds them in the hard ground at the heart of town. 'My politics are the politics of the inner city. The inner city is the same, it is *sui generis*, all over the world. It is characterized by a rawness and an energy which you do not get in the shire counties. It is like that because life is hard there. My constituency is the poorest in the country, with 80 per cent council housing and the largest number of single parents.

'There are people on the front bench who think they understand poverty, and who believe that poverty consists of an absence of money. Poverty in my constituency is not just an absence of money; it has to do with a whole pattern of social structures, and with living on the edge of violence. The other week I went to the memorial service for a policeman who was shot in Hackney. We have had four killings since June . . . all this stuff about freeing the markets means absolutely nothing around here. The place is wholly dependent on the public sector, not just for services, but for jobs as well. The last factory closed down years ago. The biggest employers are the health service and local authorities. What does it mean, to hear someone going on about competition in the market place? What they want to know is how their immediate circumstances can be helped. There are so many communities living side by side and struggling for survival, not just physically, but economically. Hackney belongs partly to the East End, which is traditionally a place of successive immigrations, whether Huguenot, Jewish or Bengali, and they stand toe to toe to ride out the poverty. It is a constant state of struggle. People in the inner cities, whatever their party politics may be, have an innate struggle against the status quo. Think of it: what *is* the status quo if you are a single mother in Hackney? It is being trapped on the fourteenth floor of a tower block with fungus and mould, trying to make the social security payments stretch.'

This all seems to come straight from the ritual chorus of the capital's Labour left. Yet even in this quarter, Ms Abbott has been the subject of controversy during her brief time at Westminster. In September 1988, activists in her constituency sought to have her de-selected on the grounds that she had been spending too much time on trips to the United States and the Caribbean, and that she had failed to champion the interests of blacks and immigrants in Hackney. Two years on, she accepts that in the three elements of a member's life as she perceives it (constituency, parliamentary and international), the first is coming to assume an increasing priority. But at the expense of what?

'There are definitely three jobs. In Hackney, as an MP, you are a sort of super social worker. People ring up and write in; they have housing problems, they are not getting the proper dole money and so on. Also, the people want to see you; they want you to come to an old people's home, or to a Greek Cypriot Christmas party, and they like to see you looking as they think an MP should look. There is a lot of making yourself visible.

'The House is something different again. Tony Banks [Labour MP for Newham North West] says the first rule of politics is to be there, by which he means being at the House, attending the debates. The conclusion I have come to, which I didn't face before, is that it is important to be around the House. When I became an MP, I didn't think I could spend as much time in the Commons as I do. But the fact is that in order to build up the relationships that you need if you are to be effective, you have to be around. But there is always the pull of the constituency. They may not know who their councillor is, but they know who their MP is.'

If there is the contrition of a member brought to heel by charges of too many jaunts, it is not showing. She still receives numerous invitations to speak in the United States, and has become well-known in Jamaica. She is also unrepentant about the attempt at a black caucus, and says that if the next elections produce even one new potential recruit in parliament she may try to revive the group. Her fellow Labour members are reluctant to speak harshly of her, even though some damn her with the faint praise of competence.

Unlike Hardy's Jude, she did attain her Christminster; in

listening to her recall those Cambridge years, in which the sense of obscurity persisted precisely because of her difference from the rest, a clear pattern emerges. For such a girl to be an undergraduate at such a place was nothing less than a dry run for what she was to experience fifteen years later. In the later case, her alienation may have been brought on by unaccepting members in the tea room; in the earlier one, it was caused by the successors of those very striped-scarved goddesses whom she had spotted on the school day trip.

'There were girls on my corridor at college, and they used to have sherry parties. They might as well have been conducting some bizarre social ritual. Academically, I was OK, and I never at any time thought about quitting the university. But the newspaper in my family had been the *Daily Mirror*, the old Hugh Cudlipp *Mirror*, which told you that basically everyone was equal.

'Sure there were upper-classes, but they were just a joke, a few people hanging out in plus fours. I can remember sitting next to a girl at dinner and listening to her talk about her family's country cottage . . . if you are working class and you go to Oxbridge, and you see one little corner of the British establishment strutting and resplendent, it can have the effect on you for the rest of your life of making you see a hurdle and be determined to clear it, whatever the odds.'

After Cambridge she bounded over the hurdle marked Home Office by telling her distinguished interviewers that she wanted power, just as she later cleared another obstacle by turning in a virtuoso performance at the Labour party's selection interview for 1987. It was the logical progression of a good examinee. In the time between graduating from Cambridge and joining parliament she went through a whole range of fairly short-lived incarnations, at the Home Office's prison department, at Lambeth's press office, at the National Council for Civil Liberties, at Westminster City Council and at TV-am. It was one of those curricula vitae which looks dynamically restless until the MP suffix suddenly justifies the sequence.

'The Home Office taught me how to write a good memo, and a great deal about office politics. Civil servants are very good at office politics because, as someone once explained to me, if you are good at that, you get to run the country. There I was, the only black woman in an eight-storey building, having to absorb the knowledge that the Home Office was intervening in black people's lives in a negative way, through the prisons, through the courts, through the immigration service. I simply did not want to become a senior black person at the top of a system acting on people's lives in this way.

'The civil servants at the Home Office are some of the nicest people I have worked for, not earning a fortune, going home to Cheam at the end of the day, and doing what seems to be their duty. Many of them, when they were new to the service, did want to see reform, but by the time they had got senior enough to implement such reforms, they had absorbed so much of the ethos of the service they were no longer capable of carrying them out.'

Even so, rather them than the creatures of the world as glimpsed from within the National Council for Civil Liberties, 'those white liberals oozing their patronizing sympathy all over me', or the cold gargoyles fashioned by television. 'When I was on *Thames News*, and you had the guests in the Green Room, you'd see these people who were absolutely high on their sense of self-importance, and they were utterly lost as human beings, with the dead eyes that come from believing all the hype.'

Despite appearances, this is no black Candide voyaging through the badlands of English public life, for she has too little ingenuousness for that, and too much ambition. That ambition, she says, consists of wanting to be a good constituency MP, not of wanting to 'get on in the party'. Were it the latter, she or it would probably have to change. 'After the election, people were saying that the great thing about the campaign was that race had not been an issue. But the whole thing about the attacks on the "loony left" was they had a clear subtext of race. And whenever people talked about the loony left in London, they fastened on to me and on to Ken; one of the "loony" things about Ken was that he spoke for black people. I was surprised at the extent to which people in my party read the *Daily Express*, and believed the stuff about the left in London, and still do. There was this strong undercurrent that London had lost us the election, and so you came in and you hit that. That was a surprise to me. I had believed that we were all comrades.'

There are at least two more specific ambitions which she acknowledges. The first is to have a family. 'Like a lot of women my age with a reasonably successful career, you're always haunted by the feeling that you may have paid a price in terms of your personal life.' The second, which she qualifies as a sub-ambition, is to return to the place of her first employer, the Home Office, only this time as a minister. There is a further aspiration, which has to do with black emancipation. As she articulates it, there are parts which could double as her own biography.

'If you take Hackney, 60 or 70 per cent are black, from Caribbean or African origin. Ten years ago, the number of blacks employed by the local authority was in single figures. Because of equal opportunities, those numbers are now up to 50 per cent. So while it is easy to sneer at equal opportunities, it is only through systematic policies that you can give black people access to jobs. Like the whole issue of feminism. Ten years ago, when we talked about it, we were sneered at and abused. Yet now we are a respectable issue in the Labour party. Maybe in ten years' time they will come round to the same position on race, and having a black representative will be something to be proud of . . . you can sweep them under the carpet in presentational terms, but the poor and the dispossessed have had a way down history of forcing themselves on to the agenda.'

6 October 1990

90

Lonely struggles of the 'third sex'

Christopher Thomas

Prancing lewdly down the street in flowing bright saris, the eunuchs of Delhi have come to celebrate the birth of a baby. Groups of giggling men mock them. Women usher their young sons indoors, out of earshot of a torrent of lurid imprecations. There is music, singing and dancing as the procession winds noisily on. Curtains are pulled back for a clearer, furtive look from a healthy distance. The eunuchs sway licentiously, blowing kisses from red-painted lips. Gold bangles sparkle from ankles and wrists, and the breeze tosses their long hair.

This spectacle is happening in a middle-class street. The eunuchs are cackling with delight and revelling in their power to shock and scare. They bang randomly on front doors, demanding money. A man haughtily orders them away, and two eunuchs chant foul rhymes at him, humiliating and taunting him. A few lift their saris to reveal terrible scars of castration. Vulgarity is a stock-in-trade.

The raucous mêlée arrives at the house where a baby has been born. The eunuchs were summoned by the father, who knows that these strange people are able to bestow good luck. They dance a well-rehearsed routine with pro-essional ease and sing in a trembling soprano. For this they will get as much as 1,000 rupees (£30), a princely sum for a few hours' work. For the harrowed father, it is a week's wages. Tomorrow the troupe has been booked at a wedding, when the fee will be twice as much. And then at last they will sink back into their private world, to count the money, give most of it to the guru, and see how many gold bangles and shiny baubles they can buy with what is left.

Just up from the Turkman Gate district of Old Delhi, locked away deep in the back streets of a teeming Muslim enclave, a eunuch called Bushpa is lounging on a mattress in a dingy room. A fan creaks overhead and an elderly deaf and dumb eunuch fusses pointlessly with a broom. A photograph of a gorgeous, pouting teenager in a woman's bathing suit adorns one wall; this was Bushpa at twenty-one. He was castrated at nineteen by a doctor who told him to come back for two more operations so that he could be taken a little closer to the womanhood he craved. But the pain was too great and he never returned.

Now fifty-two, Bushpa has the thick arms of a man, but they are completely hairless. His black hair hangs about his face. 'I am neither man nor woman,' he says. 'I am the third sex. I was cursed with a man's body. I craved to be a woman. But now, at last, I am a mother.'

Bushpa is nursing an eighteen-month-old girl, Ayesha. He paid a pregnant, unmarried woman not to have an abortion and took the child away an hour after she was born. She lies peacefully in Bushpa's lap, sleeping. 'My life is complete at last,' Bushpa says. 'I have found the most wonderful love of all. I am going to bring her up to be a priest. There are women Muslim priests in some countries, I believe. She will be educated, and I will be proud. Sometimes I can't sleep at night, I am so happy.' As Bushpa chats, other eunuchs enter the room and touch the child fondly. But they are annoyed, because a stranger is in their private world. A heavy-set eunuch, earlobes laden with gold jewellery, flops petulantly on a mattress and wags an admonishing finger at Bushpa. 'Don't talk about us to outsiders,' he says. The sanctuary has been invaded; the outside world has entered this grubby fortress.

Many eunuchs resort to prostitution with homosexuals. 'I wish I was a woman and had a man and a child,' says one. 'I would share my sorrows with him. This life is a punishment given by God.'

Indian transsexuals who decide not to be castrated are known as zenanas; eunuchs and zenanas are committed enemies, jealously protecting their territories from each other.

Bushpa, still rocking his baby, observes that men sometimes dress up in women's clothes because it fools people into believing they are eunuchs. 'They walk with swaying bodies like women and behave as we do. But they do not know the arts; they cannot dance or sing. They merely beg.'

Several doctors in Delhi are willing to conduct castrations in private clinics, charging about £60 for the first operation. The entire process takes up to four operations and may require patients to have as many as 120 stitches.

Eunuchs are surrounded by myths. It is said, wrongly, that they capture young men and forcibly have them castrated to keep the community alive. In fact, they recruit by persuasion; there is no shortage of transsexuals willing to enter the isolated world of the eunuchs. With their masculine faces and feminine gait, they are easily recognized.

Bushpa, laying his baby gently on a pillow, says eunuchs become accustomed to being laughed at. He says his sisters and brothers, whom he still visits, do not like him being a hidra, the local term for a eunuch.

'They want me to stay with them and to start dressing as a man. They offer me food and money, but I cannot stay with them. I belong here with my child and the other hidras.'

Bushpa says he would never resort to prostitution. 'I was beautiful when I was young, but I refused to do anything like that. I learnt to dance with style and grace. I am an artist. Now I know my dancing days are coming to a close. When I get old the other hidras will look after me. But now I have got my baby. She is my reason for living. It is wonderful to be a woman, and a mother.'

13 October 1990

Defying the gravity of physics

Nigel Hawkes

Stephen Hawking's body may be earthbound, but his mind sails serenely free. Cruising at a level of abstraction where the oxygen is getting thin, he juggles with notions of infinity and curved space–time, of matter falling in on itself until it disappears up its own singularity. Here, at the outer reaches of physics, where relativity and quantum theory set the rules, he feels at home. From time to time the ghost of a smile flickers across a face drawn tight by a disabling disease but still able to express pleasure at an ingenious idea or a witty aside.

Professor Hawking, who holds the Lucasian chair of mathematics at Cambridge University, is Britain's best-known scientist, a man whose reputation has burst the bounds of physics and turned him into a celebrity. His lectures are packed, his bestselling book has broken records, he is showered with honours and awards. He has even had the unwelcome experience of seeing the break-up of his marriage chronicled in the press. No scientist since Einstein has excited such a mixture of awe and incomprehension.

One reason for this is his inaccessibility. Professor Hawking is trapped in a world of silence by a progressive disease that has reduced him to a shred. He is confined to a wheelchair, and has movement only in two fingers of his left hand. He can hear but he cannot respond, except by typing words with agonizing slowness on to a computer screen, and then speaking them through a voice synthesizer that pronounces his soaring ideas in a flat monotone. Twenty years ago even this form of communication would not have been available, and he does not complain. But it means that he has not had the constant exposure by television that quickly turns so many celebrities into familiar figures. His isolation is not of his own choosing, but it preserves his mystery just the same.

Talking to Professor Hawking is an unnerving experience. In a silence broken only by the gentle click of his computer control device, one sits at his right shoulder and waits as his replies appear word by word on the screen. It is impossible to tell if he finds the questions interesting or banal. The chances are that he has answered most of them before, but when communication is so difficult there is no chance of exploring fresh leads. In almost two hours, Professor Hawking was able to answer just eight questions. At the end he kindly printed out his answers; they covered one sheet of paper.

We met in his office in Cambridge. His desk was covered with scientific papers which are held up for him by a nurse so that he can read them. Professor Hawking sits motionless in his wheelchair, his head lolling backwards against the head rest. In the corner sits the duty nurse, ready to help if needed.

Professor Hawking's image as a disembodied intelligence occupying a world of its own was brought abruptly to earth earlier this year by the news that he had left his family and set up home with one of the nurses who had been providing him with twenty-four-hour care for the past five years. Marital breakdown is hardly a novelty, but this one did come as a shock, because Jane, his wife, had always seemed an inseparable part of his success, providing the care in difficult times without which he could not have done his work.

Neither Professor Hawking nor his wife will discuss the matter publicly – he ruled out questions on his private life as a condition of this interview – but a friend of the family suggests that he was looking for, and found, the kind of uncritical admiration which few wives of twenty-five years are any longer prepared to offer. Perhaps, too, it may be less trying to live with somebody trained to deal with his disability rather than a wife who has made no secret of her past sacrifices. He would not be the first man to fall in love with his nurse, but his decision did leave in tatters the public image of the Hawkings as a productive partnership. He, after all, had written that it was only Jane's love that gave him the will to live and work at a particularly black moment of his life. While pictures of her and their three children still decorate his office, friends say that she speaks bitterly about the split, and no longer feels under any obligation, as one put it, 'to promote the greater glory of Stephen Hawking'.

For that, perhaps, he no longer has need of her. His success is assured enough to have provoked the envy and the quiet bitchiness on which university towns thrive. There are those who will mutter anonymously that he has a poor grasp of philosophy and theology, although he has ventured into both fields. Some physicists believe that his contributions to science have been overrated because of his medical condition. Certainly, it was not the ideas alone that catapulted his book, *A Brief History of Time*, into such a huge and unexpected success.

The subject of cosmology and the history of the universe had been tackled before (most notably in Steven Weinberg's *The First Three Minutes*), but Professor Hawking's book is in an entirely different league, up there with supersellers like *The Country Diary of an Edwardian Lady*. Exact sales remain a mystery, but more than two years in the bestseller lists make it an unusual science title, and its author a much richer man. Everybody has been astonished by its success. Its appeal was recognized by Mark Barty-King, the managing director of Bantam Press, but even he was aiming at a first print run of just 5,000 until his salesmen reported enormous interest in the book and he increased it to 8,000.

Professor Hawking admits to surprise at its success. 'I thought it might sell a reasonable number, but it has done about twenty times what I expected. Publishers keep asking me to write another book, but I want to concentrate on my scientific work for the moment.'

Few of the book's readers can have comprehended many of the ideas it explores, for getting to grips with relativity takes time as well as application, as Professor Hawking discovered when he was a young graduate student at Cambridge. He claims that he was not a particularly clever child, slow to learn to read and never more than about half-way up the class at school, although he admits it was a very bright class. 'When I was twelve, one of my friends bet another friend a bag of sweets that I would never come to anything,' he wrote in a short account of his life that his secretary at Cambridge provides as background material for visitors. 'I don't know if the bet was ever settled, and if so which way it was decided.'

He came from a bookish, academic background, growing up in London and St Albans. Both his parents were at Oxford, and his father worked as a research biologist in tropical diseases at the National Institute for Medical Research at Mill Hill, in northwest London. Professor Hawking was born in January 1942, in Oxford, where his mother had moved to avoid the bombs. His father, who came originally from Yorkshire, wanted his oldest son to go to Westminster to get the social polish which he felt he had lacked. But Stephen was ill at the time of the scholarship exams, failed to do himself justice, and went to St Albans School where, he says, the education was every bit as good. He resisted, too, his father's urgings towards medicine or biology, which he found too imprecise, and by the age of fourteen had resolved to become a mathematician or physicist.

He now declares that in spite of his chair in mathematics – once occupied by Sir Isaac Newton – he is a physicist whose maths stopped at A-level. As his disabilities have worsened, he has found it harder to deal in the equations that are the language of higher mathematics. Although interested in the search for a complete theory of the universe, he thinks others are more likely to discover it. 'Part of the programme to develop a complete theory of the universe is to try to write down a set of fundamental equations. There are people who are much better at that than me, because I can't write down equations. But modern physics is based on geometry and I'm better at that. I can picture it in my mind. So I concentrate on problems that can be translated into geometry.'

As an undergraduate at Oxford, he was so good at physics

that he got through with little effort. He has calculated that in three years there he did 1,000 hours of work, an average of an hour a day. 'I'm not proud of this lack of work, I'm just describing my attitude at the time, which I shared with most of my fellow students,' his autobiographical essay records. 'You were supposed to be brilliant without effort, or to accept your limitations and get a fourth-class degree.' He duly got his first, and went to Cambridge to begin his PhD.

It had been easy sailing, but now there was a terrible setback. In his final year at Oxford he had found that he was getting clumsy; twice he fell over, for no apparent reason. The next year, his first at Cambridge, his father noticed and took him to the doctor. Tests in hospital revealed that he had motor neuron disease, a rare wasting condition in which the nerves in the central nervous system that control muscular activity gradually atrophy. The doctors were vague about the details, as doctors often are, and Professor Hawking did not feel like asking for more information because he could see that it would be bad.

'The realization that I had an incurable disease that was likely to kill me in a few years was a bit of a shock. How could something like this happen to me? Why should I be cut off like this? However, while I had been in hospital I had seen a boy I vaguely knew die of leukaemia. It had not been a pretty sight. Clearly there were people who were worse off than me. At least my condition didn't make me feel sick. Whenever I feel inclined to feel sorry for myself, I remember that boy.'

The prospects were, in truth, awful. Four fifths of those diagnosed as suffering from MND will die within five years; only a tenth survive for longer than a decade. Professor Hawking has now been living on borrowed time for the better part of twenty years. He had chosen to be a theoretical physicist, which was fortunate, for solitary cerebration is one activity that remains possible for a man in his condition. But to begin with he found the going tough. He knew little of general relativity, Einstein's theory which forms the mathematical underpinning of cosmology. He feared he would not live long enough to complete his doctorate, and sank into gloom, listening for hours to Wagner and feeling sorry for himself. He denies reports of heavy drinking, however.

What would have happened to him if he had not been an extraordinary physicist? 'I do worry about what could easily have happened to me if I had not been lucky enough to be good at something that catches the public imagination, and if I had not received a great deal of help. I would probably have ended up in a home and I would not have lived very long. There must be plenty of people who are not so lucky. I think society, and that means the government, should do much more for them. They shouldn't be dependent on charity.'

Professor Hawking's help came first from his wife, who had still to complete her own degree in modern languages at Westfield College, London, when they met. Without her it is plain that he would not have got through the first few years, when his condition rapidly worsened and his name had yet to be made. Subsequently, his reputation rose as his condition declined, which encouraged the university and his college, Gonville and Caius, to give him positions that required little teaching. To begin with he could speak, though not very clearly, but a bout of pneumonia in 1985 necessitated a tracheostomy operation and his voice was lost. In due course, various foundations provided money for full-time nursing care.

He gets about Cambridge in a powered wheelchair which he drives with enthusiasm, a single hand controlling a joystick. He even insists on driving himself when negotiating the few yards from his office into the common room of the department of applied mathematics, although a male nurse is on hand. Like all scientists in British universities, Professor Hawking observes the ritual of afternoon tea, joining his colleagues in the common room. You sense that he would desperately like to join in the idle gossip of the department, but the technology that supports him, clever as it is, is a barrier to easy conversation. Nobody rushes forward for a chat.

He uses the slight movement still available in his left hand to control a computer program containing about 3,000 words. The program quickly scrolls the words past as he selects them by minute movements on a small control pad, building up sentences on the screen. His menu of words is limited, which gives his conversation a simple, almost naïve, quality. He can add words not included in the menu by spelling them out letter by letter, but this slows him down. At best he can manage about fifteen words a minute, which makes conversation slow; his research students tend to bring along something to read while he responds to their queries.

Once he has built up a sentence he can send it to a speech synthesizer mounted on his wheelchair, which pronounces it in uninflected speak-your-weight-machine tones. This enables him to give lectures, preparing them in advance, storing them on disc, then releasing them to the synthesizer sentence by sentence. He recently gave a lecture on determinism in Cambridge to a packed house. At the end, somebody politely asked a question and the whole audience sat silently for what seemed an age – actually about ten minutes – until his reply had been composed.

Professor Hawking is always on the move, refusing to allow his disability to trap him in Cambridge. In June he was in Sweden, last month in Japan and South Korea; trips to the United States are a regular event. 'I get a thrill out of travelling,' he says.

What are his most important contributions to science? Professor Hawking cites two papers, probably the same two most other cosmologists believe his reputation will ultimately rest on. The first, described by Denis Sciama, Professor Hawking's first supervisor at Cambridge, as 'one of the most beautiful in the history of physics', came as a complete surprise to everybody, including its author. Published in 1974, it showed that black holes, intense concentrations of matter so massive that nothing, including light, can escape from them, could nevertheless emit radiation. The significance of this finding was threefold. First, it was a new assessment of the nature of black holes, astronomical objects whose actual existence, although universally accepted by cosmologists, has yet to be confirmed experimentally. Second, the mechanism outlined by Professor Hawking could have implications for understanding the very first fractions of a second after the universe began in the Big Bang. Finally, by successfully applying quantum theory to black holes, Professor Hawking had begun the process of combining the two great theories of modern physics – quantum theory and general relativity.

The second paper, published in the early Eighties, is commemorated in a cartoon which hangs in Professor Hawking's office. He and his co-author, Jim Hartle of the University of California at Santa Barbara, are shown as scientists gazing at a blackboard on which a mass of equations concludes in a huge zero. The caption reads: 'No doubt about it, Hartle, we've explained the purpose of the universe. Gad, how I love the thrill of scientific discovery!'

What Professor Hawking and Mr Hartle had actually done was to propose a model of the universe that had no boundaries in space or time. Big Bang theories assume that if you go back far enough, to the very beginning of the universe, there was a moment when all cosmic matter was concentrated in a single spot, known as a singularity. The existence of such singularities is implied by general relativity, as Professor Hawking had established in collaboration with Roger Penrose many years earlier. A boundary-free universe, on the other hand, would not need to have started life as a singularity. Professor Hawking tries to explain this to non-cosmologists by visualizing the beginning of the universe as being rather like the North Pole of the earth. As one moves south, the circles of latitude grow bigger, just as the universe did at the beginning of time. At the equator the universe reaches a maximum size, before beginning to shrink again as one approaches the South Pole. In case this concept is insufficiently hard to grasp, Professor Hawking adds that one would have to measure time in terms of imaginary numbers –

that is to say, numbers that when multiplied by each other produce a negative answer, which no real number does.

A consistent theme in modern cosmology is the search for the underlying reasons why physical constants such as the strength of gravity, or the size of the electric charge on an elementary particle, have the values they actually do. It turns out that the history of the universe, and our own place in it, are critically dependent on those values. Different values might have produced a universe so thin that it simply dispersed into space without ever congealing into galaxies, or so dense that it collapsed back on itself into a gigantic black hole. If the constants were chosen at random, the chances of picking exactly the right values were infinitesimally small. To some, this finding has theological implications, for it suggests that our universe can hardly have been created by a mere fall of the dice.

Professor Hawking is now working on a theory that suggests all these quantities may be determined by a phenomenon cosmologists call wormholes. These, he says, 'are little regions of space that branch off from the region of space–time in which we live. They may join on again later, or they may carry on to another large region of the universe. Because wormholes are very small, we don't notice them joining on or branching off. But they would affect the apparent values of all physical quantities – it may be that these quantities are completely determined by wormhole effects.' Others, it must be said, are sceptical.

Philosophically, Professor Hawking is a determinist, believing that the basic laws that govern the universe are relatively simple, and that we may discover them soon. (He rates the chances of doing so in the next twenty years at 50:50.) He has no patience at all with those who search for meaning and significance behind the explanations of science, asserting that science is sufficient unto itself. In the Cambridge lecture on determinism he declared that the important point was that there should exist a set of laws that determines the evolution of the universe from its initial state.

'These laws may have been ordained by God. But it seems that he (or she) does not intervene in the universe to break the laws.'

Does this mean that the idea of free will is an illusion? If everything is determined by mathematical laws, what is left for humankind to decide for itself? Professor Hawking's answer to that is to appeal to the uncertainty principle of quantum mechanics, which declares that it is in principle impossible to know both the position and the motion of a particle; the closer you are to knowing one, the vaguer you must be about the other. This means that the basic laws cannot be used to predict the behaviour of every particle in the universe, or in the human brain, which contains a hundred million billion billion (10^{26}) particles. As a result, even a knowledge of the basic law could not be used to predict the behaviour of every human being.

He sees free will as the equivalent of the theories used in science for dealing with systems containing too many particles for each to be considered individually. An example of that is fluid mechanics, where the motions of the individual particles in a gas or a liquid are aggregated and the fluid is treated as a continuous medium. Such theories are not fundamental, but they are effective.

'I want to suggest that the concept of free will, and of moral responsibility for our actions, are really an effective theory in the sense of fluid mechanics. It may be that everything we do is determined by some Grand Unified Theory. If that theory has determined we shall die by hanging, we shall not drown. But you would have to be awfully sure that you were destined for the gallows to put to sea in a small boat during a storm. I have noticed that even people who claim that everything is predestined look before they cross the road.'

27 October 1990

103

Football's Mr Fixit

Vicki Woods

Early in the first week of the Wimbledon tennis championships, the weather was cold and the matches on the dull side. In a marquee, the invited guests of Mark McCormack included Jackie Stewart, the former world champion racing driver, and Captain Mark Phillips. Neither the weather nor the play tempted anyone to stray far from Mr McCormack's strawberries and champagne.

As the afternoon wore on, lots of noise could be heard wafting across from No 1 court, where Jo Durie, the only British presence, was battling not to lose her match, and all the famous folk in Mr McCormack's marquee began to mass around the bank of televisions and roar as well, point for point. What slightly confused me was that while the crowd on No 1 court was clearly roaring for Durie, the marquee was roaring for her opponent. Why? I asked a McCormack man. 'Because Jo Durie isn't our client,' he said, 'and Hana Mandlikova is.' I mention this because it is an example of the influence of the agent in sport.

Jon Smith is the Mark McCormack of football. He won't mind my saying so; in fact he acknowledges Mr McCormack as maestro. Mr McCormack's organization creates money for performers around the world who would be considerably less well off without him. Mr Smith has joined this super-agent league. He is one of only six who are licensed by Fifa, football's international governing body, to arrange international tours and matches anywhere in the world. Diego Maradona is his client, as is the Football Association, the England national squad, the Polish FA, the Argentine national squad, Manchester United's FA Cup Final squad

104

(Mr Smith's efforts at last year's Cup Final provided the richest ever pool: he raised more than £100,000 in two and a half weeks, to be shared between the United players). Mr Smith's company is advising the Americans on their preparations for the 1994 World Cup, and he runs an office in Buenos Aires.

He also represents the England cricket team. ('It's the first time the Test & County Cricket Board has ever made that commercial appointment, and we've already earned the team more money off the field than they got from their tour of the West Indies last year.') Graham Gooch and his team, who begin their first Test against Australia on Friday, receive a basic fee of £20,000 before Mr Smith's money rolls in.

Being the England football team agent means 'marketing' the team. Mr Smith does not act as agent for the individual England players. Gary Lineker has had his own agent (Jonathan Holmes) for years; Paul Gascoigne has a lawyer (Mel Stein) and an accountant working for him. But Mr Smith can go to 'major sponsors' (Coca-Cola, Mars, Trebor, Umbro, Top Man) and ask for large amounts of money to be paid to the England team in a pool in return for some involvement from the players. The involvement can be something as small as wearing a brand name on their chests or as large as having to spend an hour or two milling about in front of a film crew drinking Coca-Cola.

Mr Smith also arranges matches for the England team to play. He arranges publicity-worthy matches that will pull in crowds, television audiences and money. He does not set up the ordinary, scheduled matches that are part of their England commitments. But he points out that 'my role doesn't cease' when England play in Fifa- or Uefa-arranged tournaments. 'We still use those games to promote the team,' he says, 'and you'll have noticed that most of the papers on Wednesday carried pictures of Gascoigne and McMahon with Coca-Cola logos.' Mr Smith's efforts are said to have earned the England team £1 million during the 1990 World Cup. 'They're richer 365 days a year because of me,' he said.

So who is Jon Smith? He is thirty-eight, curly-headed, crinkly-eyed, sonsie-faced, warm-voiced, nattily dressed, grammar school educated, and drives a Bentley Mulsanne. He was making money cheerfully enough in California (music industry, property dealing) when a sudden and enriching thought came to him. He realized that American-promoted sports stars were as rich as rock stars, and so, it must follow, were their promoters.

Now, Mr Smith greatly loved Association Football, being a longtime Arsenal fan. So he bought the name First Artist from its previous owners, Dustin Hoffman and Barbra Streisand, and came back to London in 1986 to take football by storm.

Football, he explains, even those few short years ago and despite the efforts of Canon and the Milk Marketing Board, 'had no platform for sponsors. It wasn't marketed as a family spectacle. It didn't have the Mark McCormacks, whom I admire enormously and on whom I base my theory and practice. I wanted to commercialize footballers and make them into household names and push them into the same income bracket as the biggest pop stars of their time.'

So what was it that Mr Smith was intending to take by storm? Think back. Back to an age when footballers did not prance about the field with 'Holsten' and 'Candy' and 'C. R. Smith' and 'McEwans' on their chests. To a time when football was dead, dead, dead but wouldn't lie down. Who ran the sport, after all? Dinosaurs; men who were elected for life to preserve the freemasonry of football; men who wished they could disinvent television because it spoilt the atmosphere.

Who was it who changed all this? Luciano Pavarotti, belting out a few bars of 'Nessun dorma' during this summer's World Cup in Italy? No, it was not Signor Pavarotti, nor was it Mr 'Robert' Robson, as the Italians, with their lovely continental manners, rechristened him; nor Mr Gary Lineker, the man who picked up the prize for best-behaved boy at the World Cup; nor Mr Paul Gascoigne. Step forward Mr Jon

Smith of the First Artist Corporation, opposite Wembley Stadium! Mr Smith calls himself 'the first of the new breed of soccer agents who have become respectable'.

The infant company First Artist had two rather marvellous pieces of luck as cradle gifts. Within three weeks of setting up the company, a man called Harry Swales retired as England's team agent, and what Mr Smith calls 'the biggest pitch of all' fell vacant. All the other soccer agents pitched for England, of course, 'but we got the account'. When pressed for the reasons why his new-born company landed the prestige England account, Mr Smith says it was probably his handling of the Inland Revenue. England players used to be bedevilled by tax problems, especially on their earnings from the 'players' pool'. The pool is money that the team earns as a team: from making personal appearances, humming along to chart-topping singles, or wearing the words Umbro or Coca-Cola on their undershorts. Players often ended up, for complex reasons, being taxed twice on some of their earnings. 'We got the Inland Revenue to agree,' says Mr Smith, with breathtaking panache, 'that the players' pool should be treated for tax purposes as an "unincorporated corporation". Taxwise, this was advantageous to them. I think that was what swung it.'

The second piece of luck came only a few weeks later. Mr Smith heard that his old friend, the talented Tottenham import Osvaldo Ardiles, was thinking of going into a soccer agency, and he thought that he would arrange a chat with Mr Ardiles in hopes that there might be some mutual benefit. Meetings were fixed and cancelled, until one evening he found himself finally ensconced chez Osvaldo, enjoying a chat. Lo – the telephone rang. And extraordinarily enough, on the other end of it was Ossie's old mate Diego Maradona, who was calling long distance to moan about his agent. Could Ossie help him out and take over? No, said Ossie, but I know a man who can, and promptly interpreted non-stop between Diego (talking Spanish) and our boy Jon (talking English) on the sofa. Ten minutes later the deal was done.

'I am one of six agents licensed by Fifa,' he says, leaping up to get his Fifa passport. It shows a picture of Mr Smith looking like a disc-jockey; but it is a powerful document. 'It means I'm Mr Squeaky-Clean. It means I can organize international matches anywhere in the world.' So you could organize Brazil to play Holland in . . . Wisconsin? 'Well, we *are* talking about Brazil, but playing Italy. In New York. Next May. Next February 6, we're bringing Cameroon over to play England at Wembley. That'll be a *great* game.

'The other one I'm trying to do – this is going to be fun – and providing there are no hostilities in the Gulf it's going to work . . . ' What do you mean, no hostilities in the Gulf? 'Well, we were asked, by the Saudi Football Federation, could we show to the world that everything's normal back in Saudi. Could we put on a soccer game at the King Fahd Stadium in Riyadh? So we contacted – well, it wouldn't be fair to say who we contacted because every single one of them said no. Every major federation said, "Erm, I think we're busy that day."

'So I had this idea – why not, because we've got all the GIs over there at the moment, why not get the United States to play Saudi?' I goggle at him. 'You've got a full house,' he says. 'It'll be great; you've got these two armies sitting there; it'll be just like – remember the film *Escape to Victory*?' Oh, lord, yes. With Sylvester Stallone playing the Peter Shilton role. And I suddenly saw what the match would do for First Artist long-term, under its PR-to-the-America-Hosts-the-World-Cup-1994 hat.

You mean, it will help to teach America what football is? '*Exactly*. That's *exactly* what I'm trying to do. It promotes soccer, in America, for the World Cup in '94. Anyway, the US has said yes, Saudi has said yes, and it'll be a major televised event.'

Mr Smith has a breathtaking patriotism. 'Has there ever been a time,' he asks me, clearly expecting the answer no, 'apart from during the Falklands conflict, a time when this nation was more united than . . .' I could see he was going to say 'in the second half of the England–West Germany game at

Turin', but I say '1966', and he says 'Yes, yes', all misty-eyed at the thought of Bobby and Nobby and Bobby. 'And that just shows,' he says, 'the product that we have the responsibility of marketing. There is nothing in this country that's as big . . . for audience reaction, audience pull and audience, erm, following.'

What did you vote in the last election, Mr Smith?

'I'm a committed Maggie Thatcher fan.'

Sport and right-wing politics make a wonderful mix, as every Tory politician apart from Colin Moynihan knows to his advantage. Mr Smith enjoys the mix. 'I had dinner at the House of Commons last night,' he says. 'And we were talking to a number of ministers about how do we get England to be able to put a genuine bid in to bring over the World Cup in 1998. The FA said that they desire the World Cup to come to England. From the connections or friends I've got at Westminster, it would appear that the government would like it to happen as well. The whole aspect of it, ultimately, is going to be commercially led, corporately led.'

Now, just a second. The idea of England hosting the World Cup in 1998 is even madder than the idea of America hosting it in 1994. Americans may barely have heard of soccer, can't play soccer and won't enjoy watching soccer, but at least they have some infrastructure. They have stadiums where you can watch a ball game, eat hamburgers and take the children, and you can do all this sitting down. They may be stadiums where the field is plastic Astroturf and the ground area is actually too small to fit a football pitch inside, but they can change all that.

In Britain, how many stadiums apart from Wembley are even going to comply with the terms of the Taylor Report and become all-seater by 1995? How is anyone going to attempt to throw up half-a-dozen beautiful new ones like the stadiums they built for Italia '90? And how will you raise the £500 million (minimum) in the first place? 'One of the ways is what people like the Football Association and myself were discussing last night . . . We'll go to central government with tax-advantageous schemes for companies. Central government

cannot afford and would not fund building six or eight beautiful municipal stadiums. There is only one' – (he jerks his head
towards the window) – 'Wembley. Wembley should remain
as *the* one, because it represents the ethos of the sport itself.
What I think will happen is the commercial activity that
people like myself have started, like bringing in the Coca-
Colas and Mars and the Burton Group. They'll be the people
who say, "Let's extend our involvement in sport".' So will we
have a Coca-Cola Ground? 'You'll get something very close
to it, and it will be funded not by the company putting its hand
in its pocket and coming up with twenty or thirty million, but
by deferred tax advantages. And that's the way that I think
we'll be in a position to fund Britain's, er, *England's* campaign to bring the World Cup here in 1998.' Have you had a
word with Mrs Thatcher about this? 'I've certainly had a word
with her lieutenants, who are very, very enthusiastic. There
are people in government who care passionately about the
sport, people like John Major.' *John Major?* 'Yes, he supports Chelsea, and David Mellor – actually, he supports
Chelsea as well, by pure coincidence.'

So that's it, really. Jon Smith. Mr Squeaky-Clean, Mr
Football in the Nineties. He lives in what he calls a 'small-
holding' in Barnet, north London, with his second wife,
Janine. His first wife, Lee, died of leukaemia in 1980, after
which, he said, he 'went to live at the bottom of a whisky
bottle for a year', and he is president of the Lee Smith
Research Foundation, which works on leukaemia research at
Great Ormond Street Hospital. He and Janine have a toddler
son, Ross, who is being groomed for the mascotship of
Arsenal (though I don't think Arsenal knows yet) and a new
baby due in May. There are pet llamas, goats and a waterfowl
sanctuary at Barnet, Mr Smith says.

One other thing. As a boy, he stammered so badly that he
could not speak. At the age of fourteen, his father took him,
as a last resort, to see a man called Bill Kerr who advertised a
stammering cure in the *Daily Express*. Mr Kerr hit you if you
stammered in front of him. 'He beat me up. He beat all of us

up. He made us nod, and take a breath and say "My! Name! Is! Jon! Smith!" and if you got stuck, if you said "My! Name! Is! J-j-j-j-! J-j-j-j-!" he'd give you a real clip. He yelled at us; he was really vicious, brutal. He made us, finally, more afraid to stammer than we'd been afraid to speak. He said at the end: "Now, nothing is ever going to hurt you again as much as I've hurt you this week, so you've got nothing to be afraid of." I had a relapse once, but he came straight over and beat me up again. He holds a very special place in my heart, Bill Kerr.'

17 November 1990

A Childhood: Doris Lessing

Ray Connolly

Only in later life did Doris Lessing realize that she had grown up in the Garden of Eden, one of the world's last great wildernesses, Southern Rhodesia in the Twenties and Thirties, virgin bush country that her father put to the plough.

She was five when they arrived there in 1924, 70 miles northeast of Salisbury, in a covered wagon that carried all their belongings and was pulled by fifteen or twenty oxen, her father riding alongside on his horse. 'I can still remember the hurricane lamp swinging to and fro from the top of the cart as we made the journey,' she says. Even then she was much travelled, having been born in 1919 in Kermanshah in Persia, where her father had gone to run a branch of the Westminster Bank. Her father was a contemplative man, whose life was wrecked by the trenches of the First World War in which he lost a leg and suffered terrible shellshock.

While recovering in the Royal Free Hospital, her father, Captain Alfred Tayler, met her mother, who was a nurse. They married and her mother was very happy in Persia, particularly in Tehran, but her father was bored. In 1924 leave came and, it being too hot to take the two children back through the Red Sea, her mother decided to come home overland through the young, starving and unruly Soviet Union.

Nothing stopped her, not a Bolshevik border guard with a rifle who insisted that their papers were not in order ('Don't be silly,' he was told), not being left behind on a southern Russian platform by the train, and not the lice and the typhus on the oil tanker on the Caspian Sea.

No doubt she hoped they might stay in England, but a visit

112

to the Imperial Exhibition at Wembley, where advertisements offered the opportunity of wealth within five years in Southern Rhodesia, saw the young family back on board ship within the year.

'My father [of whom she writes sadly in the recently published *Doris Lessing Reader*] had grown up among farmers and loved the idea of farming. He couldn't have stood the idea of the bank for the rest of his life and he felt constricted by the narrowness of England.

'My mother should have married a stockbroker and stayed in England. She had no idea what she was going to and took with her a piano, curtains from Liberty's, clothes from Harrods, visiting cards and a young governess who thought it was going to be a Somerset Maugham kind of life.' (The governess lasted only a year.) The deal was that the government was selling land very cheaply to ex-servicemen in return for them 'opening up the country'.

In fact, the land for sale was land from which the Africans had recently been pushed. 'That was called bringing civilization to the benighted,' Mrs Lessing says, a theme that she worked into one of her early short stories, *The Old Chief Mshlanga*. The 1,500 acres her parents bought was in Lomagundi in what turned out to be a rich farming area where the bush teamed with wildlife. The elephants and lions had gone but everywhere there were kudu, sable, bushbuck, wild cats, snakes, hawks and eagles. With the help of dispossessed native labour the bush was stumped out, the trees burnt and the land ploughed. Home was a house built by her father in the native style, but much larger than that of the Africans – a cigar-shaped cottage built of branches lashed together into a frame around a central pole. Soil from an ant-hill, and accidentally from a native burial ground, was pounded into mud to form the walls as plaster, and then the whole was thatched, 18 inches deep.

Such a pole-and-dagga house was supposed to last about five years. For Doris Lessing's family, growing poorer rather than richer as intended, its life stretched to twenty years.

Depending upon the season, the farm might employ up to sixty native workers for a few shillings a month each. 'They lived in these terrible huts, were badly fed and badly paid and they had to work because they had to pay the poll tax – levied to get them out of their huts, otherwise they'd have just sat about enjoying themselves and we can't have that, can we? Don't forget this was when everyone took it for granted that the British Empire was the greatest thing that ever was.

'My mother was kind in that she bandaged people up and gave medicine to them but she didn't see anything wrong with the system. My father knew it was ridiculous. He used to say "In a hundred years time they'll rise up and push us all back into the sea." But that was heresy and it's not easy to stand apart from all the others.' To the two children, the bush was paradise, one continual adventure. Playing with the local African children was not even considered, but there were other expatriates' children not many miles away. She was taught by correspondence course from England and, later, at boarding schools in Salisbury.

At seven she was sent to a Catholic convent, where she was extremely unhappy. 'We were taught by nuns who should not have been allowed near children. Every night there would be a terrifying sermon. It scarred me for life.'

At thirteen she went to the high school in Salisbury. Already she was writing poems and short stories. She became ill and spent a year back on the farm, sitting around reading all the time, 'full of quinine. Then I was sent on a funded holiday to a guest house in the Vumba [a high eastern part of Rhodesia close to Mozambique] and it was while I was there, away from that terrible atmosphere of illness, that I realized that I had been brought up by hypochondriacs, through no fault of their own, and that I was not ill at all. When I went back home that was when my mother and I really quarrelled and I escaped.'

Doris left home at fourteen and took a job in Salisbury, as what would now be called an au pair. She began writing the first of her two early, unpublished and now destroyed novels. 'I'm glad I destroyed them. If I hadn't they'd have been writing theses about them now. That was no loss to humanity. I knew they were no good.'

In 1939 she married for the first time 'because the war was coming. That was why everybody married then. It was quite crazy. I saw him as a great intellectual shining light. In a way he was, an ambitious young civil servant who held, for the time and place, quite liberal ideas. I suppose I married to get away from my mother. The joke is that my daughter, Jean, will be bitter until she dies because I am not the possessive mother. My daughter should have had my mother for a mother.'

As a young mother with two children she continued to write. Some short stories appeared in South African magazines. The marriage did not survive the war and, after taking a job in a lawyer's office, she married again, a German refugee called Lessing.

'This was really neurotic behaviour.' There was another child and another broken marriage. She was now typing for parliament and select committees and having a very busy social life.

'I'd been going around saying I was a writer but then, I thought, where was the evidence for it?' So one day she gave up her job and sat down to write *The Grass is Singing*, which was published in 1950, the year after she came to Britain. For thirty years she was banned from returning to Rhodesia 'because I was a loud critic of the government and also because I was a Red'. Later, when she talked to the Rhodesian prime minister, who had also been their family doctor, he told her: 'We weren't going to have you upsetting our blacks.' Salisbury was, after all, just a small town in Africa, 'Cheltenham in the wild West', as she likes to say.

When finally she was allowed to travel back to the country of her childhood she was shocked. It had never occurred to her that it would not be the same. Though the land was still extraordinarily beautiful, the kudu and the sable now inhabited the vast national parks. The Garden of Eden had changed.

'I was very lucky in that I was of the last generation to see the bush as it was. The other thing my childhood gave me was no feeling about security. I simply don't care about it. I think the travelling as a child was the luckiest thing that could have happened to me as a writer.'

17 November 1990

Reflected future in a castle made of glass

Marcus Binney

If anyone can be termed the Grand Old Man of English architecture, it is Sir Denys Lasdun. At seventy-six he is in his office daily, and very much in evidence at all architectural occasions.

His latest building takes him into new territory: the commercial world of the City. As he says, 'The speculative office block could be designed by a computer. It's simply a question of fitting x floor space on to y land.' For him, the challenge was to produce something genuinely creative, in terms of both its public face and its functioning.

'In the Sixties and earlier I felt a sense of social responsibility about my buildings; even a sense of mission. With schools, universities and housing one felt one was helping society. In today's market economy one doesn't have such variety of input.' So how does the architect find a rationale? 'I think he exercises a sort of irony. In place of ideology you find a metaphor.' The metaphor Sir Denys has chosen at Milton Court is a castle: 'With the Barbican next door, we are, after all, in castle territory. A barbican is a fortified outer gate.'

His underlying inspiration, however, comes from Charles Rennie Mackintosh. 'For me he stands supreme in the search for a non-historical style. He derives from the castellar architecture of Scotland – from buildings which were a direct response to the elements.'

The castle analogy is most strongly evident in the towers: corner towers over the entrances in Chiswell Street and Milton Gate, complete with turrets opening on to the roofs and a great circular donjon in the centre containing the main services. With this go steeply pitched roofs (more echoes of Scotland) and, to the west, sharp setbacks in response to light restrictions, hinting at Mackintosh's Scotland Street School. The most obvious Mackintosh tribute comes in the clusters of projecting bays, guiding the eyes to the entrances. These grow out of the façade, becoming more pronounced at each level. At first sight, however, it is the glass exterior which catches the eye: not so much its colour, green tinged with blue, but its aqueous quality. You feel you are peering into water, with all the straight lines inside slightly kinked.

Over the past twenty-five years the challenge of the curtain glass wall has been to produce ever greater sleekness and refinement. By degrees, architects have eliminated every moulding, until the building rises sheer like a glacier from the pavement. But the perfect grid of architects such as Mies van der Rohe could be disturbed by a single venetian blind at the wrong angle, or glimpses of potted plants.

Mirror glass was one answer, shutting out all trace of the people and offices within, but while effective on tall buildings which reflect the sky, it can have a deadening effect at street level.

The latest solution, adopted here, is to give the building a dual skin. 'The outer glass is the architectural order of the building,' Sir Denys explains. 'It cannot be changed.' It consists of unframed glass supported from a grid within. The inner skin is also glass: not sheet glass rising sheer from floor to ceiling, but large panes set in a bold blue metal grid. The occupants can make any internal change they wish without disturbing the external perfection of the skin. Sir Denys's bays and towers introduce a pattern of diagonals across the severe Mondrian-like grid of the inner skin, creating a whole series of prismatic reflections. Particularly subtle are the bay windows, which at the top fold in and out like screens. This is a system which Sir Denys developed at the National Theatre, where a diagonal grid is laid, both vertically and horizontally, over a square matrix.

For all the visual richness the dual skin creates, it is strictly functional. First, it provides deck access for maintenance on each floor (rather in the way that passages, staircases and privies were often contrived within the thickness of castle walls in the Middle Ages). Second, it reduces solar gain and heat loss, acting as a continuous chimney which allows warm air or cooling draughts to be circulated. One reaction to modern office blocks, with their vast multi-storey atriums, is to ask how the heating of such huge spaces can be afforded. In fact, the main problem is to keep these buildings cool. Such is the heat generated by computers and special lighting that a building such as Milton Court requires only minimal heating even on the coldest day.

Sir Denys does not use the word atrium, preferring to talk of a central hall. 'Atriums in Roman architecture,' he points out, 'were always open to the sky.' His central hall is approached diagonally – once again, varying the grid – from the corner entrances, which converge on the central cylindrical donjon containing the lifts. This is entered, appropriately, across a moat.

Sir Denys's client is Land Securities, which is now completing the new Grand Buildings in Trafalgar Square. Significantly, both buildings have been pre-let to single tenants, Milton Court's 200,000sq ft to the accountants Price Waterhouse.

At Milton Court, Sir Denys says he was replacing an indifferent block of the Thirties. 'There was no clear contextual imperative.' Here, as elsewhere, he has sought to produce an elemental solution, consisting of towers, pitched roofs and the 'veil' of the glass curtain wall giving form but allowing complete flexibility within.

The most interesting aspect of Sir Denys's glass castle is that it takes him stylistically into almost new territory. Among all the modernists working in Britain, he is the one with the most identifiable style.

It is a style above all of strongly marked horizontals or planes. Not for him the carefully balanced repeating grid, but rather a forceful lateral emphasis, with each floor thrusting outwards expressively, like some great rock shelf.

This feeling emerged strongly in the elegant block of apartments at 26 St James's Place, London, which he built in 1958, next to Spencer House, overlooking Green Park. Few pieces of modern architecture have dated less. The project which has given him the most pleasure is undoubtedly the Royal College of Physicians at the bottom of Regent's Park. Here he built in the early Sixties an uncompromisingly modern building amid the Nash terraces, but with an emphasis on good manners and neighbourliness quite different from the hated Brutalism that developed over the next decade.

His most prominent commission remains the National Theatre. When completed it was a brilliant sight, seen from across the Thames, almost white in the sun. Here was an architecture of pure form, almost a giant piece of abstract sculpture which on certain days was all chiaroscuro, light and shade, with the windows lost in the shadows. But the concrete has stained with weathering and the glow, so strong in the early photographs, has gone.

None the less, it is the diamond towers at the NT which provide the direct link with the glass castle at Milton Court, both designed with diagonals laid over squares, the hallmark of his later work. He looks forward, he says, to doing one more building. 'Nothing big, but a crystallization of what I think about architecture.' He has not been invited to do much in England recently; the Prince of Wales's savage strictures on the National Theatre cannot have helped.

What Sir Denys demonstrates at Milton Court is that, for all his years, he is as capable of producing a finely-tuned high-tech building of lasting quality, elegant in every detail, as any of the young generation which has now overtaken him.

17 November 1990

Rich setting for the gems of the East

Richard Cork

When the Queen opens the resplendent Nehru Gallery at the Victoria & Albert museum next Thursday, the acrid controversy surrounding its Indian holdings may finally be silenced. Although the V&A owns the largest and most comprehensive collection of Indian art outside that subcontinent, it has never been displayed with sufficient flair and sympathetic conviction. In recent years, accusations of flagrant bias began to be hurled at the museum, particularly by Indian-born residents of this country who suspected that their native land's culture was being slighted and hidden from view.

In historical terms, they were accurate enough. Even after India became part of the empire in the mid nineteenth century, Britain's respect for Indian artistic prowess was restricted to the applied arts alone. The majority of Victorian critics and historians spurned India's immense achievements in painting and sculpture, regarding them as too paltry to be counted among the fine arts. Such ignorance and prejudice was inexcusable, particularly in view of the burgeoning Indian collection amassed by the East India Company. Established at the company's Leadenhall Street headquarters as early as 1810, the repository grew at an immense rate. By the time it was taken over by the V&A in 1879, the collection embraced an extraordinary array of agricultural models, stuffed birds and mineral products alongside jewellery, textiles and sculpture. Not until the present century, however, did scholars such as the celebrated Ananda Coomaraswamy persuade Britain to re-examine its bias against Indian art. A new generation of inventive sculptors, Jacob Epstein and Eric

Gill prominent among them, now became interested in Indian art's uninhibited emphasis on sensual delight.

At the height of his infatuation with India, Gill exclaimed in 1911 that 'the best route to Heaven is via Elephanta, and Elura [sic] and Ajanta'. But the national collection of Indian art was displayed unsatisfactorily, in former exhibition buildings at a significant distance from the V&A's premises. This geographical removal symbolized a continuing unwillingness to accord India's artistic achievement the position and respect it deserved, and worse was to come. When the buildings housing the collection were demolished in 1955, the V&A failed to find it an adequate home. Most of the items were consigned to storage, emerging only in sections for temporary displays at the museum. No wonder its critics suspected that Britain did not, fundamentally, care about Indian art. In 1946, Jawaharlal Nehru insisted that the country he was leading into independence 'has the right to reclaim in universal history the rank that ignorance has refused her for a long time'.

We were in no hurry to heed his argument, and only in 1988 did a new gallery open within the V&A to display the arts of India from 200BC to AD1500. The overdue process of reparation had begun, but the bulk of the 35,000 Indian objects owned by the museum still languished in the cellars.

Although the museum's financial crisis militated against solving the problem, its recently appointed director appreciated the overriding importance of the Indian artefacts in her care.

'With a community of nearly one million people of South Asian origin living in Britain,' Elizabeth Esteve-Coll wrote, 'it is not only time to display more of that collection, but actively to use it to explain the richness and diversity of our multi-cultural heritage.' Rightly concerned about the museum's failure to attract this Asian audience, Ms Esteve-Coll launched a £2.2 million appeal for a Nehru Gallery of Indian Art within the V&A's premises.

Intended to honour the centenary of Nehru's birth, and

bolstered by the joint patronage of Mrs Thatcher and the Indian government, the venture has so far raised £1.7 million. Many of the donations came either from India or from companies linked with that country, and work soon began on a display which would at last be worthy of the objects in the collection produced between 1550 and 1990.

Devised by Brian Griggs, the V&A's head of design, the Nehru Gallery aims above all to delight the eye. Determined that it 'should make the sort of aesthetic impact on visitors which travellers in India experience even today', Mr Griggs has used a seventeenth-century colonnade from Ajmer in Rajasthan to provide a magnificent approach to the central raised pavilion. At its heart, enclosed by traditional sandstone and marble window screens, the inner treasury will house the superb inscribed jades and jewellery made for the Mogul court.

Although this focal section includes some of the museum's most precious possessions, the Nehru Gallery takes the broadest possible view of its subject. Dr Deborah Swallow, curator of the Indian and Southeast Asian collection, emphasizes: 'We certainly don't want to imply that the Moguls came along and created art in India.' Much of its essential character had been developed in earlier periods, and the changes introduced by the Mogul dynasty and subsequent British domination were counterbalanced by the continuing strength of indigenous traditions.

When the Moguls established their rule in the mid sixteenth century, India already boasted enormously prosperous cities whose trading power gave them a cosmopolitan outlook.

Several exquisite objects in the early sections of the display derive from the era when the Portuguese became the first European presence on the subcontinent. Using Goa as their principal entrepôt, Portuguese traders gathered in goods from all over India and sent them to the West. Among the earliest and most outstanding examples of Indo-Portuguese art is the so-called Robinson casket, made from solid ivory panels and secured by a gold-fitted lock studded with sapphires. The virtuoso carvings depict biblical subjects, including the nativity and the tree of Jesse. Charged with a sinuous vitality which animates humans and animals alike, they announce the conversion to Christianity of King Dharmapala of Kotte. He probably commissioned the casket in 1558 as a present to the Portuguese court, for the conversion symbolized the king's dependence on Portugal's protection rather than reflecting a genuine change in his personal faith.

The politically fragmented India discovered by the Portuguese soon gave way, after the advent of the Moguls, to a more unified alternative. Babur, the founder of the dynasty, combined military expertise with a highly-educated appreciation of the arts. His writings often refer to the poets, artists and architects of the Islamic world, and his love of nature inspired him to write poetry. A consummate gouache and gold miniature commissioned by his grandson depicts Babur supervising the laying out of the Garden of Fidelity. Eager workmen are shown digging, tending and planting the fragrant trees and flowers with which he liked to surround himself. Channelled water flows into a pool, and high walls shut out the 'hundred disgusts and repulsions' that upset Babur when he first explored the countryside around the newly conquered Agra.

The artistic flowering initiated during his reign was interrupted after his eldest son, Humayun, succeeded him. Bitter fratricidal disputes ensued, forcing the new ruler into temporary exile. He was obliged to buy help from the shah of Iran with the Koh-i-noor diamond and equally priceless rubies. Eventually the shah provided the forces needed to regain Humayun's empire, and he was able to fortify his father's cultural innovations. The artists he brought back with him from Iran established an imperial studio in India, as well as instructing the young prince Akbar. Once Akbar began his reign, the arts in India blossomed. Under his enlightened patronage the imperial painting studio produced 14 volumes, each containing 100 densely detailed illustrations, devoted to the epic adventures of the legendary Hamza. Their style fuses Iranian and Indian influences, and the enthusiastic Akbar promptly commissioned a profusely illustrated history of the Mogul dynasty called the *Akbarnama*. No fewer than 117 miniatures from the royal copy of this prodigious work belong to the V&A. Paintings such as *Akbar's Triumphant Entry into Surat* may be propagandist, but they are also enchantingly beautiful. Akbar's artists were by now copying western art, as a *Deposition from the Cross* after a lost painting by Raphael proves. The cascade of artistic production was governed by highly sophisticated standards, and the next emperor, Jahangir, was proud of his connoisseurship. 'If there be a picture containing many portraits, and each face be the work of a different master, I can discover which face is the work of each of them,' he claimed.

Although most Indian miniatures revelled in fantastic elaboration, their makers could restrict themselves to a refined simplicity as well. The superb portrait of Jahangir's son, *Shah Jahan as a Prince*, isolates the orange-robed figure on a flower-spattered, deep green ground. Festooned with precious stones, he holds a gold turban aigrette set with a particularly sumptuous emerald and diamond. Sir Thomas Roe, James I's ambassador, was astounded by the richness of the jewel-encrusted court ceremonial, and under Shah Jahan the image of a golden age took hold. The ruler responsible for the Taj Mahal, he favoured the theme of a flowering plant – whether decorating wall-hangings, beakers, tiles or bowls. The outcome evoked a heavenly garden, and an inscription in his seductive palace complex at Delhi resoundingly declares: 'If there be Paradise on the face of the earth, it is this, it is this, it is this.'

But the Mogul Eden could not last for ever. Shah Jahan's reign ended in appalling internecine butchery, and under his successors the court art gradually lost its vitality. Greater dynamism can often be found in the court art of the Rajput kings, who ruled territories to the west of Delhi and mounted militant opposition to the Moguls. A marvellously lively gouache shows *Raja Umed Singh of Kota Hunting Lion*, and the cover of the V&A's handsome Nehru Gallery catalogue is emblazoned with a fiery painting produced in the Punjab hills. Depicting *A Lady in a Pavilion Conversing with Her Lover*, it deploys deeper colours and a more audaciously severe composition than Mogul art would have done. Its brazen strength compares favourably with the increasing stiffness of the Mogul court during its final disintegration.

The time had come for the British to assume control. Their rapid and inexorable expansion inspired the making of the most entertaining and popular object in the collection: *Tipoo's Tiger*. It was produced for Tipu, sultan of Mysore, whose determination to resist the British infidels became legendary. He saw himself as a tiger, and commissioned a large wooden model of the animal mauling a helpless European. Bellows inside the tiger make the victim emit groans, while growls are produced by turning the handle of a miniature organ keyboard on the animal's shoulder.

Tipu died a hero in battle, as he had wanted, but his mantle was quickly inherited by Maharaj Ranjit Singh – the 'lion of the Punjab'. Although small, pockmarked and partially paralysed, he excelled as a swordsman and dazzled visitors with the magnificence of his court. Covered with sheets of embossed gold, the lion's throne was especially splendid. Replete with tassels and gleaming gold cushions, it eventually passed into British hands after the annexation of the Punjab in 1846.

This empty, conquered throne could easily be seen as a symbol of the booty which flowed to this country while the Raj consolidated its authority. Even at the zenith of empire, the British never amounted to more than .5 per cent of India's population. But the schools of art they introduced to the subcontinent imposed Victorian taste on the students. Dismissing India's own fine art traditions, the policy had a disastrous effect. When current Indian art was shown at the Paris Universal Exhibition of 1878, one critic deplored the 'mongrel articles' which resulted when the British insisted on 'getting the natives all over western India to imitate the hardware jugs of Messrs Doulton'.

Ultimately, however, the Raj's influence could not destroy the resilience of indigenous tradition. And the errors committed by British paternalism are now being handsomely atoned for at the V&A. The achievements of Indian art will be disclosed by the Nehru Gallery with a splendour which should prove a revelation to many visitors. Moreover, an ambitious educational initiative has been launched alongside it, to ensure that the museum becomes a lively national centre for the study of Indian culture. Colonialist scorn is here being replaced by open-minded enthusiasm.

17 November 1990

Major: the unknown prime minister

Jamie Dettmer

Lord Blake's definitive biography of Andrew Bonar Law is entitled *The Unknown Prime Minister*. Any future historian will thus be pre-empted from using a similar title for a work on John Major, although the cap would fit as snugly.

Bonar Law's emergence as leader of the Conservatives in 1911 came about because the two main contenders, Walter Long and Austen Chamberlain, withdrew from the struggle for the sake of party unity. Bonar Law, the dark horse, was not widely known in the country and was never expected to gain the leadership.

Even a few months ago most people in Britain would probably have been hard pushed to name Mr Major as the Chancellor of the Exchequer. Michael Heseltine, a far more colourful if uneven character, was much better known, partly because of his flouncing out of cabinet during the Westland affair. Margaret Thatcher might not have been expected to win the party leadership in 1975 but she was well-known, if only in the guise of the 'milk snatcher'.

Mr Major's fame has spread only in the past few weeks. Astute political commentators began cautiously to tip Mr Major for the top in his last days as chief secretary to the Treasury. He performed well as Nigel Lawson's right-hand man, managing to keep the spending departments under tight rein without angering their ministers.

His 94 days' tenure at the foreign office was not happy. He seemed out of depth and was badly wrong-footed at a Commonwealth conference at Kuala Lumpur when he was contradicted by Downing Street. His restoration to the Treasury put him back on even ground. He proved highly effective as chancellor and steadied the City which was on the brink of going into convulsions over Mr Lawson's resignation. His autumn statement was praised by fellow Conservative MPs, in spite of the underlying bleakness of its economic message.

Mr Major's upbringing promised much less. His early life was hard, even if it was enlivened by the presence of his unusual father, Abraham Thomas Ball, alias Tom Major of the vaudeville double-act Drum and Major. His father successfully toured music halls and circuses on both sides of the Atlantic.

Mr Major has said that his father was a great influence on him. 'I still think he was the finest raconteur I have ever heard, and he had such a wealth of experience and a range of interests.' Tom Major was sixty-seven years old when his son was born but into his seventies he retained a fine humour.

Late in life, Tom Major left the stage and set up as a sculptor and manufacturer of garden gnomes. A failed investment forced the Majors to swap their home in leafy Worcester Park for a two-room flat in rundown Brixton, with a gas ring on the landing and a lavatory three floors below.

'Obviously, I was aware that we'd moved, and I could see the difference – but there was no difference in the way the family behaved or the way they treated me,' Mr Major says. 'It was a good environment to be brought up in.'

He attended the local Rutlish grammar school but performed badly. He says that he somehow turned against his teachers after feeling that he was at the bottom of the heap. All he missed was the sport, particularly his beloved cricket, when he left at sixteen.

He worked as a labourer initially, went on the dole, got a job at the Electricity Board, was turned down when he applied to become a bus conductor before joining Standard Chartered Bank. There he soon came under the wing of Anthony Barber, the former Tory chancellor, the first of a series of Conservative mentors who helped him up the greasy pole of political preferment.

Mr Major joined the Conservative party soon after leaving school. He found the attitudes of the Lambeth Labour hierarchy patronizing and offensive and at first experienced patronizing attitudes in the local Tory party as well. The young Major did not allow the snobbish attitudes of some local Tories to dissuade him from a political career. The party was beginning to change, to shift from an aristocratic, paternal vision to a meritocratic one and Mr Major was well placed to be swept along on the new wave.

His political efforts were interrupted for a short time while he went to Nigeria for the bank. It was there that he was involved in a car accident that nearly resulted in him losing his leg. His injury has stopped him playing cricket, his great passion outside politics.

His first serious political post was on Lambeth borough council. His colleagues voted him chairman of the housing committee. He has joked since that his one big regret was to have failed when housing chairman to secure the demolition of the house he and his parents had been reduced to living in after his father's business failed.

After two attempts to win St Pancras North for the Tories, he was eventually elected at Huntingdon in 1979. His rise through the Tory ranks in the Commons has been meteoric with eight different government jobs in as many years.

In January 1981, he became parliamentary private secretary to the Home Office ministers, Timothy Raison and Patrick Mayhew. In January 1983, he was appointed a whip, becoming a senior whip a year later. He spent two years as a junior minister at the then health and social security department. He was promoted within the same department a few months later. In 1987, he became chief secretary to the Treasury.

His rapid rise has not stirred rivals to envy. Mr Major is a friendly and personable man. Critics have questioned whether he has a defined political philosophy. Is he dry or wet? He has not been that forthcoming in reply. He normally tries to side-step labels. Friends say that he is hard on economics but soft on social issues. His own answer gives little clarification: 'I am a free-marketeer; I could never accept the politics of soft options, because soft options are bogus options – but beyond that, I believe in treating issues on their merits.'

The key to his philosophy lies with his wish to widen individual freedom. In a speech to the Conservative party's Radical Society last year he said that one of the questions he asked himself when deciding on a proposal was would it enlarge freedom and extend opportunity. Other questions included: would it encourage people to take more responsibility for their own lives and would it improve the lot of the worst-off.

Those questions are now going to press in on him in a much sharper way than even when he was chancellor. The final question about the man is whether he is up to the job. He has been untested by comparison with Douglas Hurd. He did look vulnerable when foreign secretary. Only proverbial time will tell.

28 November 1990

Over to Kinnock

Can Labour win? That question, so often asked when Labour is in opposition, arises with all its old insistence following the drama of the past fortnight. A weekend poll shows the party would have a much better chance led by John Smith. In the Conservative party, such a poll would already have the knives flashing.

Labour's first response to Mr Major's election has been inept. The new prime minister is no Margaret Thatcher Mark Two. At the very least, Mr Major's advent marked a stylistic U-turn. Mrs Thatcher's stridency, which was Labour's strongest asset, is removed. Mr Major makes a wholly improbable hate figure, and has electoral potential. Labour can no longer rely on the prime minister to lose the election for the Tories.

More than style has changed. Mr Major is busy shooting Labour's foxes. The poll tax no longer has a defender in Downing Street. 'Good quality and well-managed public services' figure with 'an open society of opportunity' in his vision of the future. In Europe, Britain will be 'on the pitch and playing hard'. If a few continental shins get kicked in the process, that will do the Tories no harm.

As yet, there need be no cause for Labour panic. The economy is still going Mr Kinnock's way. The recession will be deep and long. Mr Major's concern for public services will not add a penny to the tight cash limits that the government has imposed on spending in 1991–92. His enthusiasm for equal opportunities will not make it easier for Norman Lamont, his new chancellor, to cut taxes this year. ERM, as the prime minister pointed out, is a harsh discipline, especially on politicians seeking re-election. The predictable election boom is being left uncomfortably close to polling day.

Mr Kinnock's problem is the suspicion that Labour would do no better, and that it might do some things much worse. With Mrs Thatcher, Labour could hope to win on its purely negative appeal. It now needs something positive, beyond the revival of its former Big Idea, socialism, a word the party hardly dares to utter these days.

There are three pillars on which Labour could credibly construct a programme over the next year. The first is its attitude to public service. The recent British Social Attitudes survey shows growing public support for the collective provision of education and health. Labour is seen as the party that spends most; but it has become identified with looking after the providers rather than the consumers of public services. It needs to shed this image. It easily can. The recession will end; the economy will grow again. The Conservatives' policy will be to reduce public expenditure as a proportion of national income, while increasing it somewhat in real terms. Labour might get away with simply promising to spend more than the Tories, but if it wants to carry conviction with voters, it will need to supplement promises of more money with new commitments to efficiency, backed up by distancing itself from the public sector unions.

Second, Labour should return to its origins as a party of local democracy. The principle of subsidiarity – of devolving decisions to the lowest practical level – should guide its actions. There is nothing particularly socialist about this, indeed it used to be Conservative philosophy, but Mrs Thatcher so blatantly abandoned it as to leave the field open to Labour. In education, Labour could favour local autonomy. Local authorities, in turn, could hand over more control to schools and parents – though the Tories are up to the mark on this. Local government could be funded through a property tax and left alone.

Third, Labour could address itself to the new liberalism, the agenda of democratic reform which has sprung from the ashes of its Bennite years: freedom of information legislation, a bill of rights, liberalization of drugs policy, radical reform of the penal system and so on. Labour could approach all these matters with a prejudice in favour of change.

Which leaves the big question of the day: whatever the policies, or the inadequacies, of government, is Mr Kinnock a credible alternative prime minister? Whatever the polls say, his party will not waste time on this one. Unlike the Tories, Labour is ever willing to wound its leaders, but rarely strikes them dead. Not since Lansbury has a party leader been dismissed against his will. For good or ill, Mr Kinnock has one more election to lose or win. But he can no longer count on victory dropping into his lap.

3 December 1990

Britain tests a sculptor's mettle

Sarah Jane Checkland

Lynn Chadwick's tirade on greedy dealers and ignorant critics falls silent as he unlocks the door to his Gloucestershire warehouse and turns on the light. Here, bristling with spiky limbs and hammer heads, giants to the right, pygmies to the left, is a buried army of bronze forms: staggering Ned Kellys in cumbersome armour, primeval standing figures with crucified arms and beak faces, gaunt kings and queens surveying from solemn enthronement. The atmosphere is made all the more tomb-like because these are shapes dating from the post-war era; what the critic Herbert Read called the 'iconography of despair'.

We pass into the inner studio, where two female figures are in the process of being formed in armature and plaster, each stiffly ascending her personal staircase. Associations with the great Marcel Duchamp and the *Nude Descending a Staircase*, which launched his career in 1912, are interrupted by Chadwick pointing at their protruding behinds. 'Bums,' he says. 'It's a part of the anatomy not fully used.'

On the way out of his studio, we pass two majestic figures, their heads obscured by black plastic bags tied at the neck by rope. 'Waiting for the hangman,' mutters their creator. A typical one-liner from the grizzled septuagenarian, it has its own particular sting. For Chadwick is all too aware that he and his *oeuvre* are ever approaching their day of judgment.

Chadwick started his career in the Fifties as an architectural draftsman. In 1956, at the age of forty-one, he won the international prize for sculpture at the Venice Biennale. He was the youngest recipient of any important art prize since the war. But while French and German critics greeted his success with acclaim, British critics were affronted. The judges had chosen 'a gifted artist who had not shown more than his paces', Denys Sutton wrote in the *Financial Times*. At that time, the British art establishment tended to favour European art over its own.

'I was written about before I was known,' Chadwick says. 'Once I had success they stopped. Nobody will tell us why. Perhaps I smell.'

Chadwick was further torpedoed in 1958 when the seventy-four-year-old Lord Brabazon condemned a two-headed winged figure he had produced for the Air League of the British Empire as 'a diseased haddock'. The commission was cancelled. Since then, Chadwick has suffered decades of either being critically ignored, or dismissed as an imitator of Henry Moore or Alexander Calder.

Little wonder he went into retreat, working in virtual isolation, and adopting 'terrible' as his favourite word. *Contemporary Artists* refers to Chadwick in the past tense, and says 'in recent years he has rarely exhibited in London. His work, in fact, has shown little development . . . Stylistic formulas of pyramid shapes or wingspans have been reduced to anecdotal, almost sentimental symbols.'

Chadwick knows there is no point trying to defend his corner. The twentieth century is strewn with disappointed artists, who tried to prove they were first with a particular famous idea.

The irony is that, despite Britain's disdain, Chadwick has always been bought abroad, the proceeds setting him up in the stately splendour of a neo-Gothic Wyattville-designed home (sorry, 'glorified farmhouse'), with monarchs on the lawn and sheep in the peripheral fields. Apart from the warehouse, he has his own foundry.

What is more, the past decade has seen a remarkable vogue for his works. The blindfolded sculptures sell for £400,000 each, while maquettes are worth up to £15,000. Five or six important pieces have been sold to Japan in the past three years; Paris bought some for a new development in the city and Miami airport acquired another. Even the British have started to catch on.

Eva, his third wife and his manager, deserves credit for Chadwick's market success because she took control of the account books, thus relieving his longstanding dealers, Marlborough Fine Art, of their exclusive rights. 'Being freelance you get much better exposure,' she says. Chadwick is also highly productive, she says, guaranteeing about twenty works a year until his powers started fading recently. Another factor was Henry Moore's death four years ago. Chadwick is being hailed by some as the great man's heir.

Now Mrs Chadwick has persuaded Oxford University Press's Clarendon Press to produce the first complete illustrated catalogue of Chadwick's works. *Lynn Chadwick, Sculptor*, which has just been published, is both an application for a place in the art history books, and an essential precaution against fakes in the future. Short on referential monograph (unaccountably by Dennis Farr, director of the Courtauld Institute), and long on bibliography and photographs, the book comes across as a strange, somewhat joyless exercise. As a *liber veritatis*, it is of limited use because the photographs, taken by the artist, are mostly small and dark. But it is a significant start.

Typically, Chadwick has not yet bothered to inspect the book, with its brooding frontispiece photo-portrait, his weather-worn features scarcely visible due to shadow, and no sign of his one sartorial concession to fashion, a denim shirt.

'Eva did the book,' he shrugs. 'I don't know why, although it is a great help to dealers. She is terribly good at looking after the business side. I am terribly impressed.' How different Chadwick appears to have been back in the Fifties, when he accepted the role of public figure, delivering a talk entitled 'An Artist and His Public' on the Home Service. Although complaining that people 'come to see me as I might go to the zoo . . . confused if I stare soberly back at them, between bars, so to speak', he is constructive enough to chivvy people not to fear their own reactions to art.

Now Chadwick mocks all categories of humans who dare cross his path. Friends 'only go to parties if they think they will find somebody better than they've got at the moment', dealers 'smell the money' and keep the identity of buyers secret because 'otherwise people will go behind their backs and sell'; American collectors buy 'because it is a step up the social ladder', while occasional British buyers such as the Sainsburys 'bought in the early days when the work was cheap'. As for the public: 'Popular equals vulgar, you know. Basically it is the same word. Vulgate is the people,' he says. 'They cannot be expected to appreciate art in the same way that an artist does, and this artist does not care much either way.'

He professes no knowledge of contemporary trends. He scorns (inaccurately) his namesake Helen Chadwick (no relation) for 'putting used Tampax on a board. That's not sculpture.' He avoids aesthetic analysis of his work, saying the drapery was devised 'so the works can stand by themselves'. He even denies that he is a sculptor, saying such people 'take a large lump and reduce it, while I construct'.

Although the 1956 Biennale may have helped to remove Chadwick from the mainstream, there are other clues to the man and his exile. Apart from the fact that he missed out on the coterie of friends which comes with an art school training, he has never made an attempt to massage the system. He is by nature a loner, based in the country throughout his career.

Chadwick's isolation could not be more opposed to his limelight-bathed contemporaries. The big question now is: are those sculptures languishing in the warehouse a stash of masterpieces by Britain's greatest senior sculptor, or just so much scrap metal?

In the *catalogue raisonné*, Mr Farr writes that Britain's failure to buy Chadwick's works is 'much to our national shame'. Chadwick remains philosophical: 'It doesn't make any difference how I feel. I will either be appreciated or not. All I can do is go on doing what I am doing.'

8 December 1990

Centre of a tension

Richard Bassett

At first glance, the opera house at Tirana is difficult to take seriously. Surely I would be better off having dinner in the Hotel Deiti, whose kitchen was constructed by Mussolini. My 'guide', even in these days of tentative reform, clearly sensed something subversive. Would I not prefer a stroll round the Enver Hoxha mausoleum, or an excursion to the Enver Hoxha cemetery?

For some years now, it has been a steadfast principle of mine never to visit a European city without attending at least one operatic performance in the local theatre. This stems less from an obsessive passion for opera than from a curiosity to know the city well. In Tirana, the opera lover approaches the theatre with trepidation. *Cavalleria Rusticana* is a great work but, in my case, prolonged exposure to its score decades ago in the school band had left a heavy legacy of diffidence towards Mascagni's music.

Those feelings vanished when, despite an audience numbering barely thirty, the conductor arrived at the rostrum. The words of Albania's modern founder, Enver Hoxha, that are written on the walls, spurring the audience to use art in the service of socialism, disappeared as the lights dimmed.

At this point, before a note was played, before any of the singers had arrived, anticipation and curiosity were extreme. This country has the lowest standard of living in Europe, with a population existing in the way central, northern and even southern Europe last experienced more than fifty years ago; a country where fields are sown, not by machines or even horse-drawn vehicles, but by legions of white-scarved women. How could such a country have the artistic fire power to produce an opera?

There is no greater tribute to modern Albanian culture than an evening at the opera house. Once the music begins, it is clear that despite the tremendous physical and historical disadvantages Albania has experienced, its orchestra and chorus possess a musicianship worthy of Vienna.

The contrast, however, makes a serious and lasting impression. Ruled by what is, in effect, one large family of a thousand people, Albania can boast, for the first time in its history, a young intelligentsia. The average age is twenty-six and these Albanians – many of whom sing or play in the opera – often enjoy an education their parents were denied.

Writers, artists, musicians, economists and historians have developed in Albania during the past decade to a degree unrivalled anywhere else in the Balkans, with perhaps the exception of ever-sophisticated Bucharest. Such a development, however, creates strain. The young intellectuals are mentally head and shoulders above the rest of their countrymen. Not surprisingly, they want reform, and are growing more and more impatient.

At the opera house, musicians were desperate to hear recordings of other orchestras in Europe. Singers, particularly the best of them, were no less keen to have the chance to travel abroad to perform or listen to other opera stars. This frustration is repeated throughout Albanian society today.

Albania remains the most strictly controlled society in Europe, and the tensions which the presence of a new and impatient generation cause are only rarely visible to the visitor.

None the less, Tirana is a city where hints of this conflict are always to be found. Sometimes they occur in almost surreal form. Walking down the vast central boulevard after the opera, it was not surprising to see hundreds of people talking or wheeling bicycles in the fading light.

Suddenly everybody stopped. Turning their heads towards

the town council building, an imposing structure erected by the Italians in the early Forties, they were drawn by cries coming from a first-floor window. After a few seconds, without warning, a man, screaming for help, was bundled out of the building and deposited on to one of Tirana's few public buses; not a police car, but a long articulated bus which, unlit, drove hurriedly off into the night. As if nothing had happened, the crowd began talking again.

Cities on the brink of revolution offer strange insights as collective fear gradually recedes. In a large villa, a young politician explained what he and countless other Albanians fear most of all. 'It is violence which I suspect will engulf the regime,' he said, offering me a tangerine from his garden.

Nearby, in another house, an older man, also part of the city's élite, expressed the hope that reforms would come swiftly. Unfortunately, our talk was interrupted by a neighbour who, I was later told, had been sent to spy on us by the ever-present sigurime (secret police).

Although the sigurime is omnipresent, it is strangely erratic in its activities. Thanks to Albania's break with the Soviet Union in the early Sixties, it has never 'benefited' from Soviet techniques and technology. It has neither the equipment of the Czechs nor the experience of the Romanians in keeping track of hostile elements. Rather, it relies on an almost irrational system of exploiting petty jealousies among neighbours who are used to observing all around them. In this way the sigurime, unlike Ceauşescu's securitate, is not a military caste but very much, as its propagators insist, 'of the people'.

Such a system, inevitably, has weaknesses. It failed, for example, to prevent a group of westerners strolling by accident into the reception of an Albanian wedding. As the most hospitable inhabitants of the Balkans, the Albanians made the foreigners feel most welcome. It was only after some hours that two sigurime agents appeared to ask probing questions. By that time there was little to explain; after all, we had only been to the opera.

8 December 1990

Pilgrimage to a stoic's paradise

Fiona MacCarthy

William Morris went to Iceland twice, early in the 1870s. The reason for his journeys was partly professional: he was fascinated by Icelandic sagas. He had learnt Icelandic and by this time was producing the first of a sequence of translations and adaptations of the saga in his own idiosyncratic prose and verse. In this sense Morris's travels were literary pilgrimages. Morris in Iceland was described by one biographer as a combination of Johnson in the Hebrides and Byron in Greece.

Morris also went to Iceland for emotional reasons. The affair between Janey, his wife, and Dante Gabriel Rossetti, the painter and poet and Morris's friend and partner, caused him increasing anguish as it became more blatant. He was generous and stoic, taking a joint tenancy with Rossetti on Kelmscott Manor, Oxfordshire and setting off to Iceland, leaving the lovers to it. So his journeyings were also a quest, a search for solace; and it is not surprising that he chose to travel into a completely unfamiliar landscape of toothed and jagged mountains, bracing winds and lurid sunsets, as far from calm grey Kelmscott as anyone could go.

Morris first reached Iceland in mid-July. (This is still the ideal month for those who follow in his footsteps.) He arrived by the mail steamer from the Orkneys and the Faroes, sailing to Reykjavik around the south side of the island. What immediately impressed him was the endless space, the strangeness of the black and lunar landscape. He described this in his poem 'Iceland First Seen'.

Morris travelled with three friends, one of them Icelandic. This was Eiríkr Magnússon, Morris's collaborator on the sagas. They hired twenty ponies and eight packhorses in Reykjavik. The pure-bred Icelandic ponies appealed very much to Morris with his feel for native sturdiness.

They took on local guides and made some useful purchases of cherry brandy, cheese and knitted guernseys. Morris saw no reason for lingering in Reykjavik, which he considered 'not a very attractive place, yet not very bad, better than a north country town in England'. (Even now one goes to Iceland for the country, not the capital.) Morris, the impetuous, shockheaded, burly figure, who could at times appear more Icelandic than the Icelanders, was anxious to see the saga country by the sea.

Morris planned his route around the sites of the greatest of the early medieval Icelandic sagas: Njal's saga, Laxdaela saga, Egil's saga, Heimskringla and the Eyrbyggja saga. He had responded with the extrovert's sheer pleasure to those primitive soap operas recounting the events of Iceland's early years of settlement: the heroics, the bloody acts of vengeance, the life feuds.

His pursuit of the saga sites entailed a criss-cross journey through the southeast of the island, first along the southern coast, then north across the wilderness to the fiords on the northern sea, around the Snaefellsness Peninsula, returning to Reykjavik by Thingvellir, the ancient site of the lawgiving assemblies. This route took Morris six weeks, but travellers today could manage it in ten days or a fortnight.

Njal's saga is the longest and most stirring of the 'classical' sagas of the thirteenth century. It was Njal country, the area around Thorsmörk and the valley of the Markfleet, that Morris explored first. He and his entourage pitched camp at Bergthorsvoll, scene of the climax of Njal's saga: the terrible mass-slaughter as the building was first surrounded, then ignited by a hundred enemies. Morris visited Lithend, a place of mystery and magic, where Gunnar, the good warrior, rose singing from his tomb. These sites, quite recognizable and curiously brooding, excited Morris greatly, and they can still be seen.

From his first few hours in Iceland, Morris was aware of the extraordinary contrasts in the landscape. Halfway through a journey over harsh and dusty lava fields all changed 'as if by magic' to a plain of short, flowery grass. Morris noted carefully in his vivid travel diaries the way his own moods altered with the changes in the country. The instinct for survival was a part of Iceland's charm for him and seemed to symbolize the ancient saga spirit, the national tenacity. It is, in fact, quite moving to see, as Morris saw them, small bright flowers blooming strangely in vast deserts of black sand.

Moving northwards through Njal country, you come upon Keldur, where Morris cooked a dinner in the kitchen of the farmhouse, watched by twelve incredulous men, women and children. (Morris was serious about his cooking and the menu that evening centred on salt ling.) The farmhouse at Keldur has been reconstructed and visitors can see exactly why Morris was enraptured by the true organic architecture of these turf-walled buildings. They are grouped convivially, like most Icelandic farm buildings, on the emerald green hillside with a river running by. The lowering presence of the volcano Hekla dominates this region. Around it, a whole ocean of black slurry marks the extent of the centuries' eruptions. This is Iceland at its darkest and most desolate. The romantic soul of Morris – for he was a great romantic – revelled in the gloom and the queer contorted shapes of enormous lumps of lava resembling large seals or black sea monsters. The more pragmatic side of him described the types of lava with a quasi-scientific precision and detachment. It is this mixture that makes Morris such a good and an endearing guide to Iceland. The Icelanders took him to their heart; they called him Vilhjálmur Morris and the Skjald.

When Morris arrived at Geysir, he was sceptical. No writer from England had ever been to Iceland without visiting this valley of hot springs rising to great heights like enormous steaming fountains. Morris felt alarmed that he had travelled to a tourist trap. But he was won over, as anyone must be, by the whole grand surrealism of the scene. He humanized the geysers. He called them giant kettles. One can still identify the spring, a pool named Blesi (or blaze), in which Morris parboiled a joint of lamb for dinner. He camped beside the geysers and from time to time was woken by 'the thump, rumble and steam of the big Gusher'.

Morris and his party were still travelling northwards into the real wilderness of central Iceland. It was terribly hard going, through the rocky fields. At the end of the day's journey Morris's twenty ponies were cut and bleeding. Waterdale, as they approached it, was full of mist and drifting rain, and 'the wind blew up from it like knives'. In this desperate landscape, Grettir, the monster-outlaw of the Grettis saga, found a refuge. At the summit of Kaldidalur (literally Cold-dale) travellers still stop, as Morris did, and add another stone to the cairn by the roadside or leave a jokey message of encouragement.

Morris saw his best rainbow in the wasteland of the Gretla, where the fearsome Grettir lived so long in exile. The rainbows in Iceland are like rainbows nowhere else. As Morris noted, they are *flatter*. The Icelandic sunsets have a wonderful intensity sometimes glimpsed on a stormy day in England, but they turn a deeper purple and they last a lot longer. What Morris saw in Iceland was observed not with the poet's eye alone, but with the designer's. His response to the landscape is both visual and verbal. As a traveller in Iceland, Morris is original.

Over Kaldidalur, the party turned westward into very different scenery, the Laxdale of the Laxdaela saga. This is a landscape of jagged, toothlike mountains, range upon range of them, some quite low. Beneath them in the valley, the rivers, ribbon-like and glistening, wind on and on. Perhaps he was set on edge by obvious parallels between his own situation and the saga's. Laxdaela is the saga of the eternal triangle. Now, for the first time, Morris admitted he felt homesick and the minimalist landscape almost seemed to irritate him: 'a piece of turf under your feet, and the sky overhead, that's all'.

He revived when he reached the land of the berserks, and indeed this is perhaps the most enthralling scene in Iceland. We are now in the country of the Eyrbyggja saga; the places where the Eyre-Dwellers actually dwelt. Berserk-ia-hrauri itself, vast plain of lava, is named after the two wild men who hewed a path across it before suffering the worst of Icelandic fates: the two of them were boiled to death in the steam bath. A little further on, at Reykholt, you can see the bath where Morris sat so happily immersed up to his middle.

Morris the floral expert was always looking out for specimens. Near the beach at Hwammfirth he picked a horned poppy (yellow), the first of its kind he had come across in Iceland. Right out on the far western promontory, at Budir, he noticed buttercups and meadowsweet cranesbill. A few days later, at Reykholt, he observed that the whole side and part of the gable of the priest's house was covered with ox-eye daisies in full bloom. The wild flowers still bloom profusely.

He kept almost until last the site he most looked forward to. This was Thingvellir, the site of the early lawgiving, the Althing, described by Morris as 'the greatest marvel and most storied place of Iceland'. This is now a national monument, accessible to coaches; but in Morris's day the pass that approached it was so narrow that he and his companions dismounted from their ponies before descending to 'the great grey plain'. Morris acknowledged Thingvellir later, as his politics became increasingly radical, as a kind of starting point, a source of inspiration. Much more damaging than poverty was class war and social injustice. Iceland taught him that.

By the end of August, six weeks after they began, Morris was clearing up the wreck of his last cooking under a thick drizzle. Reykjavik was in sight again, and the road towards it seemed like a road in England as they swung along together, even the horses feeling they were near their journey's end. They set sail on September 3. Morris wrote a few days later: 'I thought the Scotch coast wondrous dull after all the marvels we have seen.'

People who go to Iceland return a bit obsessive. 'Iceland on the brain,' was how Richard Burton put it. W. H. Auden, who toured Iceland in the Thirties, claimed that it lingered for ever in the mind. It affected William Morris so lastingly and deeply because it was for him an experience he needed: it restored his equilibrium; brought back his old affections for the 'dear faces' of his wife, his friends, his children. It influenced his writing, it affected his design. He returned not only speaking but feeling in Icelandic and he brought his pony with him. Mouse became a much-loved figure in the land-scape around Kelmscott, growing noticeably fatter on the lush green English grass.

15 December 1990

Vulnerable, cornered Kinnock must stop and think

Robin Oakley

When David Owen abandoned his year-long flirtation with Labour for a renewed dalliance with the Tories (he is a dreadful tease: he will never join them either) it was clear that Neil Kinnock's party was in trouble.

Dr Owen may have made a few mistakes in his own political career, but he is a shrewd reader of other people's fortunes. The question being asked now is: 'Can Labour beat a compassionate Conservative party?'

Two months ago there was a certain symmetry about British politics. Both the main parties were led by people whom the supporters of the other fervently wished would continue leading them up to the next election. Neither had a new 'Big Idea' to offer for the politics of the Nineties.

Now the Conservatives have removed the leader whom they too had convinced themselves had become an electoral liability. They have discovered that if you have a new leader, you do not really need a new big idea and that the 'classless society' will do.

Labour, still bereft of their new inspirational theme, are left with the longest serving leader of the Opposition this century, greeted when he comes to the dispatch box with gleeful cries of 'Don't resign' from Tory hecklers.

Precisely a year ago I wrote up Neil Kinnock as my politician of the year on the ground that his achievements were much undervalued. In reforming the party organization, weeding out Militants, revamping policies and giving Labour back the will to win, he made his party look once more capable of government.

He has made Labour outwardly safe for social democrats to return to, marginalized the hard left and begun to loosen the trade union strings.

He deserved at least some of the credit, I argued, for Labour's emphatic lead in the opinion polls. More than that, he deserved the credit for lifting himself from the depression of 1988 when the Tories had looked invincible and the newspapers had been full of headlines about 'The leader who lost his way'.

But Mr Kinnock now faces an even greater test. Lifting a party from long-term despair when you have taken over with its fortunes at rock bottom is one thing. Lifting it again after you have seen the biggest ever opinion poll lead over the Tories melt away under your leadership and become a Labour deficit is another task altogether, especially in the face of a whispering campaign that you were never quite up to the job anyway.

There is no threat to Mr Kinnock's leadership; the cumbersome machinery sees to that. But there must be a threat to his self-confidence and to the morale of the parliamentary party.

So how are the Tories under John Major to be beaten? What does Mr Kinnock do for his next trick? More policy documents will not do the trick. Labour's policies have already had more relaunches than Dame Nellie Melba had hot dinners.

It may be frustrating for him while the honeymoon lasts, but Mr Kinnock would be wise to mute his attacks on Mr Major at this stage. The new Tory leader is an aspirin politician, a man designed for lowering the political temperature.

Labour has to stop and think. The kneejerk scorn for Michael Heseltine's offer of participation in shaping the future of local government, for example, was unwise. Mr Kinnock and Bryan Gould may not be interested: some Labour municipalities are.

Labour will have to take care too on Europe. On Europe, we just woke up one morning to find Labour announcing itself as a pro-European party. But with the pragmatic Mr Major now edging the Tories too towards speedier integration, Mr Kinnock is in danger of being pushed too far out on a limb by an attempt to sustain the 'more European than thou' title. Peter Shore and others are ensuring that the cracks in his own party are now showing on the EC. Where the Opposition surely can go after the government is on the question of public services and the quality of life. Government politicians express their concerns. But do they produce the money to support them?

Then there is the little matter of the economy. To give his party a chance of winning the election on the economy, however, Mr Kinnock will have to give maximum exposure between now and then to the shadow chancellor John Smith, the man who would be his most potent rival if he does not deliver an election victory.

That, surely, is a risk he has to take.

20 December 1990

Look back in hope

Jan Morris

Forty years ago my friend and neighbour Clough Williams
Ellis erected a plaque to commemorate a summer of particularly glorious sunshine, hoping, as he later wrote, 'that
such applause might possibly encourage an encore'. Four
decades later I feel like honouring the summer of 1990 for
quite different reasons, while also hoping for an encore. It
was also a season of fine weather, but it was far more as well,
and it has come to represent for me, as the year now comes
fitfully to its end, an allegorical moment of reconciliation; a
window, as the computer people like to say, through which all
too briefly flickered a message that the worst might be over.

High time, too, I thought, as I looked at our patch of Welsh
countryside – itself, it always seems to me, an allegorical kind
of place between the mountains and the sea. During the past
few years we had become ever more obtusely out of step with
nature. Instead of riding the organic energies, we had wilfully
crossed them. Where flowers grew in a hedgerow we murdered them in the cause of order. Where a stream ran beside a
road, we filled it in for the sake of the traffic. Wild river
reaches were given artificial fishing-pools. Mossy woodland
tracks were tidied up by community councils. Far worse,
chemical farming seemed to be making everything arid and,
as a hideous climax, Chernobyl had cast its poisonous blight
over us all, so that even poor mountain sheep were branded as
radioactive.

I had come to think of it as an irreversible process. Nature
itself seemed demoralized – half-sterilized, even. The wildlife
faded from our yard and garden, and retreated from the
beeches, sycamores, ash trees and horse chestnuts all around.

The birds were subdued, only the harsh magpies thriving. The squirrels lay uncharacteristically low. The laneside violets, shrivelled by weed killers or brutally mutilated by machinery, were hardly more than a memory. The pungent smell of silage had replaced the sweet smell of hay. Even the insects seemed to have abandoned us. I had always thought hopefully of the after-life as a comforting reunion with nature, but as the Eighties dragged on I began to feel that absorption into this loveless toxic limbo was a distinctly unenticing prospect.

Outside my yard, too, beyond the mountains, the world as a whole seemed to have lost its sap. It felt to me old, tired and desiccated. The ideologies were drained of their fire and life. The social passions of the Sixties had lost their inspiration – feminism embattled and embittered, ecology institution-alized, even jogging, that earnest of decency, going out of style. Joyless monetarism seemed the best anyone could offer in the way of radical vision, and the infantile image of the yuppie was the nearest we got to a hero of the times.

I wonder if there were ever years more ungenerous of style? Post-modern tomfooleries trivialized architecture. Auction-room prospects degraded art. Then literary fashion was reduced to the surreal or the obscurantist – Eco-esque riddles, Calvinian mysteries, meaningless magic out of Latin America. The true laureate of the Eighties was Le Carré, whose characters stumbled on, cynical and weary, through endless pointless labyrinths of deceit. Sometimes I fancied that humanity at large had been Chernobyled. Everywhere, even in the richest countries, more and more people seemed to be malformed or retarded, like unwitting victims of some unadmitted burnout. Every day the news was full of gro-tesqueries, warped unnecessary conflicts, mindless oppressions and recriminations. Diseases swirled around the planet, and while one half of the Earth starved, the other could not get rid of its surplus food. Corruption, poverty, greedy litigation, malicious gossip – in the world outside, these often seemed the very substance of the times, just as hedgerows without colour, buddleias without butterflies, symbolized those years for me in our small corner of Wales.

But in the last months of the decade, wonderful things happened, and everything seemed to change. As a mild winter slid into a benign spring, and May magnificently unfolded, I began to feel that in the summer of 1990 destiny was experiencing a change of heart. All around our house nature miraculously recovered its vigour. Far from being crowded or impotent, as I had come to think, nature revealed itself once again as irrepressible. I watched the weeks triumphantly progress as I might watch a victory march, and felt that at such a time even to be of a certain age was very Heaven.

At first, as in legend, the hedgerow flowers came back, mercifully spared the bashing of the mechanical cutters (too expensive, I suppose) and the misapplied science of agriculturists (scared of pollution charges, no doubt). Then I noticed, week by week, the return of the insects. The grasshoppers were in the long grass again – there were none the previous summer. Spiders' webs glistened once more in the dew, and draped themselves comfortably among my sitting-room beams. The bees arrived exuberantly early, and hardly had May broken than the midges were dancing above my balcony. As for the butterflies, they were like so many gorgeous prodigals coming home vindicated, wavering triumphantly all around the shrubberies, in and out of our house's ever-open doors.

Years had passed since I had seen a snake or a lizard at Trefan Morys: but here was a fine bold grass snake crossing the lane, and there a lizard scuttling across my library floor. One evening I counted 77 pipistrelle bats leaving for their twilight forage from their nests above the kitchen door. The toads, which had seemed to have deserted forever their cobbled crypt beneath the yard, were back with lively toadlets. Jenks the cat, no mighty hunter but an infallible census gatherer, reported with a rich if mangled quota of infant voles and fieldmice. Not a single nut was left to us on the hazel tree by the gate, so energetic were the squirrels again, and hardly a lettuce went unsampled by a virile slug. Whenever I looked up I seemed to see a pair of buzzards, or a heron, flapping by; a particularly resurgent robin appeared to regard my bedroom as his own.

Perhaps I fancied it, but somehow I thought the light itself had become clearer and brighter, as though a film of carbons had been washed away. On the right day, everything looked *new*. High on Yr Wyddfa the little puffs of white steam that marked the ascent of the rack railway gave me the impression, against so crystalline a sky, that they had never happened before, and the white-sailed yachts at sea looked as though they had all been bought yesterday. Once or twice during the summer we could see clear across our bay to St David's Head at the other end of Wales – seeing forever, as the song has it.

It was like a rebirth, a sudden profligate flinging of life around the place, and it came to me that we had reached some turning point in our attitudes to the natural world, the real world – that from now on it would be a long withdrawal from the awful plateau of additives, theme parks, genetic experiments, battery hens, litter and syntheticized, hedgeless meadows. It was not just that in the summer of 1990 green was fashionable, politically desirable, potentially profitable. It was more that in our part of the world, at least, humanity had begun to realize it was making a terrible mistake – a countryside which had been in all our memories true to itself, faithful to us, was being senselessly alienated. Just in time, we were turning back, or so I liked to think, and flowers, toads, snakes, lizards, spiders, grasshoppers, squirrels, butterflies, herons, buzzards and 77 pipistrelle bats were celebrating the event.

They seemed to be celebrating, too, across half the world. For a few short months before that climactic summer, the stream of humanity itself appeared to be running clear and naturally again. Will any of us ever forget that moment of innocent joy, universally shared, when the Berlin Wall was breached at last, and the young people danced and sang it into

154

oblivion? One by one, the half-dead states of eastern Europe came to life again, and terrific old cities such as Prague and Budapest rejoined the civilized community.

The Soviet Union turned out to be not an enigma at all, but an all too fallible association of human beings, like the rest of us. Nelson Mandela came out of jail, and everyone cheered. After God knows how many generations of preposterous squabbling, the nations of western Europe seemed to be growing up at last.

In my mind at least, the end of the cold war seemed, like the discovery that the world was round, to discredit many other hidebound mis-assumptions. Dogmas, shibboleths and mantras were losing their arcane power. It appeared to me, in the glow of that summer, that war could not now seriously be considered as an instrument of policy among civilized powers. To my mind nonsensical premises of organized religion were being questioned as never before. Quasi-sacred institutions like the monarchy and the law were seen at last as not sacred at all. No longer was it generally assumed that a zoo was a fit place to take a child, and even in England people began to wonder if locking people up in primitive prisons was really the best answer to society's problems. Sovereignty was no longer universally accepted as an end in itself; the rotten instruments of state supremacy, the ridiculous MI5s, CIAs and KGBs, in whose webs Le Carré's characters had been so helplessly enmeshed, were exposed as the self-perpetuating cabals they were.

Didn't we all feel like that? Wasn't there really a moment for nearly all of us, last summer, when the flowers came back?

Like one of those pale mornings that are at once tremulous and preternaturally exact, it was too beautiful to last. Even as August moved into September I began to feel the window closing once again, and the options clenching. My euphoria did not last. I waited in vain for the dolphins to appear in our bay. The salmon and seatrout were still shy of our river. The squalid advance of tourism continued, the potato-crisp packets blew around the lay-bys, and more and more often

155

the voices I heard in the lane outside my window were English rather than Welsh, reminding me of the Celtic holy man who, long ago, first heard the voices of Saxons on the far bank of the Severn, and knew that the old truths of Wales were under threat.

And consider what I see now when I look beyond the mountains. Everywhere those high hopes are betrayed already – perestroika abused, the liberated states in chaos, Mandela not the messiah after all, Martin Luther King revealed as a cheat and the British government still exploding nuclear devices under the Nevada desert.

And yet . . . perhaps, when history looks back at this ambiguous year, it will remember the hope of the summer after all, rather than the disillusioning fall. Progress comes in fits and starts, a step forwards, a step back, and at least 1990, like 1848, like 1918 even, tantalizingly showed us some noble possibilities. We saw at least the prospect of a rational, kindly world, however transient, partial or illusory. Besides, I think the summer demonstrated that we really are learning one lasting and fundamental lesson – that no matter what we do to each other, we shall be mad to continue our reckless defiance of the natural world. However the year's end lets us down, whatever next year brings us, I shall always honour the summer of 1990 with a plaque in my mind, as the season when we began our return to nature, and nature magnanimously welcomed us back.

At the seaward end of our house there is a small weeping lime, whose branches droop almost to the ground, like a tent. In the hot days of July, when I sometimes took a book or a typescript inside its shade to do some work, it suggested to me the leafy cathedral that our national poet, Dafydd ap Gwilym, once imagined for himself among the woods. Surrounded by its cool greenness, silent except for the buzzing of insects, the cawing of rooks, the occasional petulant mewing of Jenks the cat and the always welcome ringing of the cordless telephone beside me (for I am not one of your hermit naturalists), I really felt that death had lost its sting again.

156

Never mind what happened in the world outside, when the time came I should be perfectly ready after all, like Daphne before me, still in a tree to end my race.

29 December 1990

Stand-outs of an outstanding year

Simon Barnes

This column never takes sport with anything less than the full portentous seriousness it deserves. Here, then, are this year's awards for the great men and women who have made the year what it was.

The Sunil Gavaskar award for doorman of the year goes to the man at the Melbourne Cricket Ground, the MCG. He refused admittance to Andrew Peacock, then prime minister-elect *knowing full well who he was.*

The award for quixotry goes to Nathan Strange, Britain's first sumo wrestler, who fought as Hidenouki before returning, fed up with life under the sport's feudal system.

Commonwealth Games heroines: Pativaine Ainuu, a bowls player of Western Samoa, in trouble for shouting things like 'Hit it, hit it, good girl!' to her woods; and to Soma Duta, a rifle shooter from India and a double medal winner.

Team award: Liechtenstein table tennis team, with a special mention for the player who has a wooden leg.

Cricket headline of the year: 'Black Baby for Gooch'. Marrilyn Williams told the *Blast* of Trinidad that she wanted Gooch to adopt her child so that it would have 'a better life under the Queen'.

Sporting poet of the year: W. S. Cameron of Guyana, for lines like 'And Wight Cup cricket more popular and clamorous for ahwe / Than Test cricket for alas its Guyana . . . / a pee ting ting pee ting.'

Cockup of the year: the Lord's stands.

Race relations award: Brian Close, for telling the world on television: 'There's a hundred years of bloody tradition on

Yorkshire lads . . . by the time he's toddling he's got a bat in his hand. Bloody Pakistanis didn't know the damn thing.'

American football match of the year: Oxford University beat Cambridge University 60–19. The universities also have such college teams as Sidney Opera House and Jesus Saves.

Disciplinary fine of the year: Bryan Hyslop, of the Great Britain amateur rugby league side, was sent off in a match against Apia in Western Samoa. He was fined one pig.

World Cup coaching award: to Valery Nepomniachy, the Siberian coach of Cameroon: 'Today is the day for meeting the wives. Footballers are also people and if a man is in discomfort for a long time it can affect his work.'

Golfer of the year: Mikael Krantz, of Sweden. Playing the Irish Open in Dublin, he started at the first tee by hitting the ball and then falling over. He was recovering from a hangover at the time. 'I was very silly,' he said. 'I was invited to an Irish party and it went on from there.' He shot an 11-over-par 83, an excellent score in the circumstances.

Most spectacular performance in a sporting arena: the couple from the Toronto Skydome. While watching the base-ball game from the Skydome's integral hotel, they turned their attentions to each other in the mistaken impression that the glass was one-way. Did the roof move for you, honey?

Best moment of the World Cup: Maradona's penalty miss against Yugoslavia.

Sell-out of the year: the Cornhill logo on the grass at the Oval. I mean, of course, the Foster's Oval, don't I? During the Oval Test, it was announced that the left bosoms of all England shirts were on sale to the highest bidder.

Batsmen of the year: shared by Devon Malcolm and Narendra Hirwani, in honour of the Campaign for Real Number Elevens.

Sportsman of the year: Art Pease, aged twenty-three and mentally handicapped. He decided to take part in a five-mile fun run, discovered that he had accidentally lined up in the Portland Marathon, shrugged his shoulders and ran every step of the course in 4hr 18min 23sec.

Colemanballs of the year: Mike Gatting: 'I hurt my thumb and then obviously the mother-in-law died.' Runner-up: an NBC commentator: 'The Dutch boxer Ruur can speak four languages, which is amazing for someone so short.'

Sponsor of the year: Jergens skin cream broke new ground by affixing its logo to uniforms of the Memphis State University cheerleaders.

Sponsored competition of the year: TSW Printers (Scunthorpe) Lincolnshire Football League. Their league cup is the Fire Surround and Kitchen Centre Supplementary Cup.

Baseball personality of the year: Schottzie, the St Bernard owned by Marge Schott, owner of the World Series winners, Cincinnati Reds.

Boxing story of the year: Bobby Beck split with his trainer. Beck is twelve. He was trained by his father. 'We just couldn't get on,' the trainer said.

British sportsman of the year: James Lambert. He *won* a ski jumping event – in fact, a Nordic combined, which involves jumping and Nordic skiing.

Horseman of the year: the dashing rider who came third in the cross country at Potton this spring, and won £5 for doing so. This column salutes Simon Barnes.

Scorecard line of the year: Chamundeswaranagh c Balasabramaniam b Anantapadmanabhan 2.

This brings me effortlessly to my final award for Team Nightmare. It goes to Dr Feix Senanayake, who receives a bottle of Calém Colheitas 1957, an ambrosial tawny port. He offers two teams of genuine cricketers to contest a Test match: England: John D. Smith, Albert D. Smith, John F. Smith, John R. Smith, David R. Smith, John S. Smith, Charles R. Smith, John H. Smith, David F. Smith, John A. Smith, John B. Smith. 12th man: David C. Smith. India: R. Patel, A. Patel, C. Patel, D. Patel, B. Patel, S. Patel, N. Patel, M. Patel, O. Patel, X. Patel, Y. Patel. 12th man: N. Patel.

29 December 1990

Births of a nation

Catherine Sampson

Women wander the bleak corridors of Peking's obstetrics and gynaecology hospital, dressed in thick jumpers and trousers, with their pyjamas over their warm clothing as a form of identification. Even in China's largest maternity hospital, things get a little chilly in the winter. Few have brushed their hair recently, for being a mother in China means an end to the flirtatiousness of youth. None of the women looks very cheerful about the imminent miracle of birth.

An airy room at the end of one corridor is full of cribs, some occupied by babies even more thickly swaddled than the mothers-to-be, so tightly wrapped that they cannot move a limb and are impervious to cold. A dot of red dye in the centre of the forehead identifies the babies who have had their tuberculosis jabs. One pale-faced infant yells. He was born just an hour ago and, Dr Gao Feng says, patting him on the back: 'He's not used to being out here yet; he'd rather be in his mother's belly.' Their peace disturbed, none of the other babies so much as murmurs. 'In general, Chinese children are very quiet,' Dr Gao Feng says.

Forty babies are born every minute in China. Childbirth resembles more a mass production procedure than an inspiring or spiritual event. There is such a shortage of beds in China's maternity hospitals that a woman in labour may find herself sharing her bed. At this hospital, the intensive care ward for newborns sometimes gets overcrowded, and babies have to share the six incubators.

When the pain of labour gets too much, Dr Gao Feng says, 'we play soft music, use acupuncture, and try to make the women comfortable'. Acupuncture anaesthesia is routinely used for Caesarean sections. Painkillers are rarely administered. It is not clear whether this is by accident or design, but in a country of more than a billion people, it does not do to give women the idea that childbirth could be less than a nightmare. 'It hurt so much that I swore when I had my daughter I would never have another child, even if they let me,' one woman says.

Nor are women, in general, allowed the comfort of a husband's presence, because the delivery rooms are so overcrowded. Hospitals feel it would be improper for a husband to be present not only for the birth of his own child, but for the deliveries of four other women in the same room. Most of the doctors, too, are women. Husbands are allotted a small room off to the side of the delivery room in which to pace around and cross their fingers that it will be a boy. Dr Gao Feng says that her hospital has plans to install closed-circuit television, which would allow a husband to watch the birth of his child. One hospital in Tianjin, however, does allow fathers to be present, and has found that that is even better for the one-child policy. 'I could hardly bear my wife's crying caused by the pain of childbirth. For her sake, I don't want her to have another,' an official newspaper quoted a new father as saying.

Giving birth is not free in this socialist paradise. Most clinics charge about £20, or an average monthly wage, for a straightforward birth. If there are complications, or if the baby needs intensive care, it costs more. In general, if the parents work for a state-run enterprise, the cost can be reclaimed. State enterprises also give men fifteen days' paternity leave.

Seventy per cent of China's population lives in the countryside, and most of China's babies are not born in hospitals like the one in Peking, but miles from the nearest town. Here, childbirth is more basic. There are no incubators, no foetal monitors. Twenty thousand women a year die during pregnancy and childbirth, mostly in the countryside. Modern methods are slowly penetrating rural areas, but tradition and grandparents say that a newborn baby and mother should be kept for a month in a darkened room with no fresh air. The mother should not be allowed to wash for one month after childbirth. Babies are laid on their backs to sleep, because the Chinese think that a flat skull is a sign of beauty. To keep a baby from moving around and getting into trouble, some women place the baby up to his head in a bag of sand. The bag is secured around the baby's neck. In this way, the baby is anchored, and the sand acts as a disposable nappy.

It is in the countryside, too, that the most horrific tales of female infanticide surface. The jealousy and despair surrounding the birth of girls in the countryside are reflected time and again in almost incredible stories in the newspapers. Recently, one newspaper told the story of a baby thrown away by its father. The father had been told after the birth that the child was a girl and had not paused to check. A dog found the baby, picked it up in its mouth, and took it back to the family, where the father discovered it was a boy. His sister had tricked him into believing the baby was a girl and therefore into abandoning it because she herself had only a daughter and could not bear the thought of her brother having the status which comes with the birth of a son.

As early as 1988, even official Chinese newspapers were admitting that hospitals all over the country were offering ultrasound checks which would tell the parents whether the foetus was male or female. Many parents, once told that the foetus was a girl, requested an abortion and got one, the *Shanghai Evening News* said.

The number of live births in China may be frightening, but for every hundred of those live births, there are about 48 abortions. That is about 19 every minute. Abortion is simply considered another form of birth control, and women consider it part of their lot in life to have at least one abortion. Dr Gao Feng says about 15 abortions are carried out every day at her hospital. This means that the number of live births and abortions at her hospital are roughly equal, between five thousand and six thousand a year.

'The limit for the abortion of a normal foetus is seventy

days,' Dr Gao Feng says. 'If there is a severe deformity, we can do abortions in the sixth or seventh month.' Other sources say that abortions are done into the eighth month, and not always because the foetus is unhealthy. Indeed, the intended abortion sometimes produces a live and viable, if premature, baby. But what happens to that baby, nobody is prepared to say.

29 December 1990

In South Africa's crucible

Arthur Miller

What struck me strongly about Nelson Mandela in his American public appearance last summer was the absence in him of any sign of bitterness. After 27½ years with his nose against the bars, he seemed uninterested in cursing the whites who had put him there for the crime of demanding the vote in a country where his people outnumber their rulers by about ten to one.

I suppose his rather majestic poise, unmarred by rancour, lowered white defensiveness to the point where reactionaries could join with liberals in applauding his speech to Congress. But such unanimous appreciation is bound to be suspect when an honest man can hardly please everyone with his views; after all, with all his charm and civility, he was still the man who had organized the ANC's armed guerrilla force, for one thing.

But, watching from a distance, I had found him extra-ordinarily straightforward in his persistent refusal to pulver-ize his history to suit current American tastes, crediting communists for being the first whites to befriend his move-ment, sometimes at the risk of their lives. Likewise, criticizing Israel and in the same breath reminding us that perhaps 90 per cent of his earliest supporters had been Jews.

In short, he allows himself to remain complicated; he has a grandson named Gadafi (which was not his idea, however), and has written that the highest expression of democracy is the British House of Commons, and the best legal system the American with its written Bill of Rights. To me, in our interview, he said that he had never joined the Party. He did not add that he had never been a Marxist, but whether or not he thought he had been, I judge that he sees men in all their variety of character and deed in the foreground of events, rather than as shadowy creatures manipulated by forces as a Marxist usually must.

I agreed to a conversation with Mandela after much hesitation. The whole thing had begun with a London phone call from one Beverley Marcus, through whose South African English I discerned that she had proposed to the BBC that they film Mandela and me talking about life rather than politics, and that Mandela was receptive to the idea because he had called a halt to any more interviews where the same simple-minded questions would inevitably be asked.

Lacking a reporter's killer instinct or investigative techniques, I was simply very curious about the roots of this man's unusual character. How does one manage to emerge from nearly three decades in prison with such hopefulness, such inner calm?

But my main impulse came out of my New York background; a racially splintered city with over 2,000 people murdered last year, it has next to no credible black leadership, and so Mandela's success or failure seemed far from an academic question for me. If he can lead his riven country into a multi-racial democracy the ripples could rock New York, Chicago, Detroit – yes, and Europe and Russia and Israel, where the single most potentially explosive social problem is ethnicity and its unmet, often incoherent demands.

South Africa was full of surprises, the first being the fact that Beverley's younger sister, Gill, is Nelson Mandela's veritable right hand, in charge of ANC public relations, and that their father was his and Oliver Tambo's accountant. I suppose I should have felt my integrity at risk by this news, but I had never had the intention of drawing and quartering Mandela, only seeking a pathway into his nature and that of his movement. Gill, with her inside knowledge of the movement and unabashed declarations of its amateurish failings, as well as of the constantly shifting so-called tribal conflict,

166

turned out, in fact, to be of great help in my grasping the situation.

Cape Town and the Cape area, which Beverley suggested my wife, Inge Morath, and I visit for a few days to unwind from the fourteen-hour plane trip, is an unlikely place to begin preparing for a talk with a revolutionary leader, since it is as close to Beverly Hills and the California littoral as you can get without tripping over a movie studio. Balmy air, a lazy Atlantic surf lapping white beaches, swimming pools and very good fish restaurants – I felt myself beginning to sink into its lovely lethargy. Just like the steady stream of British who, with their super-valuable sterling, are buying up homes they could never afford in England.

Then one climbs a dune one hundred yards across a beach road fronting some extremely lavish homes and their tennis courts – and from the dune's ridge one looks down into a squatter-town of hundreds of cardboard and tin shacks thrown one against the other right up to the edge of the sea. Don't the rich nearby object? Not all do – some happily sell drinking water to the blacks here who have no supply of their own. But of course this shanty town in Hout Bay, near Cape Town, will have to go, for the view of the sea is superb and the sand as white as sugar, a piece of prime real estate which will not be denied its promise forever.

But one can drive the Cape and Cape Town and indeed South Africa end to end without the slightest awareness that this sanitized prosperity involves only three million of its 30 million inhabitants. The famous South African schizophrenia is not hard to understand. To be sure, the back pages of the paper display ads for razor wire with which to surround one's home, and the walls surrounding white homes show a metal sign reading 'Instant Armed Response', and in many areas you are instructed not to stop at red lights at night lest your car be hijacked. But you quickly get used to this palpable fear, just as we have in New York, where as a child in Harlem I always carried all my books and belongings with me to the blackboard or they'd be gone when I got back to my seat.

But South Africa is unique; it has state socialism for the whites – 60 per cent of all jobs are in state enterprises – and fascism for the blacks. Still, by the time we got back to Johannesburg after five days in the country, I felt the place strange but comprehensible as merely one more kingdom of denial, unusual mainly for the immense proportion of its majority ghettoized and stripped of civil rights.

Mandela's new house in the middle of Soweto has been criticized by some as one of Winnie Mandela's ostentations, standing as it does in the midst of the Soweto slum. Actually, donations built it. And there is a scattering of other quite good middle class homes in the midst of the squalor, since the few successful middle class blacks have been barred from white areas along with the poor. It is all part of the hopeless muddle of a modern technological state trying to sustain the most primitive chest-pounding Nazi master-race dogmas. So surrealism looms at every turn – the largest BMW dealership in Africa, black-owned, stands at the very edge of Soweto, a glass cube showroom exploding beams of white light toward houses yards away that have neither water nor sewers and whose occupants are no doubt unemployed and probably illiterate.

From the outside, the Mandela house seems less elaborate than odd, a large, chesty configuration of obliquely angular brick walls, an impromptu sort of construction until one is inside and realizes that it is a kind of fortress, its vulnerable dining and living rooms with their glass doors protected by a deep brick veranda extending outward some 30 ft or so. One drives into a receiving yard surrounded, as in so many other homes in this scared country, by a high wall with an electronically controlled, steel sliding door. And the doors of the main rooms are double-hinged to support a steel inner gate painted a discreet ivory to match the walls. Presumably these are barriers to an invading force.

Mandela's daughter, Zinzi, came into the living room pursuing her three-year-old son, both of them handsome, round-faced, and no doubt accustomed to crowds of strangers in the place – our crew was stringing its cables out, Gill Marcus was already on the phone, the floors and walls seemed covered with gifts, trophies, bric-à-brac, and now Winnie was here, explaining that she would not be eating with us because Nelson kept watching her calories and she liked to eat what she liked to eat. Whereupon Mandela appeared, making a round gesture with both hands referring to her weight, and saying 'Africa!', both of them laughing while she bent to lift her rampaging grandson, whom she handed to a nurse. Even in his quick glances at her, one saw Mandela's overwhelming love for his still-young wife, and she clearly basked in it. But her indictment in a murder case and impending trial seemed to hang in the air despite her tired jocularity.

Mandela was not wearing one of his formal London suits, but a collarless short-sleeved African blouse with gold-embroidered yoke, a chief's blouse, it looked to me. Gill hoped he would relax with me, and he would gradually come quite close. But he is by nature a formal, conservative man who in a peaceful country would have been chief justice of its supreme court or perhaps the head of a large law firm. And my first question to him – after we had walked out on his veranda and looked down at Soweto, the dumping ground for human beings – was how he had been raised.

He sat at first pressed against the back of his couch, somewhat on guard, having been cornered by interviewers who find it impossible to believe that he simply means what he says. He was the son of a chief – and saying it one saw how serious it was to be a chief's son; and he had been taught early on that he would have the responsibilities of governing and judging. Even now, he straightened a bit as he told with pride how, when he was ten and his father died, an uncle had taken over his education and his life. 'My father occupied a position equivalent to that of prime minister in the tribe . . . To me as a child, the Transkei was the centre of the entire world . . . The missionary tried to destroy the belief in custom and they created the perception that we have no history or culture.' And, with an amused grin, 'when the 1939 war began, we felt we were loyal subjects of the British monarch. That was the atmosphere in which we were brought up.'

'And what went on inside you when the missionary told you you had no history?'

'I'm not so sure if I knew that I had a history.' And later, 'I must confess that Africa . . . remained a dark continent in that I knew very little about it and I knew better about Europe, especially Britain.'

This meticulous specificity, and his staid, almost Victorian structure of speech and demeanour suddenly had a root and expressed an innate authority which no doubt helped to keep him together through his prison decades – Mandela, to put it simply, *is* a chief.

This may help to explain why it has been so difficult for him to deign to confer with his rival, Chief Buthelezi of the Zulus, who have recently been on the attack against Xhosa people. Buthelezi, it is felt, helped to justify apartheid by accepting the headship of a concocted homeland where his people were dumped. It is not only the equivalent of a French Maquisard guerrilla accepting political equality with a Vichy collaborator; there is a moral issue involved for Mandela, and his pride. Nevertheless, when Mandela did appear at a recent 'peace conference' with Buthelezi, the latter's people so threatened him that he was forced to leave the area.

The tribe, he insists, is basically an extended family. And in modern times there is no 'natural' conflict between tribes which are largely urbanized now, living side by side and intermarrying, joining the same unions, attending the same schools. It was the British and then the apartheid government that had always tried to tribalize Africa, pitting one against the other, setting up so-called homelands, territories that had never existed before. 'There is one Africa and there will be one,' Mandela said, creating a ball with his two hands.

The present conflict is 'simply a conflict between two political organizations', a conflict that has failed to make headway in Soweto, as one example, because it is more politically sophisticated rather than because the people are mainly Xhosa. 'But when Zulus attack they never ask whether you are Zulu or something else, like the recent attack on people in the train, who do not sit according to tribes. They attack anyone.'

And who would be interested in orchestrating these attacks?

He pauses before this answer, which goes to the heart of his hopes. 'My belief is that President de Klerk wants South Africa to take a new direction and it is therefore difficult . . . to say that the government itself is orchestrating this violence . . .'

And, finally: 'They have either lost control over certain elements of their security forces or those elements are doing precisely what the government wants . . . They want to negotiate with a weakened ANC . . . You are not dealing with tribal people from the countryside but people who are sophisticated in the use of weapons, who know how to move very swiftly with military precision . . . There are efforts now to start the Renamo movement in South Africa.' (Renamo is the Mozambiquan mercenary outfit that murdered thousands.)

I turned to his prison time. He and his comrades had originally been assured by a prison officer that they'd be out in five years because the world was so outraged by their life sentences. But five years came and went. Winnie could visit twice a year, his children were growing up with no father, and here his face showed his pain at his inability to protect his family – the helplessness desecrated his chiefly role. Government harassment of Winnie was driving her out of one job after another until 'there were certain moments when I wondered whether I had taken the correct decision of getting committed to the struggle. But at the end of these hesitations with myself I would feel that I had taken the right decision . . . The certainty of our final victory was always there. Of course I became sometimes very angry when I thought about the persecution of my wife and that I could not give her the support she needed. I felt powerless. And also my children were hounded out of one school after another . . .' His vulnerability was plain here. This was as close as he was able to come to acknowledging what must have been the loss of hope for release before he died; instead, he preferred to find something positive to emphasize. When the world began to forget him, and all black movements were suppressed, the government restated that a life sentence meant life. 'But in the English-speaking universities they came all-out to oppose these harsh measures . . . People tend to forget the contribution that was made by the National Union of South African Students, which was a white organization.'

This is not an opportune upbeat recollection, but his ultimate vision of a non-racial South Africa. It is more, I am convinced, than a tactic to recognize the future need for whites with advanced education and business prowess. It was striking how he never seemed to categorize people by race or even class, and that he spontaneously tended to cite good men even among the enemy.

'That came from my prison experience. It gets very cold in Robben Island and we had no underwear. Some warders went strictly by regulations – you were allowed two blankets. But another warder would slip you an extra one. I made some good friends among the warders, some of them visit me now.'

In fact, in the final years he ran 'Mandela University' in Robben Island, and white warders were among his pupils. But there wasn't time to talk about this. We'd scheduled two sessions and at the last minute had to settle for one because he had to rush off to deal with the murders going on all over the place and the government's inability – or unwillingness – to keep order.

On the way back to Johannesburg that night, Gill Marcus pressed the driver on no account to stop at red lights and to drive as fast as possible through the darkness.

12 January 1991

Why the consumer is king

Jonathan Clark

The Lawson boom may be dead, but it refuses to lie down. Agonizingly, with a grinding of gears and rending of metal, the highest real interest rates in living memory were required to slow down the enormous force of consumer demand. Why is the English shopper so resistant to restraint? Why will we not trim our expenditure to suit our means? Why are savings and investment so consistently squeezed by consumer spending?

We are used to thinking of England as one of the capitalist democracies. Yet neither capitalism (the priority of the producer) nor democracy (obedience to the majority) has flourished here in its pure form. Instead, we have *consumer* capitalism and *parliamentary* democracy. The English record their power in society less by how they vote than by how they spend: the high street of the English town on a Saturday afternoon is the great polling booth of the nation.

Where the newly-emancipated millions of eastern Europe take an inordinate delight in voting, the English derive their deepest satisfaction from shopping. Retail trade is more highly developed in our economy than in any other, but this means more than just consumer convenience: the individual exercises his most detailed and regular control over the world around him not by his contributions to politics, charity, the arts or voluntary societies, but by the activity of buying. Each pound spent is a vote cast, and a vote that is never wasted on a losing candidate.

Remarkably, consumerism is almost never resented: our pleasure in buying what we can afford is seldom spoilt by the enjoyment of our neighbour who buys something bigger and better. The egalitarian is scandalized by inequality and the democrat by disenfranchisement; but the unsuccessful shopper will always wait till the next sale.

Too many people called the English a nation of shop-keepers, from the American Samuel Adams and the Scot Adam Smith, for the credit to go to Napoleon. But it follows that England was as much a nation of shoppers. The debate about whether capitalist values have been accepted in England misses this point: capitalism has been accepted here for centuries, but in the form of consumerism, not heroic production. Where Stalin's beaming Russians toured their tractor factories and Japanese workers begin their day with the company song, the English prefer to go window shopping. Giant emporia stuffed with consumer durables are, to the English, the best proof that all is well with their society.

This has long been so. Historians now qualify the sense in which England ever had an industrial revolution: massive factories or forges belching flame and smoke were the exception in most sectors of the economy. Much of the technology of early industrialization was simple and cheap; it arrived gradually and patchily; national income grew slowly. It all seems very undramatic by comparison with what we learned at school.

But as scholars were abolishing one sort of revolution, they were discovering another: the consumer revolution. Eighteenth-century Englishmen developed a quite new attitude to material possessions: fashion, luxury and emulation drove them to seek the latest, smartest, best. The economy responded by developing an unprecedentedly efficient system of retail distribution and a bewildering diversity of consumer goods to tempt and flatter the customer.

Most of the techniques of modern consumerism were pioneered in eighteenth-century England, not twentieth-century America. Credit, discounts and travelling salesmen were commonplace. Aggressive selling met eager buying. Conspicuous consumption was child's play to Wedgwood;

Chippendale and Sheraton manipulated fashion with ease; newspapers were crammed with advertising.

It was this consumer revolution rather than factory production that produced a change in values and behaviour. 'All classes enjoy the accumulation of riches, luxury and pleasure,' wrote a German visitor in 1791. The social hierarchy was softened and humanized by the ability of all ranks to imitate or share in the consumption patterns of the rich. More and more people – not just landowners – were given the impression that they had 'a stake in the country'. The confident consumer eventually sought to be a voter, and with so many novelties to spend his money on, he generally voted for the cheap government and low taxes that were a hallmark of Victorian England. Adam Smith refined his remark: England was 'a nation that is governed by shopkeepers': the supremacy of commercial values, selfishness, profiteering, and delight in consumer goods are more accurately dated to 1779 than to 1979.

The term 'consumption' ceased to be pejorative in the 1690s ('capitalism' did not arrive, as a word, until the 1850s). The 'market' ceased to mean a collection of local stallholders and became a national abstraction. Increasingly from the late seventeenth century the English regarded consumer demand, not state-directed production, as the engine of economic growth.

'Consumption is the sole end and purpose of all production,' wrote Adam Smith in *The Wealth of Nations*. 'The interest of the producer ought to be attended to, only so far as it may be necessary for promoting that of the consumer.' Even today, not many societies would agree.

Paradoxically the factory, when it came, was often condemned aesthetically by the very men who consumed the products of the new industry with most relish and least conscience. By being offered capitalism as consumerism, the English were enabled to reject capitalism as industry; those cultural pundits who profited most from the workshop of the world were also those who were most mandarin in their disdain for the grubby business of making things.

So England loaded the dice in its economy. Firms flourish best that boast 'the customer is always right'; the rival philosophy of *caveat emptor* is generally left untranslated. Keynesian economics was the distillation of this ancient attitude: demand was everything. Only recently have economics textbooks shifted their emphasis to the supply side – but the dominance of the consumer is not easily dislodged.

Meanwhile, consumerism still offers a better key to our political problems than any other. Interest rates, inflation, and real disposable incomes are still the best predictors of a government's popularity: 'You've never had it so good' can be mocked, but not denied. The sovereignty of the consumer is an insight that increasingly holds good around the world. Russians may be content without the democracy they never had, but if glasnost and perestroika fail to fill the shelves, ideological rectitude on production can do little for Gorbachev. Or, we might add, for Mr Major.

12 January 1991

Pigs in the middle

The absence of wings is a design fault in the modern pig, though about the only one. If ever dogs had to stand aside as man's best friend, the family *suidae* could take over. The pig's real problem is that man, being a real swine, has not recognized his porcine benefactor for the splendid thing it is. Piggism – irrational prejudice against the creature – is rife.

Does George Orwell want a greedy animal as his ultimate farmyard bully? Does Graham Greene need a silly domestic creature to fall from a balcony? Do militants want to abuse the police; or women, men? The friendless pig will do. If pigs could sue . . .

Pigs in the natural state are friendly and intelligent creatures, all-consuming and all-consumable – and clean. Pigs and hens are to an English farmyard as bacon and eggs are to an English breakfast. But no pig ever got fat on man's gratitude for services rendered, only on the consumer appetite for lean and succulent pork with plenty of crackling.

How many votes are there in cruelty to pigs? John Gummer, not a man to be careless with his party's popularity, has just brought forward some half-hearted proposals to ease their lot. The minister of agriculture has portentously declared it is 'now time to take action', meaning, of course, a new deal for pigs in 1999. He was, in fact, merely trying to out-manoeuvre a backbencher's pro-pig private member's bill. Sir Richard Body wants parliament to legislate away pig-tethering and narrow stalls in five years' time. Mr Gummer's rival bid was eight years, so the auction seems to be going backwards (from a pig's-eye view).

When eight years of continuing 'dreadful' treatment, to use

Sir Richard's adjective, is deemed a superior offer to five, pigs have an image problem. The National Farmers' Union has bottomed them both with a bid of ten years, and demanded equality of suffering for foreign pigs.

The husbandry practices in question – confining a pig between horizontal bars or by neck-chain to the floor – were described by Mr Gummer as an 'undesirable welfare burden'. This vivid euphemism for cruelty surely would make him 'pig of the year' were it not time to stop insulting pigs. May we commend the expression 'male chauvinist gummer' in retaliation?

Notwithstanding the efforts of Sir Richard, Mr Gummer and the NFU, the time for civil treatment of these civilized animals has come. Parliament should amend the pig husbandry bill's timescale downwards, and send the new gummer regulations under the Agriculture (Miscellaneous Provisions) Act to the slaughterhouse.

12 January 1991

The Playhouse is the thing

Beryl Bainbridge

Last week the Liverpool Playhouse, the oldest repertory theatre in England, was granted an Administration Order by the High Court in Manchester. Put like that, with all those capital letters, it might appear that it has been given some sort of award; actually, it means the theatre is facing bankruptcy and cannot go on trading, not unless Mr Getty or, better still, Mr Moores, of football pools fame, gallops in at the head of the cavalry.

Who cares, I hear you say? Theatres all over the country are sinking to their knees like old bulls. I care because I was formed, informed, by the Liverpool Playhouse.

It is true I went first, aged four, to a girls' college in Formby, then to Merchant Taylors' School in Crosby, then to ballet school in Tring, Hertfordshire, but, apart from the questioning phrase, *quel dommage*, a lasting belief that geometry is a foreign language, an abiding horror of white tights and an addiction to the smell of shellac, my education, if it could be labelled as such, was provided by the Liverpool Playhouse.

I arrived there in 1949, at a time when Williamson Square still had a Clochmerle urinal made of cast iron. Of an evening, naphtha flares were lit in buckets and the square flickered in the darkness like a ship bucking at sea. The whole city, to the eyes of an adolescent, was peopled with men with missing arms, sawn off legs, burnt faces remodelled from candle wax. Years later, when I took my children to Madame Tussauds, I felt at home.

In those days one did not need an Equity card to go on the boards, nor was the vulgar subject of money mentioned. I got taken on because my father knew a man who knew a man who had gone to school with a relation of Maud Carpenter, legendary manageress of the theatre. She was unique; big, handsome, ungainly, with a bust like a bolster and an attention to detail which made the theatre a successful enterprise for forty years.

The first production of that 1949 season was Priestley's *Dangerous Corner*, during which I sat on the prompt stool with the book and wept every night because, just before the curtain fell, the cast danced to a record of 'My Foolish Heart'. I thought it was the saddest tune I had ever heard and that the actors, resplendent in dinner jackets and long dresses, were the most sophisticated beings in the world.

The second play was about a country schoolmaster discovering a mathematical genius in his rustic classroom. Just as the play was about to go into rehearsal, the Dundee authorities refused to give a performing licence to the lad who was to act the part of the swot. Within the hour the theatre consulted my mother and I was marched off to the barber for a short back and sides. Don't misunderstand me. My razoring had nothing in common with the shearing of that little sweetheart in the film of *Oliver Twist*. My haircut was of the sort given by real orphanages when nits are suspected. My mother shed a tear, and, from that day forth, I have never allowed my hair to be cut above shoulder level.

When I was not acting or understudying I was hiring props, helping to shift scenery, dabbing bits of paint on the back-cloth, and running for bacon sandwiches.

The theatre as I knew it did not survive much beyond the Sixties, when, for no good reason apart from so-called progress and innovation, the stairs were moved to the other side of the building and the paint frame and carpenter's shop enlarged. The almost Dickensian world of greasepaint and coke fumes, gas mantles hissing on the landings, cans of beans jumping in an old saucepan on the prop-room fire, vanished for ever. But then, so did the old St John's market at the back, the cobblestones and the urinal, the News

180

Theatre in Clayton Square and the oyster bar in Cases Street.

Unfortunately, most of the audience disappeared as well, preferring to find its entertainment in snooker clubs and public houses, bingo halls and sitting rooms with television boxes.

There is nothing wrong with change, but there is something wrong with the notion that because something isn't making money or showing an instant return it ought to be done away with. The Liverpool Playhouse does not need a huge amount of cash to keep it on its feet; compared with the cost of a Polaris submarine or one of those newfangled tanks which we all pay for, its annual expenditure is a drop in the ocean. And some people do keep going to the theatre, even if not in such numbers as before. It would be a pity, in this particular case, not to say a tragedy, if the apathy of the many succeeded in putting an end to the enrichment of the few.

14 January 1991

Soldiers proud to be called Rats

Henry Stanhope

The Desert Rats have returned to their habitat in the sands fifty years after their soubriquet was coined. Few British military formations have so held the imagination of the public. Like the Light Brigade, the Dam Busters and 'the Few', they have built up a mythology of their own.

Their inheritance is a broken one, however, and their identity a matter for debate. The title is usually now awarded to the 7th Armoured Brigade. But the 4th Brigade, the other fighting unit in the Gulf, has not only a legitimate claim to use it but wears an emblem which is arguably more authentic.

The term 'Desert Rats' was originally applied to the 7th Armoured Division, formed from the Mobile Division Egypt in 1940. According to Lord Carver, a former Desert Rat and a historian of the North African campaign, the new divisional commander, Major-General 'Dickie' O'Moore Creach, thought its emblem (a red circle on a white background) far too dull. So in the best tradition of gifted amateurism he commissioned his wife to design new insignia incorporating that ubiquitous local resident, the jerboa.

Whether General Creach (or Mrs Creach) deserves all the credit is disputed. According to the Ministry of Defence, his predecessor, Major-General 'Hobo' Hobart, had at least provided the inspiration. On seeing a regimental signaller's pet jerboa, he is said to have remarked: 'This little animal should become our emblem. We must learn to live as he does, the hard way, in the desert.'

The choice of a distinctive symbol was more than a mere military caprice. Military police, for instance, needed to have a rapid means of identifying army units while directing convoys along the network of barely discernible roads across the desert.

The Desert Rat was to become one of the most coveted nicknames of the war, appealing as it did to the British empathy with the underdog and the army's reputation for gritty survival under pressure.

The main components of the 7th Armoured Division in those days were the 7th and 4th Brigades, both of which adopted the new divisional motif. But when the division and its brigades separated, during and after the Western Desert campaign, each made idiosyncratic alterations.

The 7th Brigade left the desert in 1941, long before the final battle of El Alamein, and was posted to Burma where it repainted its jerboa jungle-green. The 4th Brigade moved to Sicily and then Italy, where it inexplicably recoloured the little animal jet black.

Meanwhile, the division went to Italy where it fought not with the British but alongside the American 5th Army. From there it was posted back to Britain to prepare for the Normandy landings of 1944.

The advance party which preceded it to Britain, tasked with ordering a new batch of Desert Rat signs, got the design wrong. The result was an animal which, though painted in the original red, looked more like a kangaroo, with its tail trailing between its legs.

The emblem worn by the 4th Brigade to this day, depicting a rat with its tail curled over its shoulder, is the more accurate representation of Mrs Creach's original cartoon.

All this would seem of no more than passing interest to most armies. But in Britain where the tribal system is deeply woven into the fabric of military life, regimental insignia and traditions are almost sacred. They are held to be essential to morale. Each unit jealously safeguards its colours and quirky customs, competing with others in friendly rivalry in the manner of houses in a public school. This often complicates the lives of quartermasters. While the standard barrack room garb of the modern soldier consists of dark green trousers and khaki sweater, many regiments have their own variations. The Cheshire Regiment, for instance, wears a brown sweater, the Royal Hampshire a black one, the Royal Signals dark blue, and the Intelligence Corps green.

How much this matters in wartime is debatable. The common assumption is that tribal loyalties count, especially given their territorial roots. Yorkshiremen standing shoulder to shoulder in the Green Howards or north Welshmen in the Royal Welch Fusiliers fight better because they represent a family, some of whom may have been together since early schooldays. That, anyway, is the theory.

It is perhaps true on the rugby field at Aldershot. But in wartime, when the system is supposed to prove its worth, it often breaks down. As reinforcements are dispatched to plug gaps in the front line after the first casualties have been suffered, it is virtually impossible to select men from Staffordshire for the Staffordshire Regiment or lads from Argyll for the Argyll and Sutherland Highlanders.

For similar reasons, one should be wary of Desert Rat folklore. The 7th Armoured Division spent only a few years, albeit successful ones, in the desert before moving with the action back to Europe. In 1946, when the British Army of the Rhine was carved out of the occupying forces in West Germany, its main components were two divisions, the 2nd Infantry and the Desert Rats – now facing a different enemy altogether. The 4th and 7th Brigades were eventually disbanded, the 4th not to be reformed until ten years ago. In the 1960s the 7th Armoured Division disappeared during one of the many restructurings of the Army of the Rhine and was downgraded to a new 7th Brigade.

The two brigades which proudly display the sign of the jerboa today, one in scarlet and the other in black, are only the spiritual heirs of the units which fought for a relatively short time in the desert, while the animal they look to as their mascot was the handiwork of an artistic army wife.

16 January 1991

Fine, but not private

Andrew Motion

In 1915, when he was on his way to Gallipoli, Rupert Brooke was bitten on the top lip by a mosquito, got blood poisoning, and died. He was buried on Skyros, in the northern Sporades – an island which is divided more or less neatly into two parts: the watered, populated half, and the drought-stricken, empty half. Brooke ended up in the drought-stricken bit (that's where his boat was) under a pile of stones and a wooden cross which explained, in Greek, that he had died delivering Constantinople from the Turks.

Sixty-five years later, in my last summer holiday from school, a couple of friends and I went to find him. Why? Partly because I had a crush on his poems (yes, I know, I know), and partly because it meant we could disguise having fun as something reasonably highbrow. We flew to Athens, bussed to a dump on the east coast, caught a rickety ferry, and there we were: in a thyme-smelling bay with a big iron boat rusting just off-shore, no other tourists in sight, not a map or a word of Greek between us. And at the wrong end of the island. We set off at five the next morning over the trackless scrub. It would be easy, wouldn't it? We'd ask a shepherd to show us the way to the grave – it would be fine. Twelve hours later, hopelessly lost, exhausted, our shoes disintegrating, with no food and no drink, we still hadn't met our shepherd. Instead, I had the best view of an early death anyone could ask for, and a nasty feeling there was something funny – as well as just terrible – about our plight. I could easily imagine what people at school would say. I could hear their voices, their laughter, their voices . . .

Then an old man appeared from the undergrowth. 'The

185

grave! The grave!' we shouted, and a quarter of an hour later we reached it. I've no idea what the place looks like today, but in those days it was extraordinary. Some time after the war Brooke's mother had sent out (and fixed for the Anglo-Hellenic League to build) a large, pompous, inscribed, rail-surrounded tomb, and it lay among the boulders, shaded by olive trees, like something fallen from outer space. Utterly bizarre. Utterly incomprehensible. We stared for five minutes or so, swallowing drily, and I watched a column of ants marching out of a crack in the stonework. 'They'll each be carrying away a piece of him,' I thought. I supposed it was what I wanted to do myself.

I suppose it is still what I want to do, whenever I visit a poet under the sod – and the more obscure the sod, the better chance there is of success. In Westminster Abbey the grave may be a fine place but it can't be a private one, and neither can our feelings easily remain private. They, like the poets in their corner, are too much on show; and anyway, what sort of devotion is it simply to take a journey to the middle of London? Any fool can do that. Shouldn't a real fan be made to suffer? Shouldn't admiration be *difficult*? Even Thomas Hardy in Stinsford seems available – or at least, the bit of him that is there does.

It was Skyros, of course, which made me believe this, and I felt it again a few years later when I went to look for Edward Thomas near Arras in northern France. (Thomas was killed in the trenches at Easter 1917.) I had just left university, where I had written a thesis on his poems, and I couldn't think of a bigger and better final full stop than to stare at his stone. There was – again, of course – an ulterior motive. I had just met Annick, who lived near Arras, and I reckoned I could, you know . . . It transpired that every stick of furniture she owned had previously belonged to a dentist, and whenever I sat down I thought something painful was going to happen in my mouth – so that part of the trip was a failure.

But the grave-spotting was OK. With Annick hanging out of the car window bellowing for directions, we tracked

Thomas down to a small military cemetery in the lee of a wood. It was late spring, and the cherry trees either side of the path to the front gate were shedding their blossom. Inside, we tramped soberly up and down the rows of almost-identical graves in the falling afternoon light. There were two Thomases (neither of them Edward), a handful of Germans, the long, melancholy lines of names from war memorials at home, and at last our man: P. E. Thomas, and a bush of the herb called old man growing over him. I pulled a bit off and sniffed it, just as Thomas sniffs it in his poem 'Old Man'. It smelt of chewing gum.

And the other pilgrimages, what about them? Each one has its own story. I have seen yet another war poet, Ivor Gurney, who knew and loved the Cotswolds better than most people and is buried in a hideous churchyard opposite a garage in Tigworth. I have seen the metaphysical poet Henry Vaughan, the 'swan of Usk', under a yew tree outside Abergavenny (there is no surviving portrait of Vaughan, so summoning him up requires a special effort). I have seen the shrub-covered plaque to A. E. Housman on the outside wall of the church in Shropshire, making him seem someone God won't admit. I've seen Sylvia Plath, now stoneless on her contentious, wind-driven hilltop above Heydon Bridge.

And so on, and so on. In each case, an afterlife of stories and ironies surrounds the place – an afterlife which, for those so inclined, must have something to do with religion, but for me has more to do with possession. I want to show the dead my face so that I can feel entitled to take something away from them: a sense of them clearly and definitely in my life. It is all done with a decent show of self-abnegation, but it comes down to narcissism.

As much a part of narcissism, in fact, as us pondering what will happen to ourselves when we die. You don't have to have published a line to wonder, when you take your favourite coastal walk, whether after your ashes have been scattered there someone will follow in your footsteps, trying to en-visage you. Or to speculate, as you stand on the grass beside the graves of other members of your family, about whose shadow might one day fall across your own headstone. They may seem ignoble in their selfishness, these thoughts, but they are only natural. It is myself I meet on such excursions, as well as the object of my affections – or so I tell myself. I am only doing unto others as I wish to have done unto me – and to hell with all the immodesty that implies.

19 January 1991

Mozart immortal

All over Europe the celebrations ring out. Two hundred years ago, Wolfgang Amadeus did not really die, and from Mantua to Bratislava, from Prague to London, music lovers are rejoicing in the fact, marking his birthday yesterday with a flourish. Radio 3, so long sunk in musicological elitism, rose splendidly to the occasion: a whole day of Mozart, culminating in *The Magic Flute*, his last great metaphysical opera, broadcast from Vienna. Last Friday, the English Chamber Orchestra offered up a Mozartian jewel, the rarely performed *Mitridate* under the exhilarating baton of Jeffrey Tate. The opera is surely history's most astonishing work of art by a youth not yet fifteen years old.

Mozart's career was a tribute to the concept of the pushy parent. By the age of five, he had started to compose clavier music. He was touring Europe at six. By the age of fourteen, Pope Clement XIV had awarded him the Order of the Golden Spur and he had written, directed and conducted *Mitridate*. By his death at thirty-five, by no means burnt out creatively, Mozart had produced twice as much music as many other composers twice his age.

Mozart's life, too, seems to transcend his own age. While Haydn worked happily as a servant to the Esterhazy family, Mozart broke from the Archbishop of Salzburg, rebelling against being treated on a par with a butler. He became the first great freelance, for some time relying only on commissions. He shocked the establishment with *The Marriage of Figaro*, based on a Beaumarchais play banned in Vienna for implying that servants could behave better than their masters, and thus outwit them.

Mozart died a pauper, 'his fragile, burned-out body lowered into a shabby grave'. Speculation that he was poisoned by an envious rival with lesser gifts – Salieri, perhaps, or Sussmayr – has long added lustre to a romantically burnished life. For years, his extraordinary precocity and the apparent mismatch of talent and lifestyle nourished the idea that his music was divinely inspired; he, a vessel through which the voice of God was heard.

Mozart was only fourteen years older than Beethoven. Yet his youthful work has the glorious simplicity of classicism, only hinting at the dawning romanticism of his later years. Historians enjoy reflecting that, had Mozart lived to old age, he could have capped Beethoven's Ninth and parodied the adult Richard Wagner. He would have had no need of such mischief. Of no other composer could it be said, as by Mozart's most ardent enthusiasts, that 'music began and ended with him'.

Until just a few decades ago, Beethoven was widely held to be the world's greatest composer, a Rembrandt to Mozart's Vermeer. If such odious comparison is to be made, Mozart can now (like Vermeer?) be handed the laurel. Beethoven's turbulence, his endless Germanic struggle, perhaps better caught the mood of the middle of this century. Mozart's clarity, purity and perfection are preferred today. When English National Opera devoted its 1991 season to twentieth-century opera, an exception was made for Mozart. Like Shakespeare, Mozart is rightly cast as forever of today.

28 January 1991

Little Sir Ecu

Malcolm Bradbury

Being a novelist, I have always been interested in money. This is no confession of avarice, an unwise as well as unworthy emotion in a writer of fiction. The fact is that anyone who lives in the world for gain or greed would be well advised to take up any profession or trade over writing, notwithstanding the example of Jeffrey Archer. No, my interest is in an ancient and important analogy; for novels and money have a great deal in common. Both are paper fictions, and both aim to be thought of as a form of reality. Writers have always known this, and that is why novels, especially modern ones, are filled with images of the writer as coiner, forger, counterfeiter, confidence man, someone who gives a life over to using the tricks of the imagination to create the grand illusion of reality.

But I have a special reason for taking the analogy seriously. As the older members at the back will no doubt remember, there was a time, not so long ago, when an English pound note was known by my own name: it was called a Bradbury. This was because the paper pound was a promissory note; worthless in itself, it had inscribed on it a promise to pay the bearer, on demand, the sum of one pound, and the signatory of this reckless undertaking was none other than J. S. Bradbury. John Swanwick Bradbury was joint permanent secretary to the Treasury, and he issued these paper Bradburies from 1914 to 1928.

This was, of course, a turbulent period for the modern economies. Just at the beginning of Bradbury's reign, at the outbreak of the First World War, Britain came off the gold standard, and joined the Society of Authors by turning over to paper fictions. The Treasury never again had to redeem paper for gold – not even when, between 1925 to 1931, it returned to the gold standard. Meanwhile, in Germany, the market plummeted and money went mad. The return to gold is now generally seen as a root cause of the depression of the Thirties, which really ceased only in the dollar-based world of postwar economic miracles.

So I often think of Bradbury, in his fine office in the Treasury, desperately manipulating the world of dying metal reality. I wonder what he did when the bearers of his paper promises took him at his word and knocked at his door, asking for metal goodies. I fancy he was out to lunch quite often, or else referred callers to the other joint permanent secretary, who had not been rash enough to sign any such undertaking. I suppose what he did was to exchange paper for paper – paper pounds for paper savings certificates, or longer-term promises. Whatever he did, he clearly did it well, becoming, in due course, the first Baron Bradbury.

Alas, he was no direct relation of mine. But I shall always consider him an indirect relation. After all, he was the first real fiction-maker in the family, beating Ray (author of *Fahrenheit 451*, a book about how paper burns, and also, alas, no direct relation) to it by a matter of several years. But I particularly remember J.S. when I add my own authorial signature to some new work of fiction or other – hoping, of course, that by so doing I also will authenticate it, and give its imaginary world a guarantee of true worth. As I do all this, I also reflect on my good fortune. When the public buy my mock-realities (as I hope they always will), they do so from a shelf clearly marked 'fiction'. The contract is clear; I sell lies as lies, or imaginative truths, not as absolute realities.

This cannot be so in the world of money. Here the fiscal lie must always assume the appearance of reality and value, or everything collapses. Money is protected and interpreted not by critics but by economists. It is not obtained from shelves marked 'fiction', though it should be, but from institutions named 'trust', 'bank', 'guarantee corporation', 'credit', or 'vault'. Experts explain to us that money is, like language, a language. It takes signs and symbols and creates out of the nameless chaos of the world an order, a value, a reality. It tries to pin its sign to a fixed meaning, a world of certainty, a world where words apply firmly to things, to metal, to gold, to the higher realities.

As languages go, it is a good one, and certainly a great improvement on having to exchange a donkey every time we want to buy a washing machine. It works, like all languages, on a degree of trust, a belief that when we use it there is something there. Societies that have invented money have a great advantage over those that have not, as Karl Marx failed to note in *Das Kapital*. Hence the mysterious world of eastern Europe, where countries have seventeen different rates of exchange but seem to exchange very little, or not officially, functioning largely through bribes, barter and the black economy.

But money, once invented, does need to be guaranteed. So great buildings and complex institutions arise: the Bank of England, founded in 1694, the City of London, Wall Street, the Tokyo stock exchange. As money multiplies and grows ever more complex, becoming ever more like the motorway system its various forms are named after (M1, M2, M3 and so on), ever more exotic constructs are built – usually, alas, over the top of my favourite nineteenth-century railway stations. And the less real money itself becomes, the more exotic and extravagant become the buildings.

There was a time when banks were built in the manner of the great cathedrals. Flying buttresses, marbled halls, gilded crypts and hushed and clerkly worshippers created an atmosphere of veneration to surround the inner sanctum, the vault where the ancient mystery was buried and the great transubstantiation daily occurred, base paper turning into pure gold. Nowadays – except in eastern Europe, where the grandeur of the buildings and the number of the functionaries is in precisely inverse proportion to the stability of the currency – banks have begun to seek new forms of trust.

Sobriety is out, and lightheartedness is in. Now western

banks resemble playgroups, and reassurance is provided by smiling eighteen-year-old girls with signs on them saying: 'I'm Debbie.' Why a smiling Debbie with three passes at GCSE is so reassuring economically I am not absolutely sure, except that it reflects the trend towards preferring designer signs to real substance. Just as in the novel we have moved into the realm of post-modernism – fictions which insist on their character as fiction, and insist on putting reality into quotes – so banking has clearly moved into the realm of pastiche, or post-money, with a more equivocal relation to any reality.

Perhaps, in more sophisticated times, we can allow money to deconstruct itself a little. Certainly moneymakers themselves have begun to do so. They encourage us not just to credit them but to live on credit; in fact they credit us. Our coins are shrinking almost to nothing, on their way to disappearing altogether. As metal became paper, so paper is becoming plastic, a flexible friend, a nothing with which to buy a nothing – and designer nothings are, of course, what the modern shops are full of. But soon plastic too will pass, in the way of all things. Soon we will be in the weightless era of electronic banking – computer-based intercourse, international chatter between compatible VDUs, semi-conductor fiscal fornication between consenting terminals.

And yet, just as this year's Booker Prize winner proved that we still somehow yearn for the solidity, the sense, the substantiality of the Victorian novel, with its vast illusion of reality, we still, it seems, yearn for the era of real money, the felt stuff. From time to time this produces strange paradoxes. It took several years for the British, always lovers of monetary certainty, to accept the replacement of the ten shilling note, which was pure paper, with the 50p piece, which was decimal and therefore unreliable, but did at least have the advantage that in desperate times it could be melted down to recover some of its value. Yet it seems inevitable that in our era of post-money, when chancellors of the exchequer grasp at vague Euronyms – EMS and ERM – to solve the ungovernable problems of the economy, and when the money market has become an electronic pulse somewhere in space between Tokyo and Frankfurt, this yearning for fiscal reality grows ever stronger.

It is in such circumstances that we do what so many brave souls have done before us: we lie back and think of England. For surely there was a time when reality was a sovereign reality, and sterling was truly of sterling worth. It is, of course, no accident that our primal coin was called the sovereign (it no longer exists) or that our legal tender is known as the coin of the realm. The highest honour we can do to our monarchs and potentates is to imprint his or her visage on the coin in our pocket, the paper in our wallet. This confers value in both directions, making the money the monarch and the monarch the money.

No wonder, then, that that great latter-day Keynesian, Nicholas Ridley, has so often said, quoting the words of his master: 'He who controls the currency controls the government.' This is not exactly true. The Bank of England was, after all, a private institution until it was nationalized in 1946. The pound sterling has supported us so well because it was an international rather than a national currency. It is a long time since the wealth of nations and the exchange on which it is based was confined within the borders of the national state, as Adam Smith, founder of the famous Institute, noted. Yet one understands what the man means. Let go of your franchise, and you lose the licence to print money. And it is certainly true that a national currency does more than most things to confer a national history. The coin of the realm does, quite literally, help coin a realm.

It is understandable enough, then, that we contemplate with real dismay the disappearance of the British pound sterling, which is very likely to be replaced during the Nineties by a nerveless Euro-coin which has been minted in Brussels only since 1987, mostly for ceremonial purposes, and just now buys you almost nothing, except perhaps a Swatch in Luxembourg. It is a historyless coin, its name, in English at least, signifying nothing more than another vulgar Brussels acronym – European currency unit, ecu, a coin designed by a committee. In France it all looks much better. For the *écu* is an ancient pre-revolutionary French coin, aptly described by the *Oxford English Dictionary* as 'a silver coin equivalent to an English crown'.

And that, of course, is just what we are afraid of. The crown goes, and the ecu comes. In the new world where even acronyms translate into other acronyms (the French for EAGGF is, of course, FEOGA), our base and basic reality will be translated into Eurospend. Apart from abolishing the British tea time, or bringing in a European Commission directive banning the wearing of the Burberry, the European Community could have come up with no more terrible signal of what it means to become truly European – and lose, yes, our sovereignty.

In these bleak circumstances, it is perhaps just worth reminding ourselves that even our sterling realities are actually complicated fictions. We have been here before. Sterling is what we trust; the pound, we know, is of sterling worth. And sterling is a reassuring old English word, like shilling. We might, though, remember that it was first used to describe an old French coin, minted by some medieval ancestor of Jacques Delors, who was formerly the French finance minister until Brussels called.

As the sterling *OED* explains, sterling, 'if of English origin, is descriptive of some characteristic of the new Norman penny'. The characteristic was probably a star on the Norman coin, which became a coin of the British realm when we joined European Monetary Union once before, after defeat at the battle of Hastings. In other words, sterling is an occupation currency that somehow came home to stay.

And what about the pound in our pocket, the coin that Harold Wilson said had not been devalued when he devalued it? That is not the mythic beast it often seems. It long since ceased to be the sovereign. If Wilson devalued it in 1967, it was devalued far more fundamentally in 1971, when it was gutted, gelded, eviscerated, hysterectomized or – to use a word that our age has been determined to misuse and devalue – decimated. Up to 1971, when we entered Europe, for the second time (the first time had been via the European Free Trade Association), the pound stood proudly at the apex of a vast tricolumnar edifice, a vast economic arithmetic made of pounds, shillings and pence, each in due order and balance to the other.

The complexity of l.s.d. accountancy – based on the entirely sensible principle that it takes not 100 but 240 or 12×20 units to make an effective integer – was what tested the British intelligence and made the nation great. We did not need to learn foreign languages; just to learn our own money was a sufficient education. And l.s.d. had the inestimable advantage of making British coinage, and since coins coin the country, Britain itself, totally unintelligible to foreigners.

Now the trace of the silver shilling has left us entirely; the hidden florin goes soon. The great British penny, that fine medallion of a coin, which must have protected many a thigh in the crossfire of European wars, has become mere pee. And what of the great dependent coins, the fine tuning of British commerce? The halfpenny has died, the farthing has long since flown. What a world we have lost. Think what it must have been like to be British in a time when it was possible to call on J. S. Bradbury and demand that he change a paper pound into 960 bronze farthings.

But the world has seen such agonies before. We might remember what happened when another federation of United States was attempted 200 years ago. When the American colonies won, as they thought, the war of independence and became the first new nation, they had won separation but lost a currency. It took nearly ten more years to establish the decimal dollar as an agreed currency, and battles over control of currency and a union bank lasted for nearly a further century. Like Ridley, President Andrew Jackson won (and lost) office by battling against the federal bank, although he did induce the crash of 1837. Soon after, Charles Dickens visited America, and its money problems gave him the title of his book, *American Notes for General Circulation*, in which he invented the phrase 'the Almighty Dollar'. The point was that Americans all worshipped it but nobody really trusted it. The dollar, the common currency, was a totally fictional idea.

It is our greatest human achievement that we are all creators of fiction: individually and collectively, we name the world into being and create out of its disorderly existence plot, purpose, direction, narrative and value. Being a novelist, I have always admired the makers of monetary fictions, and their skill at doing what I do myself in my own more private sphere. Like good fictions, theirs does become reality. It is money that makes the world go round, or, from time to time, stops it from doing so. It is money that makes motive and meaning, and money that keeps yuppies (though a declining number of them) in their daily Moët et Chandon.

But money is also a mythic reality, like the myths of divinity, morality, or nationality. Few of us like to see the great myths dissolve. When they do, it represents a massive withdrawal of credit, a diminishing of the general substance. And perhaps more than any other nation the British have, for historical reasons and their role in the world money markets, worshipped the weight and seriousness of their own coin of the realm. They have embellished it with dream and fantasy, fable and slang, with sovereign images, figures of Britannia, the faces of the great and the good.

Novelists know that all great myths are finally real, worth something. Perhaps the hardest price we will have to pay for becoming what we will almost inevitably become in the end, true Europeans, will be that of believing in the worth of its coin of the super realm, and coming to love the loveless ecu. It will take a very long time for that sad committee coin to acquire the mythic patina of a true and believable currency, for it to come into credit. But the history of our fictionalizing imagination also tells us that, over time, it will happen. After all, it's only money.

2 February 1991

Hear, feel, smell, buy the music

Anne McElvoy

In the beginning was the music. Then came the costume ball, the chocolates, the socks, the liquor, the Amadeus watch and the rival perfumes 'Mozart' and 'Papagena' (motto: 'Smell the music'). As a special mark of respect in this, the bicentenary of his death, there is now Mozart mayonnaise, cheese, skis and a 'Wolferl' frisbee. If the maestro really did possess the hysterical cackle with which Milos Forman's film invested him, he will probably spend 1991 in a permanent posthumous seizure of raucous mirth.

Two hundred years after his death, Wolfgang Amadeus Mozart is being marketed con brio, if not always with much attention to the score of truth. The smart black-packaged CD collection launched to mark the anniversary bears the description 'Mozart: Live in Vienna'. At the Mozart exhibition in the city, a sign informs visitors that the music accompanying the exhibits is brought to them 'By Mozart and Philips'. The latter undoubtedly feels that it has been great-hearted in the order of merit. In Vienna the year has been launched with an air of frank self-congratulation and the rustle of expensive silks.

The Figaro Ball, which opened the calendar of celebrations, was elevated to the status of the country's premier social event by the cancellation of the Opera Ball as a possible terrorist target in the light of the Gulf war. The alternative breathlessly advertised itself as, 'The night the Puritan submits to the flesh and plunges into the realm of fantasy which knows no restrictions', and then, more realistically as 'a stage for the international jet set'.

The *jeunesse dorée* of Austria and beyond squeezed itself into corsets to quadrille in the candle-lit baroque town hall and obey the traditional injunction, *Alles Walzer*. Europe's top hairdressers combined symbolism with practicality by paying homage to their fictitious Sevillian colleagues and tending the more labour-intensive head constructions frozen hopefully in hairspray at the same time. The strains of a minuet in one room merged with the thud of Bob Marley in the next. In the disco, a perfectly attired Habsburg footman in powdered wig and frock coat was getting on down with a girl wearing a body stocking to the classical anthem of Euro-trash everywhere, '*Voulez-vous couchez avec moi?*'

The return of Mozart is being celebrated without him ever having been away. Like Shakespeare, he is prone to cycles of reception which say more about the societies which produce them than about their object. He spent the nineteenth century rising to a position as the apotheosis of the genius: man as vessel for the music of the heavens, a cipher for pure creativity and godly excellence, a sublime reflection of the cultural aspirations of the emerging middle class.

After the jarring appearance of Hitler and Stalin on the world stage, however, the genius cult seemed inappropriate, culture judgments became warier. In the sober light of the post-war period, Mozart remained on his pedestal, but the spotlight of adulation was dimmed. In popular culture, he was measured instead by the bland standard of negative utilitarianism: acknowledged as the world's best composer because everybody knew him but nobody disliked him.

The musical world, led by the acid critic Wolfgang Hildesheimer, joined the trend by producing research concentrating on psychoanalytical explanations of his work. It became fashionably perverse not to like Mozart, in order to distance one's self from the *Figaro*-humming hordes. The provocative pianist Glenn Gould declared Mozart to be 'the world's most over-rated composer', and his Symphony in G minor as 'eight remarkable passages surrounded by a half hour of banality'.

It is not the protestations of the faithful, nor the imaginative machinations of the rogue producers Kupfer or Sellars which has recently changed this, but the cinema portrayal in Forman's *Amadeus*. Youth rubbed its eyes and asked what it had been missing. For here was a prototype of the new twentieth-century genius cult: the rock star. Irresponsible, giddy, chick-chasing, foul-mouthed, he lived fast and died young. He belonged in the sainted company of those who end their days at the bottom of swimming pools in their Surrey homes. The 1991 image provides a fresh nonsense, rendering him a sort of gifted everyman – an agreeable chap at one with the world, something for everyone.

Mozart has never been so accessible as this year. There is Mozart for everyone, everywhere, with or without the music. Peter Weiser, co-ordinator of Vienna's celebrations, describes his job as 'principal hinderer and refuser', as he tries to set limits to the kitsch and commerce.

'We are avoiding everything that smacks of tastelessness and absurdity,' he says, without conveying much confidence in the success of the undertaking. It is also his job to ensure that the city's venues present a balanced selection of Mozart's work in the course of the year.

'Given half a chance, every church and concert hall would stage the Requiem on December 5. They all want to do *Figaro* as well, and get upset if we suggest that sixty-eight renditions of the same work in a year is a trifle repetitive.' He has granted the Requiem to the Stephansdom, where Mozart's funeral took place, to be performed on the anniversary of his death. In Paris it will be given in Nôtre Dame, scheduled to finish at five minutes to one in the morning – the exact time of the composer's death on December 5, 1791.

For Austria, the celebration is of particular moment, giving a big boost to the small country's image and tourist trade. In Vienna they are prickly about their reputed rejection of Mozart's operas and responsibility for the meagre state of his finances on his death. The buoyant mayor, Helmut Zilk, takes any suggestion that Mozart might have been frustrated by the domination of the court's tastes and fads as a personal insult, much as if his occupancy of the grandiose town hall made him a direct successor in power and responsibility to Emperor Joseph himself.

'The story of Mozart's rejection by the court, his death on the verge of bankruptcy and his burial in a pauper's grave is a result of myths spun after his death. Vienna's reputation was a victim of the process,' he says. The theme of Mozart's liking or otherwise for the dreamy, self-satisfied, lazily beautiful city dominates talk in the coffee houses and opera intervals.

The *Beamte* – civil servants who still enjoy privileges and status akin to those their forebears had at the imperial court – have been dispatched to find and disseminate favourable references in the composer's letters and jottings. Almost daily, Zilk repeats his best find to some journalist, incorporates it in a speech, writes it in an introduction to this or that event: the passage from a letter from Mozart to his father, 'Vienna is the best place in all the world for my metier.' It has already become the slogan of Mozart Year in Vienna. Like the hoardings outside west end musicals, qualifications and criticisms are passed over with the polite deception for which the Viennese are famed.

But did Vienna really like Mozart? Does it like him now? 'It is a complicated relationship,' Weiser admits. 'I have to say that in their heart of hearts they prefer Beethoven and Strauss . . . A Beethoven concert will always sell out here before a Mozart one.' His words were borne out by the reception Zubin Mehta's conducting of the 'Jupiter' Symphony at the celebratory opening concert: a performance of such accuracy and spirit that it would have raised the roof in New York or London. The audience applauded at length but without compulsion: a calculated tribute to virtuosity rather than an outpouring of appreciation.

Sometimes Vienna is downright nasty to Mozart. The house in which he lived has been turned into a cut-price department store. On the fifth floor, amid the bicycles, weights and skis stands the only reference to the erstwhile inhabitant: a hideous glazed bust and a vase of plastic flowers.

Harald Leupold Löwenthal, president of the Austrian Freud Society, observes the fuss with the psychoanalyst's unforgiving eye. 'Here you have typically Viennese behaviour,' he says, 'the retreat of an entire city into the past and its glories. Look at how attenuated our manners are, how finely we dress, our love of balls – there is even one for psychotherapists – out of step with the times, staring past reality.'

The ancient animosity between Vienna and Salzburg has been revived with fresh intensity as capital and province strive to establish themselves as the composer's preferred milieu. In Salzburg, they have come up with a skull bearing four hairs which they would have us believe once adorned the maestro's head. The Viennese are scornful and a little annoyed that the town regularly steals its thunder by holding the best Mozart festival, and by having produced Karajan. 'Ridiculous and childish,' says Weiser of the skull claim. 'He was buried in a mass grave on a site we know only approximately and which has been dug over several times since. Trust Salzburg to come up with this.'

The vitriolic Austrian dramatist Thomas Bernhard winningly described the place as the 'thoroughly misanthropic, architectonic, archbishoply, dull-witted, national socialist, Catholic soil of death'. Such metropolitan high-handedness serves only to encourage Salzburg's defiance. It carries on oblivious to the sneers of the intellectuals, a proud, profitable shrine unencumbered with any sense of the ridiculous. At theMcDonald's they serve Mozartburgers and the Mozart Liqueur Manufacture Ltd churns out 100 million chocolate *Mozartkugeln* yearly – 'the sweet heritage of Amadeus'.

Back in Vienna, fortunately, there is generous atonement for the cloying kitsch. Lectures and congresses on the Apollonian and Dionysian debate for the learned, and a wealth of opera, concerts and open-air performances for those who are happy to let Mozart do the talking. A splendid centrepiece exhibition on Mozart in Vienna provides historical background and the most impressive array of his original letters and scores ever displayed together.

Scholars such as Volkmar Braunbehrens still cast doubt on the whole business, saying that Mozart Year simply puts Mozart in the service of the Austrian tourist board. 'All sound, fury and profit. I would be very surprised if any research of worth arose from it.' The conductor Nikolaus Harnoncourt has remarked that it is 'squashing poor Mozart like a steamroller'.

They are probably right, but does it matter? Mozart Year is grandeur and folly, tribute and insult, melody and discord in equal quantities. We can always escape the clutches of the entrepreneurs and the experts by fleeing to the sanctuary of the music, safe in the knowledge that it remains the supreme celebration of itself and its creator.

2 February 1991

How to get on in a classless society

Craig Brown

With apologies to Sir John Betjeman

    Micro the dainties, Tina,
The colleagues are soon dropping in
    For a bit of a chinwag and confab
And the bunfight's about to begin

    Are the CDs all in the cabinet?
We'll save the Lloyd Webber till pud
    We've got Country-Style Cheesecake from Sainsbury's
(Their selection is ever so good)

    Do you fancy a coffee for starters?
That's the trimphone buzzing us now
    Hi Gavin! Give us a bell soonest
Okey-dokey? Ta-ra old mate! Ciao!

    Tell you what, these eats are so super
Once started, you can't stop, don't you find?
    My waistline's gone for a burton
I've lost weight? You're just being kind

    The bleep of my watch reminds me
We're just about ready for offs
    There's red, white or lager for allsorts
And bubbly on tap for the toffs

    'Ding-Dong' the doorbell is chiming
(Ravel's Bolero in D)
    Sharon, Oh, but you shouldn't!
Darren! Long time no see!

    To the boy's room with coats and what-have-you
And then straight thru to the house
    Do mind your heads as you enter
As the lady said, Duck or Grouse!

I see Craig's brought his cam-corder
Do help yourself to cham-poo!
With *Cats* on the music centre
We're having a bit of a do

Where did you get that blazer?
What fab gold buttons it has got!
Quite casual enough for the wine bar
And sufficiently posh for As-cot

Nice to meet you again, Terry
As the actress said, put it there!
I must hand it to Nigel and Linda
They make the most fabulous pair

Your lapel badge tells me you're Andy
A computer analyst from Tring
Please excuse us for asking
But what make of saloon did you bring?

Ford! Lovely vehicle! What reg?
All the trimmings? Stereo? Phone?
Garfield? Jacket hangers? Wheel-cosy?
Come and say a big hi to Tone

Andy – Tone, Tone – Andy
Tell me, Tone, from whence dost thou hail?
T'riff for the motorway, I'd imagine
Have you met the lady wife, Gail?

Get what you were after for Yule?
Aftershave? Moccasins? Jogging gear?
A China figurine, hand-crafted?
The Chronicle Book of the Year?

Jasper Carrot's video's amazing
He always has us in fits
The wife got the new Jackie Collins
And Elaine Page's All-Time Greatest Hits

Barry! What's your poison?
Take a pew, if you'll pardon my French
A pint of best and a snowball?
Bide a while, and I'll locate the wench

Do I spy Sue over yonder?
Cooo-eee, Over here! Yoo-hoo
No top-ups for me please, I'm driving
Okey-doke, don't mind if I do

Super quiche! M&S? Can't beat 'em!
As I say, you can't help but laugh
    Whoops! I'm repeating! Beg pardon!
I've just spotted my other half

    Doesn't Jill put herself round a bit!
A smooch with Bill, then Ron, too!
    The pizza's untasted, the coleslaw's all wasted
And nobody's touched the fon-due!

    The invite said half six to eight
And it's still wall to wall beyond nine
    There are birds of the unfeathered variety
And not a bad drop of wine

    The queue for the small room is lengthy
But the blokes love to wee outdoor
    The lager is flowing, the dances are slowing
And the red wine is smooth Piat D'Or

    Cheers! 'Bye now! Take care!
Don't do anything I wouldn't do!
    Ciao! Let's have lunch! God bless!
Be good! Adios! Toodle-oo

    Now let's curl up with a hot drink
(Ovaltine's an excellent buy)
    Then soak in a luxury foam bath
And unwind with a weepie on Sky

    Mmm, nice to be under the duvet
Switching off our Snoopy light
    To dream of Panatellas in Bournemouth
Time for zizz! Ta-ra! Nighty-night!

2 February 1991

207

When the truth takes
a direct hit

Simon Jenkins

There is a point in most wars when public opinion, frustrated at the lack of swift victory, turns on its messengers. The worse the news, the more vehement the condemnation, as if attacking the media could substitute for a sudden loss of will. Thus it was last week when bombs fell on a building in Amiriya, with the death of many civilians. What happened? Was the event misreported? If not, should it have been reported at all?

After the Amiriya bombing, *The Times*, in common with most other media organizations, went to lengths to find out which was true: the Iraqi claim that the building was an air raid shelter, or the American claim that it was a command bunker. This meant risking reporters' safety, risking deception by Iraqi censors, risking the credibility of allied spokesmen and risking readers' confidence.

The alternative preferred by many MPs in Britain and congressmen in America was not to try. The media should have decided that our side of the war should always be believed and the Iraqis regarded as liars, for which thesis there was plenty of circumstantial evidence. British newspapers did not have reporters in Berlin in the Second World War. Why have them in Baghdad?

Set aside the fact that no newspaper would send a reporter to certain incarceration or death (as in Berlin during that war), modern limited wars are now conducted on two levels: fighting and politics, with its concomitant publicity. In the Amiriya case, to have suppressed the Iraqi claim would have been fruitless. It would have been all over foreign broadcasts and newspapers, in the reports of visitors. If television companies felt bound at least to give Iraqi footage, with the appropriate caveats, the public would have demanded to know if the footage was true. Hundreds dead in a shelter went beyond the normal pabulum of propaganda.

Some news organizations, including some British newspapers, have taken the view that all journalists should be withdrawn, to avoid becoming tainted by the difficult task of validating counter-claims. They have decided that no journalist can possibly work normally in Baghdad. A journalist requires two freedoms to do his or her job: freedom to move and see, and freedom to write what is seen. If both are curtailed, reporters are worse than propagandists; by their professional status they validate propaganda.

In carrying reports by two reliable correspondents in Baghdad, Richard Beeston and Marie Colvin (of the *Sunday Times*), *The Times* took a different view. We should try to give our readers the nearest we could get to the truth. Every war is a casualty to censorship. Few journalists see military action. If they do, they see only a microcosm of it. They are dependent on raw material that must come from one or other side and are plainly vulnerable to bias. Reporters who plead for an 'uncensored' war are naïve. War reporting does not start pure and become tainted by censorship. It starts censored and is an act of de-censoring. That de-censoring must take place at every stage in the journalistic process, listening, writing and editing.

'Reporting restrictions' have long surrounded news from the communist bloc and from much of Africa and Asia. Restrictions operate on journalists in Israel. Yet the media rarely mention these. After an initial burst of protest, they settle down either to working within the controls or to working round them. American journalists who sought to boycott South Africa in the mid-1980s were conceding professional defeat. They proposed no similar boycott on military news from Israel, or on 'facility trips' from their own defence department.

In war as in peace, the task of a newspaper is simple: to

make the best possible stab at the truth in the time available. No responsible newspaper gratuitously aids and abets an enemy of the state. No responsible newspaper offers its readers what it knows to be partial information from either side without the appropriate caveats. In the Gulf, censorship has been tighter from the Iraqis than from the allies, but only relatively so. Disinformation has come (in the early days) from many military sources in Saudi Arabia, including news of defecting tanks and defeated Scuds.

The Times has sought, in carrying reports from journalists whose writing was overseen by a censor, to tell readers clearly of this fact. We carry such reports only where they convey information that we and the reporter regard as likely to be true. Readers can then judge whether they feel the context is blatantly partial and make the appropriate adjustment in reading.

The extreme view was well put during the Falklands war by an admiral: 'Tell them nothing; when it's over, tell them who won.' Were such draconian censorship feasible, the silence might just help the war effort, but I doubt it. I believe the public in a democracy are better able to support a war by feeling they have been properly informed of its course, victories, defeats, mistakes, warts and all. For rulers to shield their public from the horror of war is certainly unwise. It is also immoral.

18 February 1991

Can war still create war poets?

George Hill

In the suspense before the launch of the decisive ground offensive of the desert war, three young servicemen sent out an appeal to all the troops fighting in the Middle Eastern theatre. They asked them to submit work for a new anthology of war poetry. Within three months they had been sent 3000 entries, and their initiative led eventually to an archive of 14,000 poems, a unique and moving record of the experience of war.

The desert offensive the men were waiting for was Montgomery's, at Alamein. Victor Selwyn and his two fellow-compilers of those *Oasis* anthologies in 1942 tapped a torrent of verse, mainly from individuals who published no other poetry before or after. But if the stresses faced by today's forces in the Gulf produce a similar flood, there is no comparable channel ready to collect it.

The Imperial War Museum's archives contain thousands of poems in print and manuscript from the two World Wars, and the museum regularly mounts lectures about the literature of war. But the museum is making no special plans to solicit war poetry inspired by the Gulf conflict, though it has put out a low-key general appeal for memorabilia related to the conflict. It is not the custom to send an official poet to the front line. It would be incongruous, almost impertinent, to do so. Poetry is not like that. In this century, the record has been kept most resonantly by the combatants themselves, who bear the danger and the moral stress.

We can count on it that writers on the home front will soon be stitching into their work images from the battle watched day by day with such unprecedented immediacy. In this most bloodthirsty of centuries, war has inevitably forced itself into the work of most poets in Britain, from Kipling's scathing 'The Islanders' and Eliot's 'Little Gidding' to Sylvia Plath's 'Daddy'. The Gulf conflict has done the same.

Andrew Motion's 'A Dream of Peace', printed in the *Times Literary Supplement* two weeks before the fighting began in the Gulf, has a claim to be the first published poem that refers to this war in particular. It draws a parallel between the tanks that are about to go clanking into action in the desert and the tanks in which the poet's father fought against the Germans in Normandy, to create an image of war as a repetitive process.

'Even while television shows us so much of what is going on, it has a paradoxical distancing effect,' Mr Motion says. 'It makes it more difficult to appreciate the reality of the events, because we are conditioned by what we expect to see on the screen. It tends to make a soap opera of it, as I tried to suggest in the poem – which was written quickly when it began to look inevitable that there would be fighting.'

The poem is also about war as seen by someone who has never experienced it. 'I have never put on khaki myself,' Mr Motion says. 'That is not to say that I don't have to bear witness in my own way. But war poetry written by non-combatants doesn't close with its subject in the same way as poetry written by those who were there.'

But many of those who have studied war poetry, or written it themselves, doubt whether 'those who are there' will produce a significant body of work this time. In spite of the pervasiveness of war as a theme of this century's poetry, mention of 'war poetry' still suggests predominantly the work written in one war, and in one theatre – the trenches of 1914–18.

This perception is unaffected by the mass of material collected in the *Oasis* anthologies, and by the work (familiar and excellent as some of it is) of soldier poets of the Second World War. Korea, Vietnam, the Falklands and Ulster have apparently produced still less. Public attitudes in the United States towards Vietnam were influenced by protest ballads, but these were home-grown, not voices from the battle front. The poems and diaries of David Tinker, who died in the Falklands aboard HMS *Glamorgan*, were published after his death, but what he said about the war was mainly in prose.

'Our war was a very different war from 1914,' says the poet Vernon Scannell, who served in the infantry from 1940 to 1945. 'They went into it in an extraordinary spirit of euphoria – not only Rupert Brooke talking about men going off to fight "as swimmers into cleanness leaping", but also people like Siegfried Sassoon, who became disillusioned when they saw what it really meant. My generation had no illusions of that kind to start with. It was a browned-off war from the start. We had a dour acceptance of the necessity of it.'

That disillusion of 1914 became definitive. It could crudely be claimed that there was no 'war poetry' before then, and that poets since then have had nothing to do but find new ways of saying what Sassoon, Wilfred Owen and Isaac Rosenberg said from the trenches.

The poets of the First World War, almost without exception, were articulate middle-class men who would have been unlikely in normal times to think of a military career. They bore witness not only to 'the pity of war', in Owen's phrase, but to the shock of finding war to be an impersonal machine for slaughter, having little in common with the theatre of skill and gallantry depicted in the literature of generations equipped with more limited firepower.

Owen's revulsion and contempt are unsurpassed in his account of the effects of a gas attack in 'Dulce et decorum est':

> If you could hear, at every jolt, the blood
> Come gargling from the froth-corrupted lungs,
> Obscene as cancer . . .
> My friend, you would not tell with such high zest
> To children ardent for some desperate glory,
> The old Lie: Dulce et decorum est
> Pro patria mori

Realization of this dawned slowly and painfully, especially on the home front, where there was no television to bring home images of what the conflict was really like. In a supplement of war poems issued with *The Times* in August 1915, exuberant jingoism from Henry Newbolt and William Watson stood side by side with far darker work from Thomas Hardy, Rudyard Kipling, Laurence Binyon and the Irish poet A.E., fully recognizing the dogged desperation of the conflict.

The supplement carried a poem, written four months earlier, by Julian Grenfell and still imbued with a Brooke-like conviction that war was a wonderful game:

> . . . Joy-in Battle takes
> Him by the throat, and makes him blind

By the time the supplement appeared, he was dead.

Of all the poems in the supplement, the one that most strongly captured the public imagination was Binyon's 'For the Fallen', which sets aside any talk of victory or justification, and falls back on such comfort as elegy can offer:

> They shall not grow old as we that are left grow old
> Age shall not weary them, nor the years condemn

The then Poet Laureate, Robert Bridges, contributed to the supplement an irritable little ballad, 'Wake Up England', scolding the doubtful. Since Lord Tennyson, poets laureate have not been successful in striking the note of military glory, and most have been wise enough not to try. For more than a century, the duties of the job have not involved obligatory celebrations of major political events.

By the end of the war, Kipling struck a note as harsh as anything that came from the trenches:

> If any question why we died,
> Tell them, because our fathers lied

A poem by Keith Douglas, one of the best writers of the Second World War, declares: 'Rosenberg I only repeat what you were saying.' The phrase expresses what had changed since 1914: the sense of shock had gone. Douglas voices with

paradoxical sensitiveness the insensibility, the moral numb-
ness, of being a killer ('Being damned, I am amused . . . How
easy it is to make a ghost . . .'). Henry Reed, whose 'Naming
of Parts' may be the best-known soldier's poem of the Second
World War, spoke like them as a civilian in uniform, but with
quizzical resignation rather than damning incredulity:

> Today we have naming of parts. Yesterday
> We had daily cleaning. And tomorrow morning,
> We shall have what to do after firing

Firepower has grown far greater since 1914, and 1940. Today
the enemy is scarcely seen at all, except, for the most part, as
dots glimpsed by the cameras of a laser-guided missile – scant
basis for face-to-face encounters like that in Wilfred Owen's
'Strange Meeting'. As in earlier centuries, this war has been
carried out by professionals who have enlisted, and are
trained to expect horrors and control their imaginations.

'In both the World Wars, the poets were not professional
soldiers,' says Alan Ross, the editor of the *London Magazine*,
who saw action in the arctic convoys, and wrote 'Radar', a
poem about the strangeness of combat with an unseen enemy.
'The question whether any poetry will come out of the Gulf
really depends simply on whether there are any born poets
there. The idea that amateurs can knock off worthwhile verse
is nonsense.'

Much of the verse collected in the *Oasis* anthologies is
indeed of a kind that confirms Galsworthy's wry observation
that at moments of crisis people's natural mode of expression
is cliché. Denis Healey, a polished sonneteer before he put on
khaki in 1940, believes that literary quality is not the point
about the collection. 'Its value is as a record of what these
people felt and saw, going through an experience that impelled them to write, often for the only time in their lives.
Even some of the recognized poets never wrote anything
comparable afterwards.'

Paul Fussell, professor of English at King's College,
London, who was wounded as an infantry lieutenant in 1945

and has made an extensive study of the literature of twentieth-century war, has predicted that little of literary value is likely to come out of the Gulf. One reason, he says, is that the troops are regulars, unlikely to have the habit or the skills for expressing themselves in verse. 'A short war is unlikely to produce much poetry,' he says. 'It is when things go wrong that the conditions are right – when people are suffering trauma, disillusion, disappointment, as well as a sense that they are living through the most important days of their lives.'

If this is so, we must hope for wars as little afflicted by poetry as possible.

20 February 1991

Dead and bereted

Joe Joseph

Jean-Paul Sartre and Raymond Aron may make students swoon, but they have never been much of a threat to Johnny Hallyday in the eyes of *Paris Match* editors. Some people thought that the two great *philosophes* rarely made the front cover of France's society glossies because neither could sing very well (not smoochy ballads, anyway), and because neither kept yachts on the Côte d'Azur. But the recently much-reported death of 'the French intellectual' has proved once and for all that, when it came down to a good read on the beach, even the French did not really have the stomach for another essay on the nobility of suicide.

If the French were being really honest with themselves, gloomy old Sartre was not the first person they thought of when they wanted to give their Saturday night party a little extra zip. And while the name Levi-Strauss may add cachet to your address book, when it comes to sorting out the really important things in life most people prefer the number of a good tax lawyer every time. Bully for Barthes, but what is semiotics anyway? Some kind of artificial sweetener?

Only recently it was still possible to roam the corridors of France's posher universities and not be able to see the walls for the scrawl of radical graffiti: long-faced, left-wing under-graduates appeared to have been brought up to believe that cleanliness was next to fascism. But ever since the students of St Michel heard that the young designer Philippe Starck was making a fortune from selling three-legged chairs that he designed while brushing his teeth, campus walls have been decked with sketches of improbable avant-garde furniture. Starck, who has been commissioned by François Mitterrand to redesign some of the rooms in the Elysée palace, may well have had a greater impact on the thinking of the French president than most of the philosophers on his doorstep, although Simone de Beauvoir is said to have once advised Mitterrand on the choice of a *foulard*.

What has baffled most people who are not French – a substantial portion of the world – is how and why France came to have intellectuals in the first place. And if France had not had them, would there really have been any need to invent them? When President Gorbachev visited Paris last summer, he asked for a selection of the most verbose French intellectuals to be brought before him to discuss the issues of the day. Would the Soviet leader have made the same request had he just flown in to Holland, or would he have settled for some trade union leaders, or even some opposition MPs or tulip growers?

Peter Brooks – a well-read and articulate American academic, but perhaps not quite an 'intellectual' – put his finger on the problem when he wrote recently in the *Times Literary Supplement* that: 'Even if we are not quite sure what intellectuals are, we know that the French have them. The rest of us have writers, scholars, experts, pundits many of them more or less aspiring to the status of intellectual, but only in France is the status so recognized and patented.' He can even date the species quite precisely. He says France bagged its first intellectual on January 14, 1898, the day following the publication of Emile Zola's *J'accuse* and the call for the reopening of the Dreyfus case.

Now, Brooks says, even the much-respected Bernard-Henri Levy and Alain Finkielkraut say that the French intellectual of legend is dead. Since Levy and Finkielkraut rank as two of France's most glamorous intellectuals of the moment, their newly announced death sentence raises the philosophical teaser that if intellectuals are dead, then Levy and Finkielkraut may be dead, too: and if they are, why should we trust their views on the fate and whereabouts of the French intellectual? But we digress. How did it all come to this?

Perhaps nobody symbolizes the dizzy rise and fall of the French intellectual more than Jean-Pierre Levy, who shot to glory with his thesis, explored in his book, *Impedimenta* (published in London by Bodley Head in 1941 as *In My Feet*), that if Cleopatra's toes had been longer, the whole history of the world would have been different. Levy was one of those Parisian intellectuals who lived in that twilight between being and nothingness. For all his lasting achievements, he may well be thought by future generations never to have lived at all. Was it really true, they will ask, that Jean Genet would cry on his shoulder when his men friends were being testy? Did Eugene Ionesco, a long-time friend of Levy, really immortalize their friendship in his play, *The Lesson*, when he inserted the now-famous line, 'The French for Jean-Pierre is Jean-Pierre'? And why did the line disappear in the published version of the play?

'I knew that Paris had changed when Parisians became more proud of their new chairs than their old intellectuals, like me,' Levy says now.

Levy sprang from that grand tradition of French thinkers who could think of three new reasons to commit suicide or sign a petition before breakfast. They made their names by sneering even more than the average Parisian. Many of them also made their names by picking three, in any permutation, from a list that included Charles, Henri, Paul, Levi, Pierre, Sartre, Bernard, Jean, Claude and Buffy.

Every day, over coffee in Les Deux Magots and Brasserie Lipp, Pierre-Henri Charles and Levi-Claude Sartre would quibble about *ennui* and *engagement* with Charles-Paul Pierre and Jean-Pierre Levy. If nobody was getting engaged they would quibble about something else, like why nobody ever chose the name Buffy, or how it was that cats had two holes in their coats just where their eyes happened to be. Tourists would often ask them to autograph their hotel copies of the *Paris Tax-free Shopping Guide*. They would ask the tourists to commit suicide or, perhaps, sign a petition. Tourists would reply that they were under the firm impression that Emile

Durkheim had rather taken the punch out of suicide by suggesting, in his classic work, *Le Suicide*, that even taking one's own life was not the ultimate act of individual will but was an action essentially determined by the society in which one lived, or at the very least the size of one's overdraft.

'I remember one afternoon when one such cheeky tourist found a *fourmi*, how you say, an ant, in his café crème and was violently sick, giving Sartre the idea for *La Nausée*,' says Levy, who retains the intellectual's skill of speaking to you as if you were a tailor who had made his trousers too short. 'Hence the line in that novel: "Three o'clock is always too late or too early for anything you want to do." If Sartre had not been there at the café at three o'clock that afternoon, so bored out of his mind that he stooped to playing a childish prank on a tourist, he might never have had the germ for this novel. This is what gave left bank café society its spice and intellectual energy.'

Levy, now seventy-four, and still living in the apartment he took over many years ago from Marcel Duchamp, with a white urinal installed conveniently in every room, vividly remembers the day he stopped calling himself Claude Dubois, published his gloomy doctoral dissertation (which was only partly about suicide), and began drinking pastis.

'Why has the intellectual died?' he asks with the familiar manner of someone who was been asking perplexing, often unanswerable, questions all his life. 'It is, essentially, a question of changing tastes. Pascal said, *"Le coeur a ses raisons que la raison ne connait point"*, which means, loosely translated, "Some people like fruit cake, others do not". It was his way of saying that tastes differ, that philosophical fashions change, that you cannot dip your finger into the same cake-mix twice. Consider, if you will, that when he had this little pensée the first French intellectual was still officially 250 years into the future, and Zola and Dreyfus had not even been born. It shows you what a genius he was. Only France can produce such men. Or, at least, it used to.

'I, myself, made my name in the au contraire school of

thought. The philosophical premise was merely to oppose the latest theory by a rival intellectual. This kept issues alive and prompted publishers to commission books on the growing debate that had been manufactured. Thus, for example, when Louis Althusser developed a theory of Marxism, which sought to free what he called the scientific Marx from some Stalinist distortions, and also from some Feuerbachian and Hegelian traits reassigned to Marx by neo-Marxist theory, I published my infamous rebuttal, *Phooey Louis*, which argued that the Feuerbachian and Hegelian traits must stay.

'But then Althusser decided that Marxism was philosophy as the "practice of the production of concepts" or the "theory of theoretical practice". I toyed with the idea of arguing that, in fact, Marxism was "production as the concept of practice" or "the practice of theoretical theory". It was a form of analysis I picked up from Tristan Tzara, who would often take another philosopher's latest work, cut it up with a pair of scissors and paste it together again to see if it made any more, or any less, sense, or, indeed, if anyone noticed: with Althusser it was often difficult to distinguish between the original and the Tzara-ized version. This also, unfortunately, meant that people understood my counterattack even less than they understood Althusser.

'One thing in his favour, Althusser had cracked the art of being humourless. There are no jokes, well, no very good ones, in his book *Reading Capital*. If a soi-disant French intellectual makes you even smirk a little, chances are you've got a fake on your hands. Of course, Althusser was not only humourless. He was also very unpredictable. Ten years ago he was committed to a mental asylum after he strangled his poor wife. I realized then that he was too dangerous to tangle with, even with a pair of scissors and a tube of Uhu. Now, of course, he is dead, along with Marx and Marxism, which has put an end to his crazy rantings once and for all.'

How did one enter the charmed circle, those who could always secure a table at the right restaurants, those who could settle their bills by scribbling a newly minted aphorism on their gingham napkin? Enter a Parisian café which has framed napkins on the wall and you can be sure you have entered either an old intellectuals' hangout or a new bistro designed by Philippe Starck.

Levy says entry into the fold was mostly by a process of heart-searching self-interrogation. It was a questionnaire, published many years ago in a philosophers special collectors' edition of French *Cosmopolitan*, that has become the litmus test of intellectual aspirants. He himself passed the test on his second attempt, barring him from adopting a full sneer for his first five years of intellectual life. For those who wonder whether they might have made the grade, here are a few of the questions that everyone from Apollinaire to Sartre had to answer before being allowed to buy their first black roll-neck sweater.

1. *I think it is always important to speak . . .*
   - (a) well of someone
   - (b) for a fee
   - (c) extempore
   - (d) French

2. *I tend to beg . . .*
   - (a) forgiveness
   - (b) indulgence
   - (c) for my supper
   - (d) to differ

3. *I like my friends to be . . .*
   - (a) convivial
   - (b) humorous
   - (c) generous
   - (d) existentialists

4. *I prefer to start with . . .*
   - (a) caviare
   - (b) an advance against royalties
   - (c) a premise

5. *I'm never short of . . .*
   - (a) money
   - (b) time

(c) energy

(d) an opposing theory

6. *I like to remember . . .*
   (a) people's birthdays
   (b) to wear a tie
   (c) appointments
   (d) things past

7. *If I had to describe myself in just one word, that word would be . . .*
   (a) friendly
   (b) sporty
   (c) frolicsome
   (d) superior

8. *Complete this word or phrase. Dial . . .*
   (a) M for Murder
   (b) ogue
   (c) ysis
   (d) ectics

9. *I like overhearing . . .*
   (a) a good argument
   (b) social gossip
   (c) people's salaries
   (d) my name

10. *I'm never happier than when offering . . .*
    (a) a lift
    (b) a drink
    (c) an opinion

'Of course,' Levy says, 'I am very sad that they have killed and buried the French intellectual. We were never rich – I remember once, soon after everyone thought that Levi-Strauss had licensed his name to a jeans company, that André Gide was so jealous he approached a famous laxative with the idea of marketing a new potion with the slogan, "*Vous serrez vide avec une dose de Gide*": they spurned him and Gide instead sat down to write *Straight is the Gate* – but we were happy. And useful in our way. There are still questions to be asked and maybe even answered. Every day I think of more.

'This morning, for example, I sat up in bed and it suddenly occurred to me that if we are certain that something is impossible, can we really be certain, without at the same time assuring ourselves that we are not uncertain, that it is possible? In other words, is the possibility of certainty a valid parameter for any individual's action when we cannot, with any logical or methodological justification, be sure that the sun will rise tomorrow morning without first satisfactorily proving that its disappearance tonight is not simply the result of everyone drawing their curtains at the same time? What do you think?'

2 March 1991

What is terror?

Conor Gearty

There are few more complex problems confronting the West than what we have become used to calling 'terrorism'. Its impact on our lives is enormous and is likely to increase. The end of the Gulf war has already given rise to anxieties about a resurgence of 'international terrorism' and the sporadic violence of groups like the Irish Republican Army, the Basque separatists Eta, the Red Army Faction and the Sikh extremists seems sometimes to suggest that a 'terrorist problem' has become one of the emblems of democratic freedom.

Despite this pervasiveness, the meaning of 'terrorism' is less clear than the atmosphere of irrational evil that surrounds it. The moment we try to define what we mean, embarrassing ethical conundrums stray in from the edges to contaminate the purity of our moral certainty. Were George Washington and Oliver Cromwell terrorists? And where do casually uttered clichés, such as eco-terrorism, consumer terrorism, and narco-terrorism, fit in?

Scrupulous sub-editors avoid these questions by omitting the term altogether, just as many writers and journalists jettison it as hopelessly compromised. Academics produce very broad definitions while suggesting that to call something 'terrorism' is not necessarily to condemn it. But this misses an important point. It is value-laden; once a group is successfully so described, its further involvement in politics becomes impossible. Individuals on whom the dreadful badge is pinned are pushed beyond the pale of civilized life. We need only to remember the Guildford four and the Maguire seven to realize the tragic consequences that flow from such mis-labelling.

These were ugly mistakes. But governments justify many of their most unseemly acts – the bombing of Tripoli, the prevention of terrorism legislation, the Gibraltar shootings, the invasion of Lebanon – by invoking the umbrella of 'counter-terrorism'. Since they are by definition upholders of the status quo, they can be relied upon constantly both to use and to widen the meaning of such a convenient insult. It is, therefore, irresponsible to buy linguistic purity by abdicating to governments a monopoly of power over definition.

The first step in our quest for a definition lies in putting the terror back into terrorism. When the police described the IRA mortar attack in Whitehall as 'cowardly and indiscriminate', it was not only the IRA that winced, but many who care about words. We may not like the fact, but it was neither. The bombing at Victoria station, however, shared both these characteristics, and the differences between the two tell us a great deal about what the word should describe. Whitehall was a targeted attack on what, in another context, we might call a 'command and control' centre. Ordinary people may have been appalled and angered – but they were not terrified. It was subversive violence, certainly, but not *terror* violence.

The distinction is an important one. The legitimacy of the former depends on the context in which it occurs. The history of the country, the nature of the regime that is being attacked and the political and economic institutions of the state being subverted are all important factors in the analysis. In this respect the Palestine Liberation Organization and the African National Congress may well differ markedly from the IRA. Victoria, on the other hand, involved the deliberate infliction of severe violence. When committed against civilians, these are the trademark of the true terrorists. Such deaths and injuries are not rare in contemporary society. The genuine political terrorist differs from the criminal because of his or her motive. The purpose is not personal gain, but political advantage. This dimension is an essential part of terrorism, and is what separates its exponents from the hoodlum and the drug baron, both of whose terror is but a brutal side effect of what is little more than a selfish and extreme form of criminality. The political message, with its subtext of subversion, is one of the reasons why free societies view the violence of such terrorists with particular dread: the crook merely wants to benefit from society, whereas the rebel wants to destroy it.

The means these core terrorists are prepared to employ to achieve their ends mark them out as special. The violence is inflicted in a place of leisure, travel or tranquillity – a bar, an Olympic village, an airport. It occurs in peaceful, liberal, democratic societies, far away from any front line. The claims of such societies to have matured beyond the violent settlement of political disputes are mocked by such bloody interventions. What is more, the victims are not responsible for the hurt that compels these terrorists to act. Their 'crime' is to belong to, or even merely to live in, a country which the subversives despise. In the case of the attacks by the Popular Front for the Liberation of Palestine (PFLP) on airports and the IRA's campaign of pub bombings, it was enough that the victims should have been in the wrong place at the wrong time; it did not matter who they were. A pure terrorist act results in everyone recoiling in horror, with the words, 'It could have been me,' etched on their mind. It is, therefore, the indiscriminate nature of its victims which gives the act of terror its powerful impact. It disfigures a settled community with abnormalities and uncertainties, in the wake of which follow disruption, fear and anxiety. We are all victims of a successful terrorist attack.

The opportunity for reaching the wider audience that terror violence achieves is, of course, one of the main reasons it occurs in the first place. Society wonders who will be next and, thus weakened, is more susceptible to the political message of the moment: why are the British troops in Ireland? Why are those Palestinians in Israeli jails? Without this type of terrorism, these questions would not be posed; with each new act of violence, they have to be answered afresh. In this way, such terrorism springboards issues into public debate. It uses fear to jump the queue of ideas waiting for public attention.

The publicity achieved by terror is fleeting, however, and the attention it draws soon wanders. A whole campaign of terror, therefore, is required to reduce the risk of media neglect. But systematic violence is not enough. Terror cannot afford to be repetitive, for the public is not much moved by an atrocity which, in an earlier incarnation, has already distressed them. Thus, as with a television soap desperate to keep its ratings, the producers of terror dramas have to escalate their actions with each episode. In this respect, as in others, they are not as strong as they appear.

Despite its noisy and newsy impact, terror is the weapon of the weak. The practitioners of this form of violence lash out because they have no other more efficient means of fighting. As they do not enjoy statehood, they have no access to the authorized and mechanized killing efficiency of armies. They do not even pass the test of the guerrilla leader, who must develop a rapport with the local people in whose communities his forces wish to operate. Many pure terrorists, like the Tupamaros in Uruguay and the Montoneros in Argentina, merely provoked their governments to excesses of counter-violence.

But if terrorism is most effective as a way of communicating a political grievance, this in turn begs an important question: what is all the publicity for? Here we come to the central paradox of terror. The methods terrorists use to get attention mean the public learns of their aims, but invariably rejects what they stand for. Yet, if they had not used terror, their plight might never have been noticed. Having used it, their condition no longer goes unremarked upon, but they are still ignored, this time because their methods make them political untouchables. The IRA is further away than ever from a united Ireland, and the international terror between 1968 and

1974 brought an independent Palestine no nearer. It is extra-ordinarily difficult for a group to break out of this trap of its own making. For, if it attempts to eschew terror, it will undoubtedly split its own ranks and see a militant wing spin off to continue the fight. This has been the experience of Fatah, the IRA and Eta. Disavowal of violence is not enough to protect subversive groups from political opponents who, for their own reasons, will long continue to accuse them of using it; the reformed terrorist must face a long penance of mislabelling. If, on the other hand, the group perseveres with terror, the violence gradually takes on a less political air, becoming little more than a type of existential self-assertion, a childlike demand for attention. Where once the plea behind the violence was 'listen to me', with long running terror groups, the message eventually becomes the shrill cry, 'I'm still here'.

Our reward for being strict about definitions is that we can see that subversive terror poses much less of a threat than we might otherwise have thought. Not only is it morally wrong, but it is also, as far as its grander ambitions are concerned, invariably a failure. Described in this way, it is immediately apparent that subversive terror is different in kind from the guerrilla-style violence that accompanied the liberation of the formerly colonized world. It does not necessarily embrace the activities of popularly supported groups like the PLO and the ANC, in so far as their actions form part of a carefully controlled struggle against illegal occupation or racist oppression. The morality of violent subversion which does not involve the use of terror depends on a careful analysis of the political, legal and historical context within which it occurs. 'Terror' and 'terrorism' are simply beside the point in such cases, and function merely as terms of abuse. Precision along these lines should assist in the quest for an international consensus on terrorism, a search that will fail as long as the word is seen as a subset of American foreign policy – as it has become in the Reagan and Bush presidencies.

229

There is one awkward consequence in this linguistic integrity. It takes us back to Whitehall and Victoria, and to the meaning of terrorism in UK law and politics. The Prevention of Terrorism Act defines the word as 'the use of violence for political ends', including 'any use of violence for the purpose of putting the public or any section of the public in fear'. The Victoria attack fits squarely within this, as well as within the more precise definitions we have been discussing. No one celebrated the assault, just as no one (not even the IRA) rejoiced over Enniskillen or the Harrods bomb. These were pure terror atrocities. If this was all the IRA did, it would long since have disappeared, rejected by its supporters and the communities from which it draws its following.

But it is not all that it does. The Whitehall mortar attack may be 'terrorism' as defined by the law, but it falls well short of being pure terror in the mould of Victoria. Legislation alone cannot obscure the fact that many British citizens living in west Belfast and elsewhere in Northern Ireland saw the assault on the war cabinet as part of the IRA's quasi-military campaign against the British state. Targeted actions of this sort enjoy a degree of community support in areas of deprivation and alienation in Northern Ireland; they have only the Provos to boast about and (as they see it) stand up for them. Many of their councillors are Sinn Fein, and they regularly elect as their MP a man who shares the goals and the methodology of the IRA.

It may be emotionally satisfying and morally invigorating to call the whole place and its people 'terrorist', and leave it at that. Such loose language hides the fact that the problem is more serious than that which would be posed by mere terror. There is no guerrilla-style insurgency, of course, but there is at least some violence which is not terror based.

In the early years, the IRA fed on the explicitly military atmosphere engendered by a massive army presence, by internment and by interrogation practices which were later condemned by the European Court of Human Rights. The switch in emphasis to a policy of criminalization in the mid-

Seventies appeared at first sight to represent a move away from the obsession with the 'terrorist' threat. The new icon was the supremacy of the 'rule of law'. Suspects were no longer interned, but were arrested by the police, interrogated and, if the evidence was sufficient, charged and tried in court with serious but, in an important sense, ordinary offences.

The message behind this policy, that the IRA was no more than a bunch of crooks, was aimed not only at international audiences but also, and most importantly, at the nationalist communities themselves. To be successful, it was essential that the rule of law and the legal system being utilized in this way were seen to be impartial. This was always going to be difficult, given the suspicions that had built up over the years of Unionist hegemony. If it had been achieved, who knows how the IRA might now be regarded. In fact it has proved to be impossible. The authorities may now channel their opponents through the criminal courts, but they still label all of them terrorists, and use the potency of this stigma to twist the rules of the game. The designation criminal may have become a useful public relations insult, but it has been purchased at the price of the integrity of the system, and the cumulative effect of the changes that have been introduced has been to confirm and to deepen the target communities in their sense of disillusionment with British rule.

First, there have been the substantive changes in the law. The emergency provisions and terrorism legislation give the police and army such wide powers that it is a very attenuated 'rule of law' under which they are being required to operate. The law permits wide powers of stop and search, of entry and seizure and of arrest, all based on the open-ended definition of terrorism to be found in the Prevention of Terrorism Act, and all too often exercised against persons who have little or no paramilitary involvement.

Secondly, apart from the substance of the law, there have been dramatic changes in procedure. Under the Prevention of Terrorism Act, suspects may be arrested and held without charge for up to seven days. They may be denied access to legal advice throughout the first forty-eight hours. When this seven-day detention period was struck down by the European Court as an infringement of human rights, the government chose not to obey the ruling, claiming that a 'public emergency threatening the life of the nation' justified its stance. The suspect's right to silence has also been emasculated, and a failure to answer questions may now be used as evidence against an accused in a Northern Ireland court. Many trials in the province are before a judge, without a jury, and many witnesses give their evidence in secret. These changes are not restricted to terrorist trials, they have quickly settled down to become part of the legal landscape. Those convicted under this system look with cynicism at the record of investigation into killings by the police and army. Despite numerous controversial deaths, the same rule of law has delivered only one conviction for murder against a member of the security forces while on duty – and the private involved was free within three-and-a-half years. The rules governing coroners' inquests have been interpreted by the House of Lords, overruling Belfast's Court of Appeal, so that the soldiers and police officers doing the killing do not even have to turn up at the subsequent inquests to explain their actions.

Thirdly, there are the administrative powers which have been invoked in the name of 'terrorism', not against the IRA as such, but against the lawful political parties and the nationalist communities on the periphery of militant republicanism. Foremost amongst these are the exclusion order procedures, a system of banishment similar to the internal exile practised by the Soviet Union in its darkest days, and the media ban, under which expression of political opinion is prohibited from radio and television on account of the unacceptability to the authorities of the message that would be conveyed.

Just as it is dangerously misleading to label the IRA as nothing more than a terror gang, so is it also self-defeating to describe it as a gang of criminals, where this stigma is purchased at a price of even further disaffection in the communities from which it comes. The rule of law has a vital role in fostering a culture of reconciliation in the province by being demonstrably fair, even handed and responsive to the community in which it is applied. On the other hand, a policy of criminalization which separates 'law and order' and 'the fight against terrorism' from politics, and changes the law to suit its ends, hinders the ending of sectarian divisions by appearing to confirm the partisanship of British law. In such circumstances, measures aimed at tackling subversion in fact compound it.

9 March 1991

The Liberal record in a pact House

Vernon Bogdanor

Liberals have traditionally seen Labour as the competition, but the Conservatives as the enemy. In his campaign for party leadership in 1988, Paddy Ashdown spoke of his party replacing Labour as the standard-bearer of the Left, the position from which the Liberals were displaced by Labour in the 1920s.

The reality, however, given Labour's recovery, is that the best the Liberal Democrats can hope for is a hung parliament. Their bargaining position would be maximized if they could deal with either main party. Cinderella must be prepared to go to the ball with either of the Ugly Sisters. This is why Mr Ashdown's speech to the Liberal conference yesterday, in which he indicated that he might do a deal with a post-Thatcher Conservative government, is so significant. Were the Conservatives to remain the largest political party after the general election, but without an overall majority, Labour (unless it conceded the key issue of proportional representation) could still be kept out of office.

Since 1922, when they ceased to be a leading party, Liberals have dreamed of holding the balance of power in the Commons. Yet in 1923–4 and 1929 the Conservatives preferred to let Labour minority governments take office rather than negotiate with the slippery Lloyd George. Nor was Labour more sympathetic. For the Labour stalwart, the Liberals simply muddied the great divide between socialist and capitalist. In 1924, Ramsay MacDonald, Labour's first prime minister, told C. P. Scott of his 'dislike and distrust of the Liberals. He could get on with the Tories . . . They were gentlemen, but the Liberals were cads.' MacDonald preferred short-lived Labour minority governments to a progressive alliance which might have given the Left five years of power. The consequence was almost uninterrupted Conservative government between the wars.

Yet Liberal difficulties have also been the result of divisions among Liberals themselves. In 1931, faced with the prospect of coalition, they split three ways. The main body of the party supported the national government only so long as free trade was preserved, resigning from it in September 1932, and moving into opposition in November 1933. Another group, the Liberal Nationals, led by Sir John Simon, remained in the government, merging with the Conservatives in 1966. A third, smaller group, led by Lloyd George, sought co-operation with Labour. 'If I am to die,' Lloyd George said, 'I would rather die fighting on the Left.'

More than forty years later, Edward Heath asked the Liberals to join a coalition after the March 1974 election had failed to produce a decisive verdict. The Liberals proved unable to respond constructively, and, as in the 1920s, a Labour minority government was able to take office. It won a narrow majority in October 1974.

By 1977, however, by-election reverses had deprived Labour of its majority, and the Liberals agreed to cooperate to sustain the government. The Lib-Lab pact, which lasted until the summer of 1978, fell short of formal coalition, and the Liberals remained on the opposition benches. Yet they gained participation in the legislative process through an inter-party consultative committee.

David Steel, the Liberal leader, hoped that the pact would give the Liberals credibility, and perhaps prove the forerunner of a new style of multi-party politics. Yet the Liberals were blamed for propping up an unpopular Labour government, without being able to implement many Liberal policies. It is for this reason, no doubt, that Mr Ashdown seeks, not another pact, but full participation in government if the next election yields another hung parliament.

Experience shows, however, that constitutional conventions favour the leading parties. A minority government, as Harold Wilson proved in 1974, can choose the right moment for a tactical dissolution to secure an overall majority. If he is to break with the pattern of the past, Paddy Ashdown will have to ensure that his party remains more united and self-disciplined than its Liberal predecessors in 1931 or the 1970s.

18 March 1991

The child is always father to the manual

Libby Purves

The call was from Denmark, in faultless English. Would I comment, please, on systems of toilet-training for a magazine? Or could the relevant paragraphs of my book, in Danish translation, be reprinted? I thankfully took the second option and hung up with a shaking hand. What next? Italian *Vogue* demanding a quote on the tooth fairy? The *Frankfurter Allgemeine Zeitung* straw-polling about smacking?

At least I was safe from transatlantic enquiries: the Americans will not publish my books about children because they are not 'positive' enough. The titles *How Not to be a Perfect Mother* and *How Not to Raise a Perfect Child* do not chime well with the culture which invented 'having it all'. The first twenty minutes of motherhood having convinced me that there is no chance whatsoever of having it all, my tone is probably closer to 'having-mislaid-it-somewhere-owing-to-lack-of-sleep-but-never-mind'. This goes down fine in Europe, but will not do for the States.

Anyway, I never meant to become a childcare guru, and the role fills me with some dismay. Especially since the whole process began with a heartfelt conviction that there are far too many childcare gurus already. Eight years ago, as a shell-shocked new mother with a wakeful baby and flat nipples, I was overshadowed by Benjamin Spock, confused by Drs Jolly and Stanway, irritated by Miriam Stoppard and made to feel alternately idealistic and hopeless by the lucid perfectionism of Penelope Leach. It is, perhaps, lucky that the experience of motherhood came early enough for me to avoid being patronized by Paula Yates.

There is good in all the books: it was just that in my uncertainty I took them too seriously. One particular night sticks in my mind, when I searched my entire library in the hope of finding the printed sentence: 'Some babies, sometimes, need to cry themselves to sleep. It does no lasting harm.' Failing to find it, I picked up my son, and paced, and fed, and paced, and wept.

So why choose to swell the torrent of advice on childrearing which has flowed from Jean-Jacques Rousseau to Mrs Bob Geldof? What inspired me was reading earlier generations' gurus, a pursuit inspired by Christina Hardyment's history of childcare manuals, *Dream Babies* (Cape, 1983). As I surveyed the diversity and barminess of advice down the decades, I realized that anybody could join in.

After all, once you know that Rousseau favoured dipping babies in icy water to harden them up, that Mrs Sydney Frankenburg believed you should never point out things to a toddler because it diverts blood to the brain which should be going to building healthy teeth, and that John B. Watson argued, in the Twenties, that you must never hug or kiss a child (shaking hands in the morning is enough), you are healthily inoculated against gullibility. Alone with your baby and your pile of books, you give up searching for Holy Writ and accept that every childcare book is the product of a particular personality and culture. If the Thirties and Forties saw women advised to leave babies in prams down the garden all day, might it not be partly because that was when houses shrank and housemaids became extinct? If Dr Truby King was obsessive about feeding by the clock, should we not remember how, as superintendent of the Seacliff lunatic asylum in New Zealand, he experimented on the asylum farm with the 'scientific rearing' of bucket-fed calves?

So, clearly, pinches of salt should equally be applied to the writings of the current authors. Look hard and you can see who has read too much psychology, who is enthused by feminism or reacting against it, who is a Sixties child in search of 'natural' behaviour, and who is a tight, over-controlled

238

Seventies person obsessed with career and style. It is a fair bet that future generations will get as many laughs out of 'quality time' or early infant education as we do out of Watson and Frankenburg.

So I joined the bossy chorus. Not being a doctor made me feel an impostor at first; but then the trouble with books by doctors is that, because one defers to their knowledge of spots, one is too slow to question their parental qualifications. Yet what does a medical degree teach you about bedtime, television watching, or discipline? There are as many un-balanced doctors as there are laymen. And psychologists. Just ask their children.

I resolved to speak from the front line. Rather than wait ten years and write in a quiet tidy room, I would do it quickly, before my younger child reached three, thus ensuring that the main influences on me would not be theoretical but small and grubby. Not a page of the first book – up to age three – was completed without a child under the desk filling my shoes with Sticklebricks, or a baby snuffling ominously in a basket alongside. Every observation was cross-checked with ques-tionnaires filled in (often, they caustically observed, in the small hours) by other mothers of mixed ages and class; every piece of advice qualified by an account of someone else's system which also seems to work. It was an assault on theory.

I had not yet heard Bruno Bettelheim's phrase about 'good-enough' mothering, but that was roughly it: ways to get by without much style but without guilt either, to love without illusions and to arrange family life so that poor mummy got out for the odd game of darts. Then I swore never to write on the subject again.

Five years on I had to, because the goalposts moved. Still knee-deep in the subject, I discovered that the years from three to eight were a totally different subject. The traditional '0 to 5' baby book had always seemed nonsense: a child changes so radically at about three that an eight-year-old has more in common with a four-year-old than the four-year-old does with a baby. Without nappies or broken nights the challenges became intellectual: explaining death and war, helping children to handle friendship, money, strangers, school, pets . . . other mothers, writing in, provided checks and balances (the hazard of being a childcare guru is galloping opinionatedness). I wrote the chapter about illness and accidents sitting beside a small hospital bed, and the one about toys knee-deep in broken ones.

So there was plenty of input. Re-reading the book after six months, I notice that it appeared to draw advice also from Saki, George Orwell, *The Pilgrim's Progress*, Terry Waite and Vesta Tilley. At least such openness about my cultural influences will assist the next generation in its duty of throwing me aside.

Because it will. I have learnt humility. I now know the problems of the childcare writer: inability to decide whether to say 'he' or 'she', terror of accidental ambiguities which might betray a hasty reader into doing something dangerous, and fits of Stygian gloom when the chapter on discipline cannot be put off any longer. I know what it is to hammer out 1000 words on the importance of listening to your child, while ignoring a monologue about Ninja turtles from the floor alongside.

In the end, all I can do is offer my contribution to the genre as a grudging sort of tribute to all the rest. What we are all doing, in our different ways, is acknowledging the extraordinary and perennial power that children have to remodel their parents: and hoping that, as they grow older, the path towards enlightenment will wind just a little bit further upwards.

20 March 1991

A Childhood: Lord Soper

Judy Goodkin

Donald Soper was eighteen when his childhood peace was shattered with such force that the memory of it haunts him to this day. 'It was the summer of 1921 and the drought had baked the playing fields dry. I was a fast bowler as a boy. My father was and he insisted that I should be too. So he used to take me out on Streatham Common to practise bowling and I was very fast.

'I opened the bowling for my school team but the third ball kicked and I hit the batsman above the heart; he died on the pitch in front of me. It was a dreadful shock. It wasn't my fault, he'd got a bad heart to begin with, but I was so young and it is so traumatic to be responsible for killing someone.'

Pacifist and socialist, Soper received a peerage in 1965 for his work among down-and-outs, prostitutes and homeless at the West London Mission during his forty-year ministry. In his maiden speech in the Lords, he referred to the House as a 'testimony to the reality of life after death'. He was chairman of Shelter for four years and received the Methodist Peace Award in 1981. Now in his eighty-ninth year, he can still be seen every week encouraging a 'fellowship of controversy' at Speakers' Corner and Tower Hill.

Soper was born with a wealth of gifts: he was handsome, musical, had a blotting paper memory and was captain of sports at Haberdashers' Aske's School, in southeast London. 'I had a beautiful soprano voice – no credit to me – and won a number of competitions. As a family we weren't ugly, although my sister Millicent was rather plump. I was reasonably adept at games and I was the sort of boy who would be captain of the team. I don't want to sound arrogant, but I was the type that stood out in a crowd. Normally, older boys would not have anything to do with a much younger boy like me, but because I played the game as well as them, I was an equal. It gave me an experience of leadership not shared by boys of my age.'

He was the eldest of three children born, in close succession, to a dynamic but diminutive headmistress, and raised by a string of 'aunties' (more headmistresses) who shared the Sopers' Wandsworth house. His home life combined moral certainties with sound educational principles. His father was a devout Wesleyan and a campaigning moralist whose job as an insurance adjuster took second place to his life's passion: teetotalism.

'We all used to go along to hear my father's lectures at the Band of Hope, an offshoot of the Sunday school, as an expression of our abhorrence of "the Devil in solution". He used empty bottles with exaggerated labels as props.' This symbolism had a profound effect. 'I was so badly concussed at soccer one day that my team mates took me to see the trainer who said: "A drop of brandy should pull him through." Well, the word brandy alone was enough to shock me awake. I sat bolt upright and said: "I refuse to touch a drop of that stuff." My father was inordinately proud. Perhaps his moral discipline was extravagant but I don't resent it. I'm grateful for it now. I'm still a teetotaller – not through any great effort on my part. I have lapsed in many ways, but never into drinking or gambling.' Years later, Soper pioneered a hostel for alcoholics.

'Our house was strict but never stifling. Music was an important outlet as well as a major cohesive factor. My brother played the fiddle, my sister had a good soprano voice, my mother sang contralto and my father insisted on singing songs about the sea. One summer at Minehead, we heard a pierrot troupe performing on the prom. As we listened, my father would be busy remembering the words while I was remembering the tune. We appropriated many songs that way. I had an amazing ear for music. I've got carpal tunnel

242

syndrome now which has affected my wrists, but I can still knock out the hymns for Sunday morning communion. At one time we really weren't too bad. Together with my brother Meredith Ross, known to us as Sos, we would play Vivaldi, making it up as we went along. We took care to avoid wrong notes, at any rate. It was a primitive kind of fun but its value lay in bringing us close together.' Sos died of diabetes in 1926, aged twenty-eight. 'It is a great sorrow to me still.'

Soper's politics grew out of the annual family holiday. 'They were always thoroughly planned in advance by my parents as a corporate activity for the good of the family. When I look back to those days, I still discern the heartbeat of the socialist faith I hold. The environment, with its unity and group spirit, largely engineered my own convictions about society. A week before leaving, we would fill a trunk full of sporting equipment and send it on ahead to our boarding house. It contained tennis rackets and our own net, bathing suits and sturdy walking gear.'

Sport was in the blood – Soper's grandfather was one of the three men in *Three Men in a Boat*, a 'great Thames man' who won many cups for swimming. But vigorous exercise did more than uphold a family tradition; it acted as a foil against the dangers of time wasting.

'Part of my father's Nonconformist ethic was that if you're not doing anything, you're probably in sin. "Go look for Jimmy, find out what he's doing and tell him not to . . .", probably sums it up. My time was so highly organized that I could never get away entirely from my parents' sphere of influence. When I went to church on Sundays they would all be there too. At one stage, my mother was a headmistress, my father was my church superintendent and my "Aunt" Nellie, who lived with us, was my Sunday school teacher. I didn't take too kindly to it and got into trouble very often. I still have the impression that for quite a lot of the time, I was under suspicion for not behaving quite well enough.'

Armistice Day 1920 was the first in a series of transforming experiences. 'The son of a local communist wouldn't observe the minute's silence. As head prefect, it was my job to make him behave. He wasn't a friend of mine but he was being bullied, so I stood by him and I'm glad I did. It was a crisis for me because I expressed something which had not surfaced. It was the start of a recognition that he represented something I didn't share but which I had to respect. It showed me tolerance.'

This unease, closely followed by the violent cricketing tragedy and his departure to read history at Cambridge, threatened his childhood certainties. Many of the attitudes for which he later became famous find echoes in this period. 'I had been shielded and nurtured all my life and suddenly I was confronted with all sorts of things for which I had not been prepared. My father was not very loquacious, what he required was discipline. I assumed Christianity was true because it was obviously true for my parents and it had given me such a happy life. Here, all alone for the first time, I found intellectual problems I had not anticipated and which threatened all my religious values. No mother, no father, no church, it was a critical time for me. Suddenly, I found I didn't believe anything.'

His secure Methodist childhood had contained no warning of the isolation of his atheism. 'I had contracted to teach a Sunday school class at the local Methodist church and I was forced to go to the superintendent and tell him that I was now an atheist. He saw the problem right away. But I did say I would still play the piano for him, and that was a very important matter. It sounds bizarre, but I saw no reason to leave the church just because I was an atheist. I still felt I belonged in the church and that was where I wanted to be.

'I stayed in the church all the time I was recovering my faith. It was a very different kind of faith this time. The Christianity that I hold now, and which I have never lost, is a more rational one. I have learnt to express it in pacifist and socialist terms rather than in laying off the liquor and not betting on the horses.' His childhood was over.

'My second grown-up experience was getting married [they

244

have four daughters] and then taking charge of a church.' In 1926, the young probationary minister was sent to the South London Mission, Old Kent Road, and soon after began his unique open air ministry at Tower Hill.

'I don't suppose I do it anything like John Wesley but I keep going because there are not many opportunities for personal confrontation any more, they have all been swallowed up by public relations. The great thing about preaching is consistency. Don't think I'm painting the holy hero, but people know that whatever the weather, I'll be there.'

23 March 1991

Oxford's triumph sullied by their arrogance

David Miller

Oxford University dispelled, historically, two perceptions of the Boat Race: that it is between amateur sportsmen, and that technique is fundamental to success. For the eighteenth time in the last twenty-three races, Oxford demonstrated that strength-through-weight is more critical than refinement, the latter a quality also absent in their street-gang-style prancing in victory.

Duncan Clegg, the chief administrator of the race, must be wondering today how far his sponsor, Beefeater, will be willing to maintain its commercial loyalty to this national event if it becomes just another vehicle for loutish manners masquerading as professionalism.

Hampton School can be proud of the way Rupert Obholzer stroked Oxford to another outstanding victory, but it should be ashamed of the way one of its sons then denigrated the defeated.

Obholzer gestured dismissively at the shattered Cambridge crew after it had crossed the finishing line almost five lengths behind. Oxford were visibly gloating; Michels, their No. 2, had sarcastically shouted at Justicz, his fellow American at No. 3 for Cambridge, 'See you at the finish' as Oxford bulldozed past Cambridge's early vain lead.

After receiving the trophy from the Princess Royal, Obholzer continued to belittle the opposition on account of its 'pretty haircuts, shades [dark glasses] and poncey clothes'. Such trivial, gratuitous insults ill become someone whose own hairstyle suggests that any minute he may begin to intone

'Bubble, bubble, toil and trouble', never mind that he is an established international oarsman.

It may well be that Cambridge, in their ghastly lime-tinged gear that was supposed to be light-blue, did posture a bit before the race in their search for the self-confidence that is necessary if they are to terminate the hold which Oxford have established on the race. It *is* an intense, goldfish bowl event that generates motivation that most of the oarsmen will never experience elsewhere; and Oxford, fearful lest they became remembered as the Oxford crew that *lost*, had been nettled by pre-race claims that Cambridge were the more competent.

Determined to inflict the heaviest possible defeat – a result that hung on a hair's breadth for half a mile down Fulham Reach – was one thing; to remain fired by psychological arrogance when victory was completed was another.

The borderline between amateur and professional is narrow in emotions, as rugby union is painfully discovering; and once the Boat Race crosses that border too far, the traditional appeal will perish. It is as much Oxford's responsibility to combine with Cambridge in preserving that tradition as to win the race, yet the problem for both crews is that professionalism is tending to outstrip traditionally-mannered amateur management.

How much finer sportsmen would Oxford have appeared, how much more subtly crushing would victory have been, had they shaken hands as mortified Cambridge stepped ashore? Michels put his finger on the truth, when, attempting to explain away the misplaced hate-campaign, he admitted: 'Without Cambridge, there is no race. The beauty of the event is the personal conflict, and that is what brings out the crowds.'

The Boat Race will not survive if it loses its *Chariots of Fire* concept, any more than it would if other universities were to be embraced. This is not an event that can be competitively 'balanced', as with European involvement in the once exclusive Britain v United States Ryder Cup. London University, for example, can call on 100,000 students from a huge range of polytechnics, many of whom would fail Oxbridge academic entrance standards. The ancient Boat Race is about Oxford and Cambridge and sportsmanship, or it is nothing.

When asked, as Oxford president, if this was his greatest day, Obholzer said no. It is commendable that he has ambitions for the Olympic Games, and unquestionably his physical contribution to Oxford's victory was immeasurable. Yet he and Pinsent and other exceptional rowers must not be allowed to lose sight of the fact that the Boat Race is more than a race.

This one will be remembered for its fascinating tactical balance, for Cambridge's unsustainable burn at the start, for Oxford's enormous power through the water that found coherence on the day for the first time. They may not have been worried about refinement of their blades out of the water. They should be more worried about the refinement of their personalities once out of the boat.

Aggression in the water is fine. 'I've got five, give me four' [meaning the opposite number is overhauled] is a cox's common cry. 'I've got five, give me Bolshaw' the Cambridge cox bellowed twenty years ago, regarding a feared Oxford rower. Oxford have now carried motivation a shade too far.

1 April 1991

Saving the Kurds

Leader

No sooner were the people of Kuwait released from occupation by the forces of President Saddam Hussein than other subject peoples of Iraq, Kurdish and Shia, found themselves in a similar inferno. The Kurds, who had some 4000 of their villages razed by Saddam only three years ago and were viciously gassed, are proving especially vulnerable. Their fears of Iraqi brutality are based on bitter experience. Hence the panic-stricken exodus of thousands of people towards Syria, Iran and, above all, Turkey.

Military action that might have defended Kurdistan from the Baghdad regime existed only in the minds of those far distant from that benighted land, not in the realm of practicality. The urgent need now is for a huge humanitarian effort.

Turkey and Iran, as the states adjacent to northern Iraq, have a simple humanitarian responsibility to these refugees. Iran is already burdened with tens of thousands of Shias who fled across the border from the Republican Guards in southern Iraq. Turkey is clearly reluctant to increase the separatist aspirations of its own Kurdish minority. That is too bad. Ankara must relent from its intransigence, order its troops not to shoot at the refugees, and set up proper camps. If Turkey has any doubts about this, it should remember its oft-expressed desire to be judged by European standards.

The United Nations must play its part, both in providing relief for the victims and in putting pressure on Baghdad to halt the slaughter. The question is, how? President Mitterrand yesterday gave his answer: there should be a UN resolution, condemning Iraqi atrocities and maintaining sanctions until Saddam's troops stop behaving abominably. The British and American response to this was cool. They see great obstacles to obtaining security council unanimity for such a resolution. The present ceasefire resolution has taken more than a month to draft. It is likely to be the last for some time. To have entered at this stage into protracted negotiations on incorporating the Kurdish issue into the resolution would have been unrealistic. A UN relief effort must not be delayed.

Organizing a relief effort is more tractable, even if the logistics are complex. But the Gulf conflict has created refugee problems before, notably last autumn when thousands of Asian refugees poured into Jordan from Iraq and Kuwait. The relief agencies should have absorbed the lessons of coping with that flood of unwilling travellers. The Kurds are in a worse state: the Asians who fled to Jordan had not been bombed and shelled.

In addition to relieving the plight of Saddam's Kurdish victims, the international community must find new ways of forcing the Iraqi leader to stop what appear to be genocidal attacks on his own population with the huge arsenal at his disposal, including armour, warplanes and helicopter gunships. Saddam is clearly aware that international opinion does impose some constraints on him. His failure to use poison gas, either against the coalition or against the Kurds, seems to reflect this awareness.

Sanctions imposed on August 6 remain in place. If amending Resolution 661 to require Saddam to stop persecuting his Kurds or Shia Muslims is impractical, the UN should remind Baghdad forcibly that 661, and indeed the other UN resolutions on the Gulf crisis, refer repeatedly to the need to maintain international peace and security in the region.

Hundreds of thousands of Kurdish refugees are gathering on Iraq's borders and confronting Turkish troops. Their plight is an international issue as well as an international outrage. The UN, the European Community, the American and the British governments must devote themselves both to the starving, dying refugees and to all feasible sanctions that might curb Saddam's excesses.

4 April 1991

Exodus adds to the Kurds' long history of suffering

Michael Binyon

Like a line of ants, the trail of human misery snaked down the side of the gorge to the rickety suspension bridge over the brown and swollen Zap river. A Turkish soldier guarded the entrance to the bridge, allowing the Kurds across in groups of about twenty.

They shuffled over, weary, ragged and clutching a few sacks of possessions, all they could salvage for the six-day trek across the mountains. Relief was waiting on the other side, lorries parked on the shingle beside the river distributing cheap rubber shoes, bread, water, biscuits and whatever supplies fellow Kurds from nearby Hakkari could get down to their desperate Iraqi kinsmen.

The scene was one of overwhelming turmoil and wretchedness.

People set themselves down in weary groups by the river; the unshaven men in dirty, torn jackets and baggy trousers or long, striped garments like outsize pyjamas; women in billowing, coloured dresses with shawls and overalls; children in garish, party dresses that were torn and mud-caked. Others milled around among the stubby thorn trees, calling out for friends and relatives clustering around the lorries, trying on shoes and opening bags of biscuits. Some just stood there smoking, confused, exhausted, their will destroyed.

One or two people spoke a smattering of English, and many more could speak passable Arabic. They had no idea what the world would do for them, but there was an expression of hopelessness and devastation on their dark faces as they pressed around, anxious to tell any Westerners of their sufferings.

Most had come from Dahuk, four days' walk away and now apparently a ghost town. One man showed his lacerated, bare feet, the hardened skin cracked and raw from the long march.

'My mother, my father, my brother – all gone,' he said. 'There were ten in my family. Only I am left.' He presumed they were all dead, but they could have just gone missing in the exodus.

Another man, eager to give his name as Salih Abid Haji, was also alone. 'Saddam Hussein's soldiers took my mother and father and brother,' he said. He proudly admitted he was a member of the Kurdish resistance forces.

All insisted that chemical bombs had been dropped on the fleeing refugees. There were aircraft, helicopters and soldiers firing in the hills. The accounts were rambling and confused, and seemed to repeat incidents that are fast becoming the tragic folklore of the suffering Kurdish people.

Among a cluster of rocks, a toothless grandmother in black headscarf and shawl had settled herself and spread out a blanket. Children jumped around, nibbling bread and biscuits, chattering and laughing. It could almost have been a picnic. The sun shone, the cliffs rose high and jagged on either side with little, yellow flowers peeping out among the craggy overhangs. But on the far side, way, way up, there was an endless line of people slowly moving along a precipitous track – little blobs of colour patiently zigzagging down in an endless stream.

The riverbank was filling up quickly. The refugees had begun to arrive only a short time earlier, having found a short cut from Iraq that skirted the camp, hard on the border, where thousands are now confined, guarded by Turkish soldiers and likely to stay within yards of the country they abandoned until some international relief brings them to more permanent settlement.

A city administrator from Van, the only big city in this

desolate region, six hours away over the mountain roads, was attempting to assess the flow of refugees.

The Turks are clearly overwhelmed by the influx, but are reluctant to allow the Kurds in Turkey to make the refugees really welcome. Local villagers spoke of Turkish army patrols preventing them from bringing cheese or fruit to the refugees. But like all stories here, this was hard to verify.

The local administration has begun a massive relief effort, and lorries with bread and other emergency rations were streaming down to the border throughout the night. A few miles on, Cukurca was cut off by a recent landslip. Bulldozers were trying to re-open the vital link. The few soldiers on the road to the town were making no attempt to halt the refugees' push to get deeper into Turkey, although some people were being helped into lorries and taken away – probably to another makeshift camp.

American embassy staff have been down here, wading through muddy tracks to see for themselves the conditions of the refugees and to try to assess what is needed. And all day, more and more keep coming, the long, thin line of a nation fleeing this latest and most bitter collapse of the long struggle for a free and independent Kurdistan.

8 April 1991

B flat?

From Dr G. B. R. Walkey

Sir, Two years ago, in a letter which you published on 3 April, 1989, I reported to you that the note of the buzz of the bumble bee (*Bombus terrestris*) on 27 March that year was C sharp below middle C.

Today I had the opportunity to listen to the note struck by the same kind of bumble bee and its pitch was a semitone higher, the D below middle C. A year ago I noted it to be the same on 3 April, while the note of a slightly smaller bumble bee was three semitones higher, i.e., F.

12 April 1991

From Mr Bruce Garner

Sir, I note your heading (B flat?) to Dr Walkey's letter today, and recall the humming bee (*Bombus terrestris*, no doubt) that settled on my arm one summer day and, in response to my playful overtures, stung me. I forget now the pitch of its hum, but the sting was certainly B sharp.

From Mr Tony Pristavec

Sir, I was intrigued to read that the bumble bee appears to have changed its pitch from C sharp below middle C to D below middle C.

It is obvious that the humble creature has given up the annoying practice of performing at 'baroque' pitch. We can only hope it has set a precedent.

16 April 1991

From Mr R. G. Lofting

Sir, The bumble bee's buzz note reported by Dr Walkey is presumably related to its wing beat. Memories from my flying days tell me that any flying machine must produce more lift than its weight in a climb and less in a descent.

I assume *Bombus* knows this, too, and therefore varies its wing beat. Perhaps Dr Walkey could extend his research into the creature's 'flight envelope' and come up with a bombiform scale?

18 April 1991

From Mr Paul Pickerill

Sir, Which method does Dr Walkey use to ascertain the notes produced by his seemingly homing bumble bees?

Is he blessed with perfect pitch, or does he have to compare the notes with those of a piano? If the latter, has he considered that it may not necessarily be the pitch of the bees that is sharpening, but rather, that of his piano flattening?

19 April 1991

From Mr S. C. Littlewood

Sir, It has been said that, because of its physical characteristics (huge body, narrow wings, etc), the bumble bee should not, aerodynamically speaking, be capable of flight.

Is it not therefore conceivable that, in keeping with modern technology, this amiable insect has increased its engine power, with a consequent rise in pitch?

From Mr H. F. Smith

Sir, When I was living in Madras, in 1934, I heard tell of a military funeral being savagely dispersed by wild bees disturbed from their abode near the

256

top of the cathedral. Apparently the creatures had been angered by the band playing the 'Dead March' in *Saul*.

22 April 1991

From Mr Michael Horne
Sir, I would suggest a stringed instrument (possibly a viol?) as being more suitable to Dr Walkey's researches among bumble bees than the piano postulated in Mr Paul Pickerill's letter. The relative ease of transportation would make it more convenient for use, and a claim for its efficacy is historically documented.

Pepys's diary, 8 August, 1666:

> . . . discoursed with Mr Hooke a little, whom we met in the street, about the nature of Sounds, and he did make me understand the nature of Musicall sounds made by Strings, mighty prettily; and told me that having come to a certain Number of Vibracions proper to make any tone, he is able to tell how many strokes a fly makes with her wings (those flies that hum in their flying) by the note that it answers to in Musique during their flying. That, I suppose, is a little too much raffined; but his discourse in general of sound was mighty fine.

From Mrs Iduna Hawkey
Sir, In a letter written to the Hon Daines Barrington, dated 12 February, 1771, Gilbert White of Selborne records that his brother, the Reverend Henry White, found that all the owls in his neighbourhood (Fyfield in Hampshire) hooted in B flat. He used a pitch pipe tuned to concert pitch. (I have had the same result, using a recorder.)

His neighbour, who was reputed to have a 'nice ear', found that the owls in his village hooted in three different keys: G flat, A flat and B flat.

From Dr G. B. R. Walkey
Sir, Mr Paul Pickerill asks how I determined the buzz note of *Bombus terrestris*. I did so by means of a Hohner pitch pipe, which contains the chromatic scale for an octave ascending from middle C.

From Mr Anthony M. R. Adlard
Sir, Might I respectfully suggest that, rather than continuing to wax lyrical on the musical attributes of *Bombus terrestris*, your correspondents find an alternative subject about which to drone?

25 April 1991

Sir David Lean

Towards the end of his life David Lean was fond of quoting a piece of advice given him by Noël Coward early in his career. The two men, both master craftsmen and master entertainers, had come together to direct *In Which We Serve*, a film likely to appear a bit jingoistic today but which in 1942 did much to raise patriotic morale in war-buffeted Britain. 'Do what pleases you,' said Coward, 'and if what pleases you does not please the public, then get out of show business.'

Lean remembered those words and followed them. He had joined Gaumont British as a tea boy when he was nineteen. Over sixty years later, when he was well into his eighties, Lean was still obsessed with the cinema and planning the film of *Nostromo* based on Conrad's novel. In the meantime he had pleased himself, despite a tendency to be disparaging about his own work, and he had mightily pleased the public. He had also made a lot of money.

Many critics admired him most for some of his early films, *Brief Encounter* and *Great Expectations*; the public all over the world adored him for the blockbusters which became the Lean hallmark: *The Bridge on the River Kwai*, *Lawrence of Arabia* and, financially the most successful of all, *Dr Zhivago*. He had his setbacks: *Ryan's Daughter* received a critical mauling which wounded him more than he would ever admit, even though it did run for a year at the Empire, Leicester Square. He failed to get his project *Mutiny on the Bounty* to the screen. But Lean was tough enough and carried sufficient weight to bounce back with *A Passage to India* after over a decade of silence.

Lean regarded himself as a storyteller, albeit of those

invented by others. That was why he so often turned to the great novelists of the nineteenth and twentieth centuries. There were Dickens (*Great Expectations* and *Oliver Twist*), Pasternak (*Dr Zhivago*) and Forster (*A Passage to India*). Carol Reed, whose best films unrolled their plots with economy and precision, was an early influence, so were the great French directors of the Thirties and Forties such as Carné, Renoir and Duvivier. Lean claimed not to be an intellectual but he gave his scriptwriters a hard time. Christopher Hampton, a mild mannered man, worked for a year on *Nostromo* before he could take it no longer and Lean returned to his old and trusted collaborator, Robert Bolt.

Lean's other obsession was landscape, which played an increasing part as his films became larger and longer. Stories abounded during the filming of *Ryan's Daughter* of camera crews and stars alike being left kicking their heels until just the right cloud formation arrived on the horizon. He explored the world to find precisely the right locations for the next project in hand and this was one of the reasons for his rootlessness. He had his houses, quite recently in London's Docklands and then in the South of France when he despaired of the parsimony and gutlessness of the British film industry. But his natural habitat was much more likely to be a hotel suite in whichever city happened to be catering for his immediate cinematic needs. Off the set Lean's manner was patrician in a way designed to hide a certain shyness and a lack of interest in the small talk and the gossip of the film industry. His nose was aquiline, a boyish lock of hair tended to fall over his brow as he spoke, but his face was dominated by the eyes which fixed on their subject with a steady, almost intimidating gaze. Nothing gave away David Lean's quite modest upbringing among a Quaker family in a London suburb.

He was born in south London and the strict religious observance of his parents, whose good looks he was to inherit, kept him somewhat apart from other children. Cinema-going was not encouraged and the young Lean had to slide secretly away from his Quaker school, at which on his own admission he was an indifferent pupil, to the pictures. An illicit visit to a silent version of *The Hound of the Baskervilles* gave him a taste of the magic the screen could produce and made him determined not to work in the staider profession of accountancy, which is what his parents, now separated, had in mind for him.

From being a tea boy at Gaumont British he progressed to the cutting room, working initially on the newsreels that were part of the diet of cinema programmes in those days. Lean's prowess with the scissors, sharpening such pictures as *Pygmalion*, became known and the technical mastery he was acquiring served him well. Audiences seeing *Great Expectations* (1946) were as terrified as young Pip himself at the sudden cut to Magwitch looming out of the Essex fog.

He worked with Michael Powell on wartime dramas such as *One of Our Aircraft is Missing* before the invitation came from Noël Coward to co-direct *In Which We Serve*. The film helped forge a number of Lean partnerships: he worked several times with its star, John Mills, and was to marry (as his second wife) the actress Kay Walsh, who was also in the cast. Then there was Coward himself. Lean was to work with him on *This Happy Breed*, *Blithe Spirit* and, most importantly, *Brief Encounter* with Trevor Howard and Celia Johnson. Some regard the latter as Lean's most perfectly shaped film. Certainly the theme of love in approaching middle age was one that fascinated him and he was to return to it, rather more opulently and less successfully, in 1955 with *Midsummer Madness*, starring Katharine Hepburn and Rossano Brazzi.

During the 1940s and 1950s Lean was highly productive. There were stylish adaptations such as *Oliver Twist* and *Great Expectations*, contemporary subjects including *The Sound Barrier* and one or two films, *Madeleine* and *The Passionate Friends* among them, which have almost disappeared from memory. *Midsummer Madness* marked a turning point: thereafter Lean was to devote himself to epic movies. The gaps between films grew longer and longer as the finance became ever more complex to arrange. Lean the perfectionist became ever more dominant as he demanded the perfect shot and was prepared to spend money and keep everyone waiting while it was achieved.

His reward was world-wide success and plenty of prizes. *The Bridge on the River Kwai* won seven Oscars, including one for Lean as best director. *Lawrence of Arabia* equalled that tally, including another for Lean, and no one seemed to mind too much that it ran for close on four hours. *Dr Zhivago* was less garlanded, but made MGM more money than any film since *Gone with the Wind*. With *Lawrence* and *Zhivago* Lean owed quite a lot to a young English schoolmaster turned playwright called Robert Bolt. The partnership was to continue in good times and in those when the going was considerably tougher. Together they had to take the critical savaging sustained by *Ryan's Daughter*. Lean, although he did not say too much in public, was wounded by the reception, not least because the advance publicity, with battalions of journalists descending on Co. Kerry where much of the shooting was done, had promised a masterpiece.

Another fourteen years were to pass before Lean was to make his next film, *A Passage to India*, based on E. M. Forster's novel. This was a period of disappointment. Lean planned a film on Gandhi, but his rival Richard Attenborough beat him to it. Years were spent on a project to remake *Mutiny on the Bounty*, with Bolt heavily involved as screenwriter despite the fact that he had suffered a severe stroke. But *Bounty* was never to take to the high seas: there were quarrels with the producer, Dino De Laurentiis, over the cost and scope of the film. Its abandonment caused Lean the same disenchantment with the world of movie making as had the attacks on *Ryan's Daughter*.

His pride was restored by *A Passage to India*. The usual stories, some true and some false, emerged from the locations of wrangles, notably with the temperamental Australian actress, Judy Davis, playing the part of Adela Quested. Any Lean film was news and his first in a decade and a half was something special. When *Passage* was eventually screened there was criticism of the casting of Alec Guinness, but the consensus was that Lean had lost none of his skill as a storyteller and none of his eye for a landscape with which to embroider it.

He had hinted that this would be his last film but as he turned eighty he was already embroiled in Conrad's *Nostromo*, searching out locations in Mexico and mocking the studios for lining up 'reserve' directors in case his health failed him.

There is confusion about the number of his marriages, but he is known with certainty to have been married five times and he leaves his widow, Sandra.

17 April 1991

Muck, moans and magic

Paul Heiney

So there I was, forking muck on a balmy spring afternoon, arm muscles settling into the gentle rhythm of the swing of the fork, mind unwinding under the hypnotic influence of repetitive work. Organic farmers like muck and are always happiest close to it. I was very close: I could savour every nutritious forkful, inhale each pocket of invigorating gas ruptured by my fork and, when pausing for breath, see newborn lambs at play, cows ruminating, fields becoming ever greener under the warming sun.

Then the precious moment was shattered. The woman came nosing into the farmyard, having spied the lambs. I had spotted her earlier, striding down the lane with the air of someone who owned the place. The only people round here who strut as if they own it invariably do not – except at weekends. 'How pretty; aren't they lovely,' she cooed. Like all proud fathers, I fell for the flattery. 'If you want to see more lambs,' I offered, 'have a stroll up to the meadow.'

I expected a word of thanks, but instead got a mouthful.

'What *are* those?' she asked, pointing in disgust at the growing piglets.

'Pigs,' I replied.

'But what sort?' she snorted.

'Large Black pigs.'

'Well,' she said, 'they don't look very large to me.'

Muck-flinging dulls the reactions, so I was unable to wither her with a barbed reply.

'Why do we see all these pigs in fields these days?' she continued. 'Have you farmers just discovered bacon?'

I opened my mouth, but no words came. She strode off,

264

heading for the lambs, no doubt to frighten them as well. I think I remembered to warn her about the electric fence. Ah well, perhaps I forgot.

Still bearing the scars, I was wary when the next visitors turned up. It was a party of schoolchildren, and it is well known that no creature can cut you to the quick as precisely as a child. But I was pleased to have them, and their headmistress was relieved, too: taking children on farm visits these days must be a near impossible task. At some stage they have to learn that eggs come from hens and sausages from pigs, but you could hardly expose six-year-olds to battery chicken units or intensive pig-fattening sheds. Better they tickle Alice's ears or hunt for stray eggs. Modern farms are not safe places for children. The machinery is too unforgiving. Like an old music hall turn, I have a set patter for school visits. I start by showing children the harness, choosing the biggest horse collar and asking if any of them would like to try wearing it round their necks, as the horse has to. None of them can even lift it. Then I tell the smallest child to walk through it, which they usually can, without stooping.

Then I say I'm off to get the horse. By now they are bursting with anticipation, expecting a cross between Black Beauty and Nellie the Elephant. I pick the biggest horse. The children gasp; a carthorse close up is an awesome sight.

I remember a letter from a woman whose little boy had seen his first Suffolk Punch. The lad stared at the big brown horse, sensing its might and majesty, overcome by the shimmering brilliance of it, and said: 'He looks like the sun.'

You may think this is all sentimental twaddle, an educational diversion, but if farmers want to be loved again they would do well to follow my example and start working up an act. As my nosy woman visitor demonstrated, no amount of public relations is going to convince hard-bitten adults that farmers have any good in them. Our only hope is the children. Anyway, children are always worth encouraging just for the thank you letters and poems that arrive a few days later.

It was lovely to see,
Close to me,
A Suffolk Punch
Which had just had its lunch.
He lived on a farm with some Red Polls
And a family of pigs as black as moles.
There were sheep too in a pen.
I'd love to go back – but when?

A lot sooner than some I could mention, is the answer.

20 April 1991

People who knead people

Richard Holmes

Biography, like love, begins in passionate curiosity. Where it ends – or should end – has become a matter of dispute in the boom of book sales and advances. In fact, the British, with their bristling sense of privacy, have long been a nation of biographers; and if there really is a boom in the form, it began 200 years ago with the publication on 16 May, 1791 of James Boswell's *Life of Samuel Johnson LLD*.

The two enormous quarto volumes sold out in eighteen months, earning its author spectacular profits of £1,555 18s 2d and bringing praise and condemnation with equal extravagance.

Boswell is the godfather of English biography, in both the literary and the mafia sense. He championed the art, and he launched the business. Nobody before him had reconstructed another life on such an epic scale (modern editions run to 1500 pages) or with such relentless, brilliant intimacy. He spent almost twenty years on research (unveiling his project to Johnson by degrees in 1772) and six years writing up his material after Johnson's death in 1784.

He persisted obsessively through periods of extreme depression, alcoholism (and, worse, teetotalism) and the death of his beloved wife Margaret. He wrote up thousands of pages of conversations recorded in his private journals; collected hundreds of letters; interviewed bishops, actresses, philosophers, booksellers, blue-stockings, childhood friends and household servants. (Johnson's black servant, Francis Barber, was sent a detailed questionnaire; while Johnson's confidante, Mrs Desmoulins, was carefully cross-questioned about cuddling sessions in Hampstead.) Boswell deftly explored Johnson's lifelong melancholia, delving deep in his private diaries, prayers and annals. He minutely observed the Great Cham's nervous tics and religious terrors, his Rabelaisian eating habits, and his fondness for cats.

Finally, he wrote proudly in his preface: 'I will venture to say that he will be seen in this work more completely than any man who has ever yet lived. And he will be seen as he really was; for I profess to write not his panegyrick, which must be all praise, but his Life.' This, in effect, was the manifesto of modern biography.

In one of his moments of manic optimism, Boswell even considered applying for a royal endorsement, 'By Appointment to His Majesty, Biographer of Samuel Johnson', for the second edition title page, as if his work was a pot of successful marmalade on the breakfast tables of *le tout monde*.

In fact, reactions to his labours were divided in a way now familiar to contemporary biographers. Dr Charles Burney, the distinguished musicologist, considered he had achieved a noble work of memorial art, as Xenophon had done for Socrates. Mrs Barbauld, the novelist, reckoned he had produced a fascinating but cheap piece of popular gossip: 'It is like going to Ranelagh pleasure-gardens; you meet all your acquaintance: but it is a base and a mean thing to bring thus every idle word into judgment.'

Modern doubts about biography – particularly raised by the peculiar form of anti-hagiography in recent 'celebrity lives' of Picasso, John Lennon and Nancy Reagan – run much along these lines. The biographer is seen as a type of predator, grave-snatcher or gossip driven by commercial instincts; the stock-in-trade is betrayal, invasion of privacy and superficial scandal; the biographical method is shallow and can say little about the deep springs of character or the profoundly inward process of the creation of a work of art; and biography, so flourishing in Britain, is at best a productive part of the heritage industry, a pungent but malodorous mushroom of the nostalgia culture. In short, the 'boom' is a hollow, passing drum, beaten by industrious clowns.

Well, maybe some of it is. But the bicentenary of Boswell's masterpiece, which has remained one of the most widely read and reprinted books in the English language, should give us pause for reflection. Why *is* biography so popular? Why does it, at best, seem to fulfil Dr Johnson's own epitome of fine literature, that balances entertainment with instruction, and helps us the better to enjoy life or to endure it? And, indeed, why did Johnson himself, no literary lightweight, consistently say that biography was the part of literature that he 'loved best'?

Boswell seems to have bequeathed us not a technique of exploitation, but an idea, even an *ideal*, of truth-telling. Conceived within a calm, noble culture of Augustan enlightenment – 'the proper study of mankind, is man' – it has burnt ever more brightly in the dark *Sturm und Drang* that has followed. In our own age of scepticism, discredited ideologies and disabling self-doubt, the possibility and the desirability of knowing our fellow man and woman – how we really are beyond the masks of fame, success, obscurity, or even ordinariness – has remained extraordinarily constant. And biography has gradually become a prime instrument, an important artistic form, of that essentially humane, courageous, and curiously cheering epistemology.

Its arrival has certainly been gradual. Boswell did not, with rare exceptions, convert the Victorians, although his book was almost canonized by Macaulay and Carlyle in famous essays. Instead, the protectionism of the 'authorized' biographer, such as Dickens's friend John Forster, or A. P. Stanley, Arnold's one-time pupil, drew a cloak of respectability and family pieties around the eminent subject. It hardened, as Edmund Gosse (significantly, an inspired autobiographer) observed, into the marbled monuments of multi-volumed 'life and letters', massive, shapeless, stainless and sepulchrally concealing. Indeed, Victorian biography, in the hands of Sir Leslie Stephen, ended by erecting a Great Wall of China, the *Dictionary of National Biography*, around the outposts of public truth-telling: thus far and no further may civil knowledge go.

Of course, there were exceptions, notably Mrs Gaskell's vividly empathetic *Life of Charlotte Brontë* (one novelist upon another); or Froude's grimly honest exposé of, ironically, Carlyle's own marriage. And Victorian biography is at last beginning to receive study, in the work of A.O.J. Cockshut, or the recent Clark lectures of Professor Christopher Ricks. One can now see how its restrictions have, paradoxically, given modern biographers something to work *against*; in William St Clair's striking analogy, like huge archaeological sites to be patiently redug and redefined.

Perhaps Boswell's first true heir was Lytton Strachey, whose *Eminent Victorians* (1918) – four short lives of Cardinal Manning, Florence Nightingale, Dr Arnold and General Gordon, each elegantly pierced and mocked – breached the Great Wall of respectability for ever. It was the end of Empire in several ways. Strachey was, perhaps, less of a truth-teller than a destroyer of illusions and a liberator of forms. What he released was a generation of brilliant experimenters in biographical narrative, who at last began to ask *how* lives can be genuinely reconstructed: what is memory, what is time, what is character, what is 'evidence' in a human story?

Thus, Virginia Woolf (daughter of Stephen, or 'rebellious daughter of DNB', as Julia Briggs has called her) wondered how to describe the twenty or so personalities a single life may contain. She produced a fictional biography of her friend Vita Sackville-West, covering several centuries and a change of sex, in *Orlando*; and presented the Browning household through the biography of Elizabeth Barrett's dog, *Flush*.

Many other writers, such as the former actor Hesketh Pearson, contributed to this flexing and exercising of Boswell's grand ideal. What it meant was that the monumental form lost its rigidity and was recognized at last as a subtle, responsive art as various as the lives it contained.

Our own generation has seen literary biography, especially, freed of Victorian inhibitions and allowed to rise to power as a virtually new genre.

The appeal of such a genre to a wide public has also become more evident than perhaps it was to Boswell's startled contemporaries. The partial collapse of the large, naturalistic novel – precisely the form invented by Boswell's peers such as Fielding and Richardson, and continued from Dickens to Lawrence – has left an immense hunger for the large, naturalistic biography, with its solid, architectural colonnade of beginning, middle and end. (Peter Ackroyd has remarked that his highly successful *Dickens* was originally conceived in the exact form of such a Victorian novel.)

A similar collapse of academic literary criticism into the dry ruins of deconstructionism, has left the old, humane Arnoldian form of commentary at the disposal of biographers and their readers. Jon Stallworthy, both an academic and biographer, superbly deployed this critical tradition in his *Wilfred Owen*, a matchless account of the war poet; and recently observed that the finest critical work on Joyce remains Ellmann's *Life*.

At another level, much modern biography has something of the inescapable tension, and steady unfolding, of the classic detective story: with the psychological promise of some sort of 'revelation' (not of a crime solved, but of a human mystery at least partially resolved). The resolution often appears not in narrative, but in figurative form, which a skilful biographer can sometimes give with almost poetic force. Boswell had already divined this art, and central to his revelation of Johnson's innermost struggles is not a conversational exchange, but an embattled image.

'His mind resembled the vast amphitheatre, the Colosseum at Rome. In the centre stood his judgment which, like a mighty gladiator, combatted those apprehensions that, like the wild beasts of the Arena, were all around in cells, ready to be let out upon him. After a conflict, he drove them back into their dens; but not killing them, they were still assailing him.'

This image has such power that it resonates through the

entire biography, representative not simply of Johnson's moral struggles, but of a whole Augustan culture soon to be beset by the wild beasts of romanticism, of Rousseau and his hirsute crew.

It may also suggest how biography offers a shapely doorway back into history, seen on a human scale. Carlyle called history the sum of innumerable biographies; a view profoundly opposed to the current statistical sweepings of economic history and sociology. Even the most recherché fields can be illuminated by light from this human doorway: the complex development of romantic music in David Cairns's rumbustious *Berlioz*, or the arcana of early twentieth-century philosophy and logic in Ray Monk's patient, limpid *Ludwig Wittgenstein*. It does tell us something crucial about the delphic, regimented and numbered propositions of Wittgenstein's *Tractatus*, to discover it being drafted in the forward observation post of the Austrian artillery on the Russian front in the summer of 1916.

But above all, modern biography continues the Boswellian enquiry into the quiddity of human nature: what motivates us, what forms or splinters character, what gives self-identity, what brings intimacy. At a recent biography conference at Oxford, I was asked by a marriage counsellor how well the biographer could ever discover the truth about married couples when she herself often wondered, after extensive interviews, if two partners were living with the same spouses, so different were their accounts of each other.

This provoked animated discussion, which Margaret Boswell and Tetty Johnson would have enjoyed. But the short answer was to read something like Nigel Nicolson's account of his parents in *Portrait of a Marriage*, followed by Victoria Glendinning's generous, all-embracing life of *Victoria Sackville-West*. Such biographies, with the comprehending perspective of time, and the multiple intelligence of diaries, letters, memoirs, autobiographical fiction from both sides (and from outside) move far beyond banal bedroom truths about a relationship. The biographer may simply be in the position to know more, and more variously. In this subtlety, and this relativity, biography is post-Freud and post-Einstein. Indeed, biography can provide a kind of ethical mirror in which we can see ourselves and our lives from new angles, with sudden force. Such mirrors can have great influence over current movements: it is impossible to imagine the development of feminism over the past twenty-five years without the rediscovery and reinterpretation of such exemplary existences as those of Mary Wollstonecraft, Aphra Behn, Dorothy Wordsworth, Zelda Fitzgerald, or, indeed, Vita Sackville-West.

Nor is the biographic form itself static. Boswell had already tried many narrative modes to bring Johnson to vivid, complex, front-of-stage life. His dramatized conversations drew on the conventions of the Restoration comedy of manners (often using himself as foil and butt); his handling of Johnson's correspondence is partly inspired by Richardson's epistolary novels; his use of the diaries and prayers establishes a Johnsonian inner voice drawn from the Protestant tradition of solemn meditation.

Similarly, modern biographers experiment with the modes and conventions of truth-telling. Andrew Motion used the Forsythian interplay of a family saga to present three generations of *The Lamberts*. Ian Hamilton explored the limits of journalistic investigation and legal confrontation when actually blocked by his own subject, in the sardonic, self-questioning, cautionary tale *In Search of J.D. Salinger*. Peter Parker sensitively used a minor, tangential life of *J.R. Ackerley* to illuminate a whole literary period (and also another dog's life).

Marina Warner re-examined a celebrated historical figure in terms of the legends and archetypes, transforming her through centuries, in *Joan of Arc*. Alan Judd brought his skills as a novelist to bear on the enormous series of displaced, fictional autobiographies that made up the apparently impenetrable, shape-shifting, comic epic of the life, or lives, of *Ford Madox Ford*. My own *Footsteps* is an attempt to explore the vertiginous experience of biographical research itself, through perilous time-warps of self-projection, solitary travel, and the infatuations of the wandering scholar.

Finally, it is an unmistakable sign of the times that modern novelists have themselves begun to respond to this challenge of the biographer invading new territories, so close to their fictional heartlands. The biographer has become a recognizable fictional type, often rapacious or self-deluded, but treading close upon the heels of the novelist in the search for shy, retreating, human truth.

In Julian Barnes's *Flaubert's Parrot*, in Penelope Lively's *According to Mark*, in William Golding's *The Paper Men*, or in A. S. Byatt's aptly named *Possession*, fictional biographers pant along the trail of fleeing authors – physically breathless and metaphysically outmanoeuvred – but memorably alive and relentless. Some even have fast cars. Here parody and polemic are surely a form of grudging tribute: the biographer has come of age, and demands the keys to the house of literature.

And that age, in my view, is still a golden one. The good sons and daughters of Boswell have reason to be modestly rampant. Boswell once announced, in another of his delirious moments (he was in Cornwall, under heavy rain), that he preferred to be known as plain 'Mr B the biographer', than as 'Sir James B the High Court Judge' (which, indeed, he never was). A delusion of grandeur, no doubt. But in celebrating his bicentenary, many readers may indulgently agree with him.

11 May 1991

Index